W9-CLP-917

A Nation of Women
An Early Feminist Speaks Out

* * *

Mi opinión
sobre las libertades, derechos
y deberes de la mujer

Recovering the U.S. Hispanic Literary Heritage

Board of Editorial Advisors

José F. Aranda, Jr.
Rice University

Alejandra Balestra
University of New Mexico

Aviva Ben-Ur
University of Massachusetts, Amherst

Antonia Castañeda
St. Mary's University

Rodolfo J. Cortina
University of Houston

Kenya Dworkin y Méndez
Carnegie Mellon University

José B. Fernández
University of Central Florida

Juan Flores
Hunter College of CUNY

Erlinda Gonzales-Berry
Oregon State University

Laura Gutierrez-Witt
University of Texas at Austin

Luis Leal
University of California at Santa Barbara

Clara Lomas
The Colorado College

Francisco A. Lomelí
University of California at Santa Barbara

Agnes Lugo-Ortiz
University of Chicago

Gabriel Meléndez
University of New Mexico

Genaro Padilla
University of California at Berkeley

Raymond Paredes
State of Texas, Commission of Higher Education

Nélida Pérez
Hunter College of CUNY

Gerald Poyo
St. Mary's University

José M. Irizarry Rodríguez
Universidad de Puerto Rico, Mayagüez

Antonio Saborit
Instituto Nacional de Antropología e Historia

Rosaura Sánchez
University of California at San Diego

Virginia Sánchez Korrol
Brooklyn College of CUNY

Charles Tatum
University of Arizona

Silvio Torres-Saillant
Syracuse University

Roberto G. Trujillo
Stanford University

A Nation of Women
An Early Feminist Speaks Out

* * *

Mi opinión
sobre las libertades, derechos y deberes de la mujer

by Luisa Capetillo

Edited, with an Introduction, by Félix V. Matos Rodríguez

English Translation by Alan West-Durán

Arte Público Press
Houston, Texas

This volume is made possible through grants from the City of Houston through The Cultural Arts Council of Houston, Harris County.

Recovering the past, creating the future

Arte Público Press
University of Houston
452 Cullen Performance Hall
Houston, Texas 77204-2004

Cover design by James F. Brisson
Cover photo courtesy of Biblioteca Nacional José Martí,
La Habana, Cuba

Capetillo, Luisa.
    A Nation of Women: An Early Feminist Speaks Out = Mi opinión sobre las libertades, derechos y deberes de la mujer / by Luisa Capetillo ; English translation by Alan West-Durán ; introduction by Félix V. Matos Rodríguez.
    p.   cm.
    ISBN-10: 1-55885-427-4 (trade pbk. : alk. paper)
    ISBN-13: 978-1-55885-427-7 (trade pbk. : alk. paper)
    1. Feminism. 2. Women—Social conditions. 3. Capetillo, Luisa, 1879–1922. I. Title: Mi opinión sobre las libertades, derechos y deberes de la mujer. II. Matos Rodríguez, Félix V., 1962–   III. Title
HQ1214.C26   2004
305.42′097295—dc22   2004052188
                                                                    CIP

♾ The paper used in this publication meets the requirements of the American National Standard for Information Sciences—Permanence of Paper for Printed Library Materials, ANSI Z39.48-1984.

© 2004 by Luisa Capetillo
Printed in the United States of America

4 5 6 7 8 9 0 1 2 3   10 9 8 7 6 5 4 3 2 1

Contents

Mi opinión sobre las libertades, derechos y deberes de la mujer

"Mi patria es la libertad": Context and Introduction to Puerto Rico's First Feminist Treatise.[1]

Preface and acknowledgments

It is not uncommon for academics working on a historical figure such as feminist and anarchist writer Luisa Capetillo (1879–1922) to be shocked by the fact that some of the author's work has never been translated or reprinted. One is often convinced that the writings of notables like Capetillo have not received substantial public attention and analysis. This has been my experience with Luisa Capetillo since I became familiar with her work as a graduate student in the late 1980s. It was inconceivable to me that the author of Puerto Rico's earliest feminist treatise and one of the most fascinating political and literary figures of early twentieth century Puerto Rico had received such limited scholarly attention. It was downright appalling to find out that her four books—including *Mi opinión acerca de las libertades, derechos y deberes de la mujer*—published between 1907 and 1917 had never been reprinted in Puerto Rico or elsewhere in Latin America for that matter. As I continued my own research on Puerto Rican women's history, I still could not believe that Capetillo's works were not easily available to students and general audiences in Puerto Rico. Convinced that such an obvious omission was due to attract the attention or interest of one of my many fine literary or humanities colleagues in Puerto Rico, I decided to focus on making Capetillo's most important work available to readers in English.[2]

The purpose of this book project was to translate the first feminist treatise in Puerto Rico's history and also one of the earliest book-length statements of feminist thought in Latin America and the Caribbean: Luisa Capetillo's *Mi opinión acerca de las libertades, derechos y deberes de la mujer*. The book was published in 1911 and reprinted in 1913, making it an early example of twentieth-century feminist and labor writing in the Caribbean. In this edition, besides Alan West-Duran's fine translation of *Mi opinión*, I have also included an introductory essay discussing some of the implications of Capetillo's work to the study of early twentieth-century US, Latin American and Caribbean labor and migration history, as well as women's cultural and intellectual history. Fortunately for readers of *Mi opinión*, Capetillo's work is so rich and multi-layered that it speaks to all of these subjects.

I am very pleased that this translation will make accessible this pioneering example of early twentieth century written for the first time since 1913 when *Mi opinión* was last printed. The book is currently available in only four non-circulating libraries in the US and Puerto Rico.[3] The historical interest in this project cannot be overestimated. A feminist, union organizer, journalist, activist for social justice, Capetillo's voice argued for non-conformism premised on a profound sense of natural harmony, gender and social equality. She often questioned deeply held social, sexual, political, and economic assumptions of her time. I am hopeful that this translation will introduce future audiences to Capetillo's achievements and work, since only a few bibliographic references about her are currently available in English (Quintero Rivera 1976; Romero-Cesáreo 1994; Sánchez González 1996, and 2001; Suárez Findlay 1999; Valle Ferrer 2003). I am also hopeful that it will encourage more research and debate on Capetillo's work and her politics.

The early twentieth century was a time of profound economic and social dislocation in the United States and the Caribbean as what many consider a second industrial revolution swept through the hemisphere. Capital, labor and political power in both the Caribbean and the US experienced profound transformations in the period between the 1890s and the 1920s (Ayala 1999). Some of the consequences of these transformations were labor and social unrest, new waves of immigrant labor in the US and the Caribbean, a surge of new social actors in civil society, economic dislocation, and emerging competing political and cultural ideologies. Many of these issues are explored in *Mi opinión*.

I have noted already that two editions of *Mi opinión* were published by Capetillo: the original one, published in San Juan, in 1911, and an expanded edition published in Tampa in 1913. I decided to have the 1911 edition translated for several reasons. First, I wanted to make available Capetillo's earlier text. The 1911 edition of *Mi opinión* was the first time that a feminist treatise was published in Puerto Rico, so I wanted to accentuate the significance of this event. Its 1911 publication date also makes among the first such feminists texts in the Caribbean and Latin America. Second, practical considerations also played a role in my decision. The copy available at the Centro de Estudios Puertorriqueños' library is of the 1911 edition, so working with this edition was easier for me. Finally, the 1911 edition is the one most often reproduced in anthologies and the one most commonly quoted by scholars.[4]

Although the 1913 edition will not be the one used for this translation, a few comments about it are warranted given that this edition has remained mostly unexamined by Capetillo scholars. Only Norma Valle Ferrer (83–84) has commented on the 1913 edition, briefly stating that Capetillo corrected some mistakes, polished its prose, and got a fellow anarchist, Jaime Vidal, to write a preface. Although a detailed discussion of the differences between the 1911 and 1913 editions deserves a separate article, it should be clear that the 1913 edition is not a mere rewritten and better polished version of the original book. Capetillo engaged in significant rewriting and included new materials on key aspects of her thinking such as spiritualism, prostitution, education, hygiene, nutrition, and female suffrage. The 1913 edition also deletes important selections highlighting Puerto Rican individuals and events (such as the often-quoted section on her participation in the Partido Socialista's proselytizing campaign, the

"Cruzada del Ideal") and adds Cuban personalities and themes instead. Except for a brief reference to her Spanish culture and language, the 1913 edition has very scant references to Puerto Rico.[5] In the 1913 edition, Capetillo is more direct in her feminist challenges—the book opens with an "Introduction to the study of women," instead of the 1911 opening "Women in the home, in the family and in government;" sections entitled "Varieties" in 1911 are more clearly renamed "Women in government;" and a new section entitled "Refuting the advocates of the inferiority of women" takes aim at figures such as Schopenhauer, for example—and demonstrates less ambiguity about her political positions.[6] There is also new material on the need of being an "educated person" which seems to signal a different relationship for Capetillo with the bourgeois literati and with the practice of writing and publishing, although she remains critical of formulaic academic writing.[7] Finally, one could also comment on the authoritative picture of Capetillo sitting in front of a writing desk, which is included only in the 1913 edition; the change in the author's dedication from the original edition (her compatriots, workers, her children, Manuel Ledesma, and her mother) to the more austere 1913 edition (to all women and workers in general); and the much shortened 1913 preface; an indication that the 1913 text is worth exploring and might yield material that might challenge some elements of the current interpretations of Capetillo's work.[8] The scholarship on Luisa Capetillo will undoubtedly benefit from a more profound analysis of the 1913 edition particularly in comparison with the edition that we are currently presenting, but that task is clearly beyond the limits of this project.

Any scholar working on Luisa Capetillo's writings has a profound debt of gratitude to two scholars who have labored hard to research and make available Capetillo's life and writings for future generations: Norma Valle Ferrer and Julio Ramos. Their texts provide the cornerstones of any scholarly work done on Capetillo. I also want to thank two different—although not always mutually exclusive—generations of scholars who have studied and analyzed the impact and significance of Luisa Capetillo's writings. The first generation includes some of the scholars who started to document, analyze and disseminate the contributions of working-class and feminists writers during the early 1970s and 1980s: Ángel Quintero Rivera, Rubén Dávila Santiago, Isabel Picó, and Yamila Azize, among others I have listed in the bibliography. I also want to express my gratitude to a second generation of scholars whose recent reinterpretations of Capetillo's writings have proven of great value to me: Lisa Sánchez González, Eileen Suárez Findlay and Ivette M. Rivera-Giusti.

It has been a pleasure working with Alan West-Durán, who has produced a first-rate translation of Capetillo's work. I want to thank him for being a generous colleague and for accepting my invitation to work on this project. He is an excellent translator. His expertise in Puerto Rican and Caribbean history and literature and his sensitivity to women's and gender studies certainly enhanced his ability to approach and translate Capetillo's prose. Alan also provided me with excellent comments on an earlier draft of this introduction. My thanks and appreciation also go to my colleagues at Centro de Estudios Puertorriqueños at Hunter College (CUNY)—particularly the Centro's Library staff and the Research Group—for their support and encouragement. José Camacho, the Centro's library cataloguer, deserves special thanks for helping me track the libraries that held copies of Capetillo's books. I also want to thank Nélida Pérez, Xavier Totti, and Esther Shapiro for their comments and critiques. My deep appreciation also goes to Juan José Baldrich who read one of the earliest drafts of the introduction, provided very valuable feedback, and suggested additional reading and sources during my research. Also, the participants of the "Gender and History Seminar" sponsored by the History Department at the University of Connecticut at Storrs—particularly Blanca Silvestrini and Karen Spalding—offered constructive comments and insights during a presentation in the Spring 2003. Melissa Colón must be thanked for her help as a research assistant on the early stages of this project. Jillian Baez and Raquel Otheguy also helped with library research and proofreading towards the end of the project. The funding for the translation was provided by a grant from the

Recovering the U.S. Hispanic Literary Heritage Program at Arte Público Press and the University of Houston. At Arte Público Press, my most sincere gratitude goes to publisher and scholar Nicolás Kanellos. His personal interest in seeing the work of Luisa Capetillo translated into English made it possible to obtain the matching funds needed to complete the translation of *Mi opinión*. Nicolás encouragement and understanding have been important reasons why this project has been completed. At Arte Público, I also want to thank Alejandra Balestra for all her logistical support with the mechanics of the Recovery grant. I also want to thank my family for all their love and support, especially my son Lucas Andrés, who learned to walk and run as I worked on this introduction and the recently born Juan Carlos. Finally, I want to thank my wife, Liliana M. Arabía, who loses sleep every time I miss a deadline—her sleep deprivation levels have increased significantly since I joined the Centro!—and thus encourages me to get my work done on time and with pride.

Luisa Capetillo (1879–1922): Short Biographical Sketch

Although Luisa Capetillo was recognized in her lifetime as an important labor and feminist pioneer in the Americas—one of her essays was included in a 1921 anthology of leading international feminist and radical figures, such as Clara Zetkin, Roxa Luxemburg, and Emma Goldman, published in Argentina—there has been little historical writing about her life and work.[9] Currently, for instance, there is only one biography of Capetillo available (Valle Ferrer, *Historia*).[10] Most of what we know about Capetillo's life comes from three decades of research by Norma Valle Ferrer and from several autobiographical passages found in *Mi opinión* and in other of Capetillo's writings.

Luisa Capetillo was born out of wedlock in the northern town of Arecibo, Puerto Rico, on October 28, 1879.[11] Arecibo was one of the largest urban enclaves in the island at the time and its port was the key outlet for the sugar and coffee exported from Puerto Rico's northern municipalities throughout the last three decades of the nineteenth century (Cubano 1990). Capetillo's mother, Luisa Margarita Perone, was a domestic of French ancestry. Her father was Luis Capetillo Echevarria, an unskilled worker born in northern Spain. Perone initially came to Puerto Rico to work as a nanny or governess for the wealthy Zeno family in Arecibo. She later stopped working for the Zeno's and became a domestic. Luis Capetillo, who came from a financially stable family, tried fortune administering a traveling fair or bazaar company.[12] He was unsuccessful in this venture and continued to earn a living as a journeyman in agriculture, the dockyards, and construction. As a domestic, Perone did laundry for hire among Arecibo's wealthy families. Although we do not have much information regarding how the couple fell in love, they remained together—if unmarried—until 1901 and raised their only daughter, Luisa.

Capetillo's mother made sure that her daughter received a solid education at home and encouraged her interest in literature. Although both of Capetillo's parents were workers, they retained from their European ancestry a desire to partake in literary affairs. Perone religiously attended a daily literary *tertulia* held at the Café Misisipi in Arecibo (Valle Ferrer, *Historia* 44). Foreshadowing some of her daughter's future experiences, Perone was the only woman in attendance at those literary gatherings and was recognized by the participants as an extraordinary woman. Both Perone and Luis Capetillo instilled in their daughter Luisa a passion for books and took great pride in teaching her arithmetic, reading, and grammar at a time when the education for girls, if available, was focused on preparing them for domestic chores. In Arecibo, Capetillo attended a school for girls run by María Sierra Soler, where she won numerous student awards (Valle Ferrer, *Historia* 46). Still, it was her parents who encouraged Capetillo to read European writers such as Victor Hugo, Leo Tolstoy, and Emile Zola at an early age. When away from her books, an adolescent Capetillo accompanied her mother to the homes of well-to-do families in Arecibo assisting in her domestic chores. The combination of life experience and exposure to world literature provided some of the foundations for Capetillo's later thoughts on class, gender, and power and would serve as Capetillo's source of knowledge and authority in her writings.

In 1898, at the age of nineteen, Capetillo gave birth to her first-born, Manuela. Since her teenage days, Capetillo had been courted by Manuel Ledesma, son of one the wealthiest families in Arecibo. Ledesma was the son of Gregorio Ledesma, marquis of Arecibo, and leader of the pro-Spanish conservative party, the Partido Incondicional Español, in Arecibo. Capetillo probably met the young Ledesma while accompanying her mother in one of the many rounds of laundry work that Margarita Perone performed among elite Arecibo families. According to Capetillo's biographer, Ledesma and Capetillo had become lovers by 1897 (Valle Ferrer, *Historia* 54). The couple never married, but had another baby son, Gregorio, in 1900. By all accounts, it seems that Capetillo and Ledesma had a relationship constructed along the traditional gender roles of the time. Capetillo's writings made references to both her deep frustration with playing the traditional wife role and also her profound love for Ledesma, who insisted on her staying home even while he meandered at night with friends and mistresses (Suárez Findlay 159). Because of her lower-class status, Capetillo was never accepted by Ledesma's family. Ledesma's mother seems to have been particularly opposed to the relationship (Capetillo 1911 186). After the couple broke up, Capetillo and her two children continued to live in Margarita Perone's house. This arrangement continued on as Capetillo became more active in the worker's movement and was forced often to be away from her children attending political and labor activities.

Capetillo and Ledesma had definitely separated by 1901. Still, Ledesma, who later became mayor of Arecibo, legally recognized both Manuela and Gregorio and provided financially for them (Valle Ferrer, *Historia* 56). As Capetillo became more involved in labor and political affairs, the children remained under the care of their maternal grandmother Margarita Perone. In spite of this, Manuela and Gregorio throughout their lives interacted with both sides of their family and were not marginalized by Ledesma's relatives. Capetillo worked in the garment industry during this stage of her life.

Puerto Rico ceased being a Spanish colony after the 1898 war. Although Puerto Ricans were never clear about the U.S. intentions for the island, they had high expectations with regard to the changes that the new imperial power would facilitate for them. Most, irrespective of their political ideology, were initially disappointed at the consolidation of a colonial government in the island and subsequently frustrated at the lack of attention and respect that the U.S. government seemed to give to Puerto Rican affairs (Picó, *La guerra;* Cabán). The U.S. did make sure that Puerto Rico's financial and commercial infrastructure would be upgraded to facilitate the growth and export of two crops in high demand: sugar and tobacco. Although other improvements followed in those early decades of the twentieth century, social and economic indicators pointed to persistent poverty, violence, and stagnation for the average Puerto Rican (Picó, *Los gallos;* Santiago-Valles). Still, one of the most significant developments of the new U.S. colonial regime in Puerto Rico after the 1898 invasion was the rise and prominence of organized labor.

Capetillo became active in the Federación Libre de Trabajadores (FLT—Free Federation of Workers) since its inception in 1899. The FLT was Puerto Rico's most important labor organization throughout the first three decades of the twentieth century, and Capetillo figured as one of its more prominent leaders. Although workers were dissatisfied with working conditions and wages, they were able to organize unions under the new colonial regime, something that had been prohibited by law under Spanish rule. Organized labor—represented mostly by artisans and skilled workers, such as cigar makers—took advantage of U.S. laws and quickly organized the Federación Regional de Trabajadores in 1898. This organization split in 1899 and the Federación Libre de Trabajadores was born under the leadership of Santiago Iglesias Pantín. The FLT did not want political parties meddling with labor unions, so they created their own party, the Partido Obrero Socialista (POS—Socialist Workers' Party) as a buffer against partisan politics. Both the FLT and the party became aligned with the Socialist Labor Party in the U.S. and with the American Federation of Labor. Iglesias Pantín became a key ally of Samuel Gompers and his representative in Puerto Rico and Cuba. In 1915, the FLT decided to reorganize its political arm and the Partido Socialista (PS) was founded. Both the FLT and Partido Socialista played a key role in Puerto Rico's political life during the first three decades of the twentieth century. Several Socialist leaders were elected to positions in local government and Iglesias Pantín even served as Resident Commissioner in Washington DC—Puerto Rico's non-voting delegate in the U.S. House of Representatives—between 1933–39 (Quintero Rivera and García, Azize, Cabán, Bird Carmona).

At that time, Capetillo worked in cigar factories in Arecibo. Arecibo was one of the towns in Puerto Rico with the highest percentage of unions and union members and was one of the municipalities where the POS and the Socialist Party managed to win several elections (Valle Ferrer, *Historia* 67). In Arecibo and in other cigar factories throughout the Island, it was not uncommon to find female workers. Besides domestic work, employment in cigar factories as stemstrippers or leaf strippers became the second most important source of work for Puerto Rican women in the early decades of the twentieth-century (Baldrich 108–109). Women had been working in this industry in small cigar factories or in smaller family-operated shops since the nineteenth century (Matos Rodríguez, *Women* 81). So, while it was not unusual to find women working in cigar factories, it was not usual to have women as "readers" in the factories. Capetillo became one such reader in Arecibo's factories, paid by cigar-workers to read novels, philosophical and political essays, and other writings aloud as they prepared the cigars. The reader job was among the most prestigious ones among turn-of-the-century cigar workers in the US and the Caribbean.

Scholars such as Julio Ramos have stressed the importance of Capetillo's role as a reader to understanding and valuing the contributions of her writing and its role in early twentieth century Puerto Rican literature. Being a reader was an extremely prestigious public role for a worker and one that immediately placed them among the worker's elite (Rodríguez). Readers also had to face factory owners who historically disdained them and tried to either eliminate their positions or to severely limit the number of hours they could read (Ramos 24–27). The reader's job required the ability to project one's voice for several hours in cigar factories that were big in size and housed large numbers of workers. It is not surprising then that Capetillo became such a feisty and sought-after public speaker at political rallies, since her experience as a reader seasoned her oratory skills. Capetillo's role as a reader also put her in contact with some of the most important political, philosophical, and literary works coming from Europe and other parts of the world, as well as with local news and world events that the cigar workers wanted to be informed about immediately. This body of readings helped to form the core of Capetillo's theoretical and political thinking. Some of the authors who either appear quoted or were clearly influential in her writing include Kropotkin, Bakunin, Tolstoy, Malatesta, Zola, Voltaire, Maupassant, Vernet, Kardec, and Malato, to name a few (Dávila Santiago, *Teatro;* Valle Ferrer, *Historia,* Ramos).

When she was not reading to her fellow "tabaqueros" in the factory, Capetillo was out helping to organize workers, attending and speaking at rallies, and participating in strikes. She was active in a 1905 strike by agricultural workers in Arecibo and other northern municipalities organized by the FLT (Valle Ferrer, *Historia* 62). She gained the respect and trust of fellow labor leaders by her relentless activism, fiery oratory skills, and her proselytizing work. Throughout her life, Capetillo continued to travel across the island to participate in rallies, meetings, and strikes. In 1909, for example, she was very active in "La Cruzada del Ideal" a massive FLT-driven initiative to gain workers' support through meetings and events that introduced workers to the union's policies and objectives. It was also a recruitment drive for the FLT. During the crusade, Capetillo was manhandled and beaten by the police at several of the strikes or rallies she participated in. Several years later, in 1917, she was clubbed by police agents in Patillas who tried to break a strike by agricultural workers in which Capetillo played a leading role. Capetillo was also beaten and arrested when she participated—she was a political organizer in the towns on Puerto Rico's eastern side—in the massive agricultural strike of 1918, one that caused sizeable concern among U.S. colonial officials in Puerto Rico (Valle Ferrer 1990: 91). A strike in Vieques in 1919 also won Capetillo several beatings by scabs hired by the owners of the sugar mills.

In 1904, Capetillo started what later became a lifelong endeavor: writing short pieces for labor newspapers and magazines. She became a frequent collaborator in the important working-class newspaper *Unión Obrera* (Valle Ferrer, *Historia* 63). Capetillo's first book, *Ensayos libertarios,* was published in 1907 and combined many of the themes Capetillo had been addressing in her articles and in her work as an FLT organizer. The book engaged the socialist and anarchist discourses familiar to the Puerto Rican and international working class and displayed her views on a just society free from capitalist and sexual exploitation. Capetillo argued that the most effective tool for workers to enact real change was union organizing and activism. Other themes that will be more developed in Capetillo's subsequent writings are already present in *Ensayos libertinos*: anti-clericalism; spiritist beliefs; internationalism; and free love. Through her life, Capetillo continued her activism and writing on behalf of the FLT, which she considered the most effective vehicle for the achievement of working-class goals. In 1909, she founded a short-lived feminist working-class magazine called *La Mujer* and moved to Puerto Rico's capital, San Juan. Unfortunately, researchers have not been able to find any remaining copies of the magazine (Ramos 34).

In 1910, Capetillo published a utopian book *La humanidad del futuro* that contains two essays. The first and lengthier of the essays is the one that gives the book its title and was written as a way to raise funds for Capetillo's struggling magazine, *La Mujer* (Valle Ferrer, *Historia* 70). The essay is centered on the concept of a general strike as developed by anarchists and syndicalists. It presents a utopian modern society that emerged out of a general strike initiated by a small group of workers and peasants and then managed by a Strike Committee and sustained on the basis of mutual aid and cooperatives. The second and shorter essay of the book is entitled "La educación moderna" and addresses the issue of what a modern, scientific education should be based on. Also in 1910, Capetillo wrote

Verdad y justicia; cuento de Navidad para niños, a Christmas children's story denouncing social injustice for the working classes, according to literary historian Josefina Rivera de Álvarez (291–92). Although none of the secondary sources reviewed for this study makes a reference to this children's story, Capetillo alludes to having written this for her children while traveling in the FLT's "Cruzada del Ideal" (Capetillo, 1911 179).

Capetillo published her most important and influential book, *Mi opinión* in 1911. This book is considered the first feminist treatise in Puerto Rico and one of the very first in Latin America and the Caribbean.[13] I will comment more on the book's content and impact on the last section of this introductory essay. By the second decade of the century, Capetillo was a well-known figure both in Puerto Rico's labor movement and also among literary and feminist circles. She exchanged ideas, for example, with fellow writer and suffragist Ana Roqué. Although they found some common ground on the issues of suffrage and equality in the workplace, Capetillo was disappointed at Roqué's rejection of free love and sexual equality doctrines.[14] Still, even while Capetillo had access to the Island's intelligentsia, she felt frustrated by the lack of attention to her ideas by both members of organized labor and by feminists (Suárez Findlay. 164).

Besides the central focus of *Mi opinión*—the need for a workers' revolution and ending the exploitation and subordination of women—one of the other important features in the book was its defense of "espiritismo" (spiritualism). Recent studies have shown that spiritist's ideas—particularly those influenced by the French writer Allan Kardec—were widely disseminated in Puerto Rico during the early decades of the twentieth century. Furthermore, women played an important role in Puerto Rico's spiritist movement and used it to advance their feminist agenda and to increase their visibility on the public sphere (Herzig Shannon). Spiritists in Puerto Rico were also on the side of many modernizing "reform" agendas such as prison reform, opposition to the death penalty, and prohibition, among many others (Herzig Shannon 62–70). One of the key features of the spiritist doctrine—which certainly struck a cord in

Capetillo's own thinking—was its demand for accentuating women's prominent role and special mission as vehicles for the improvement of the family and thus of society.

It is interesting that although Capetillo probably produced the first systematic publishing regarding women's rights and emancipation in Puerto Rico's history, she was not in the forefront of one of the more visible feminists crusades of the early twentieth century: female suffrage. This issue captured most of the energies and attention of many early twentieth century feminists in Puerto Rico. Capetillo was on record as a supporter of universal women's suffrage. In 1908, in a FLT general assembly held in Arecibo, she strongly defended the inclusion of universal female suffrage as one of the causes to be included and advocated for in the union's agenda (Valle Ferrer, *Historia* 68). She rejected the idea of limited suffrage based on education and/or income that was supported by many professional and upper-class women and men in Puerto Rico at the time. Still, while fellow working-class feminists and bourgeois feminists met on several occasions to advance the cause of female suffrage— although not agreeing on whether to pursue a more or less inclusive type of suffrage—Capetillo always managed to be absent at these conventions, including the first "Congreso de Mujeres Trabajadoras" (Congress of Working Women) in 1919. Capetillo also failed to address the issue of female suffrage in most of her writings. The only two references I have found to female suffrage are in the 1913 edition of *Mi opinión*. The first reference is to European suffragists burning museums and art galleries because these institutions were founded upon and perpetuated sexist values. The second is a brief reference to a conversation with Ana Roqué.[15] For Capetillo, the key struggle was waged through the efforts of the labor movement and that is why female suffrage is underplayed in her writings. Capetillo, influenced by anarchist beliefs in the ineffectiveness of voting, concentrated her efforts on organizing strikes and disseminating propaganda.[16] Literate women got the right to vote in Puerto Rico in 1929 and universal suffrage was finally enacted in 1935.

In 1912, Capetillo began her work as an international labor intellectual and organizer. She moved to New York and worked closely with the Hispanic labor press and publications such as *Brazo y Cerebro* and *Fuerza Consciente*.[17] Capetillo's move to New York coincided with a systematic repression of anarchists orchestrated by the local Puerto Rican government between 1911 and 1912 (Suárez Findlay 165). Anarchist leaders were imprisoned, study centers were closed, and printed materials were confiscated during these repressive years. Capetillo probably joined many anarchist leaders who were forced to migrate in order to avoid being arrested or harassed. In New York, a small but growing Puerto Rican community existed since the mid-nineteenth century comprised of individuals displaced by a combination of the existing commercial ties between the city and the island and the vicissitudes of an anti-colonial struggle against Spain. Some of the initial Puerto Rican enclaves in New York City included the Navy Yard and Borough Hall areas in Brooklyn, the Lower East Side, Chelsea, sections of the West Side, and East Harlem. A significant part of that community was made up by Puerto Rican cigar workers who worked in factories sprinkled throughout Manhattan (Vega).

Capetillo's commitment to working class issues led her in 1912 to collaborate with Cuban, Spanish, Italian, and African-American cigar workers in Ybor City and Tampa. The Tampa region had seen several migratory waves of Cubans—and Spaniards and Puerto Ricans in lesser numbers—since the Ten Year's War (1868–78) seriously disrupted the Cuban economy (Poyo, Hewitt, Pozetta). Also, many Cuban and Spanish cigar factory owners moved their operations to Tampa to avoid the economic and political uncertainty, to be closer to main markets for Cuban cigars in the Northeastern cities of the US, and to avoid paying punitive tariffs imposed by the US government on foreign cigars. As a result of this migration, a large number of Cuban cigar workers lived in Tampa and were very active in the labor movement and in socialist and anarchist politics in the Spanish Caribbean. In Tampa, female cigar workers had played an important role in the labor movement since the last decade of the nineteenth century. In a 1910 strike, for example, six women were arrested for blocking the entrance of strikebreakers and their case attracted significant attention in the US labor press (Hewitt, "Voice" 156). Capetillo was probably drawn to Tampa in 1913 for its mix of radical anarchist politics, its strong Latin population, the presence of cigar factories, and the strong reputation of female workers. Capetillo worked as a reader in a cigar factory and roomed in the house of a German family on Lamar Avenue, a few blocks away from Ybor City and Tampa's African-American business and commercial district (Hewitt, *Southern* 215).

Capetillo used her stay in Tampa to work on her writings, among other projects. She polished and significantly rewrote sections of *Mi opinión*, culminating in the 1913 edition of the book. The second edition contains several new sections dedicated to Cuban and Spanish personalities—including poet Ms. Eugenia Villalonga and baritone Abelardo Galindo—whom she met as a result of her stay in Tampa.[xviii] It is clear that her involvement in Tampa's intellectual and labor circles introduced Capetillo to numerous contacts in the Cuban community that would facilitate her subsequent trips to Cuba. While in Tampa, Capetillo also reworked the materials that would be published as *Influencias de las ideas modernas*, even when the book's anchor piece was originally written in Puerto Rico in 1907 (Sánchez González, *Boricua* 34).

In 1915, Capetillo moved to Havana, Cuba. During her stay in Cuba, Capetillo traveled through the country participating in numerous strikes and political rallies (Valle Ferrer, *Historia* 84–85). These were years of intense labor organizing in Cuba—the first National Workers Congress was held in Havana in 1914—and of opposition to the unconstitutional attempts by conservative President Mario G. Menocal to obtain a second term in office (Pérez 216–28, 241). While in Cuba, Capetillo experienced an incident that would seal her notoriety among the Spanish Caribbean world. On July 24, 1915 Capetillo was arrested and subsequently acquitted for wearing trousers in public, considered at the time to be exclusively men's clothing. This should not have been surprising, since Capetillo had advocated in her writings for the practice of women using trousers and pants as a sign of female progress (1911 150). Shortly after her arrest, the judge had to accept that no law existed that barred Capetillo from wearing trousers and was forced to set Capetillo free (Valle Ferrer, *Historia* 85). One of Cuba's leading newspapers, *El Día*, published a picture of Capetillo wearing her "male" outfit prior to her arrest (Ramos 11). Capetillo continued the practice of wearing men's trousers in public events—a practice she had started prior to this incident in Havana—as a result of the publicity generated by her experience in Havana. In 1916, Capetillo was deported by President Menocal for her syndicalist and anarchist activities in Cuba.

Back in Puerto Rico, Capetillo published her fourth and final book, *Influencias de las ideas modernas. Notas y Apuntes. Escenas de la vida.* Although the book was published in Puerto Rico in 1916, the project had been gestating since her days in Tampa. The book's goal is "to continue my propaganda on behalf of women's freedom in all its manifestations in life." It reinforces and expands on many of the themes explored in *Mi opinión. Influencias* is composed of a three-act play "Influencia de las ideas modernas," (The Influence of Modern Ideas) a section of notes and reflections; an exchange of letters with a Panamanian anarchist; another play entitled "La corrupción de los ricos y la de los pobres" (The corruption of rich and poor); a short play "En el campo, amor libre" (In the Countryside: Free Love); and, a final comedy called "Después de muerta"(After Death). The book was intended to help raise funds for her Escuela Granja Agrícola (Agricultural School/Farm).

Throughout the 1910's, Capetillo became very interested in developing an education project she had conceptualized during her years as a labor organizer. She called the project Escuela Granja Agrícola and its objective was to create educational camps for children where they would be trained in agricultural skills while developing leadership expertise and receiving a traditional education (Rivera de Álvarez 290–91). Capetillo hoped that this project would help to ameliorate poverty and lack of educational and work opportunities faced by rural children. Her vision for the project was a pan-Caribbean one, as she saw "granjas" being established not only in

Puerto Rico, but also in Cuba and the Dominican Republic. In her prologue to *Influencias de las ideas modernas,* Capetillo announced that any funds generated from her writing and other activities would be destined for the project (4). She tried to convince U.S. labor leader Samuel Gompers and Puerto Rican labor leader Santiago Iglesias Pantín to support the project, but neither showed much interest in Capetillo's idea (Valle Ferrer, *Historia* 94). Ultimately, Capetillo was unsuccessful in attracting philanthropic and political support for her project.

As mentioned before, between 1916 and 1919 Capetillo very actively organized and participated in strikes and collaborated with working-class newspapers and magazines. These were years of significant labor unrest on the Island. In the cigar industry, for example, there were a significant number of strikes between 1917–18 caused by the changes in the industry and the attempts by owners to decrease real wages and decimate traditional union leadership (Rivera-Giusti, Baldrich 110–120). Between 1917–1918, for example, some forty-five thousand workers from the sugar industry, cigar-manufacturing industry, and the dockyards were involved in approximately eighty-eight strikes or stoppages throughout the island. Between 1919 and 1921, some thirty-two thousand workers participated in more than one hundred strikes (Santiago-Valles 117–118).

Capetillo was also vigorously promoting her books during those years. In 1917, for example, the editors from the newspaper *Brisas del Caribe* in Guánica reported—under the heading "Luisa Capetillo: Tireless Propagandist and Defender of Women"—on a visit by Capetillo to their offices to promote *Influencias* and her Escuela Granja Agrícola project. The editors were pleased to be visited by someone they described as a "tireless defender of women." Still, after a lengthy conversation between Capetillo and the newspaper's editorial staff, the editors from *Brisas del Caribe* wished her well on "her noble enterprise" while clarifying that they "did not agree at all" with any of Capetillo's ideas.[19]

Capetillo's visit to Guánica—an area of substantial labor organizing and mobilization—also prompted a three part series written by

Brisas del Caribe's editor in response to her writings. In the second article, although the editor agrees that women have made considerable advances in joining the professional ranks, he objects to Capetillo's suggestion that women should be active in politics.[20] Women's feminine side would be corrupted and ruined if she participated in the viciousness of political life. It would also take away from her role as key guardian of the family and home life, according to the editors. In the third and final article, *Brisas del Caribe's* editor attacks Capetillo's notion of "free love." For him, only prostitutes would be persuaded by Capetillo's calls for women to be able to express their sexuality more openly and to have more egalitarian structures in marriage. For the editor, women were "free in society, only a slave to duty; embodiment of the household, the procreation of the family, and devotion to her husband."[21] Capetillo issued a brief response to the articles on the newspaper's April twenty-fifth issue. In an article entitled "For Women: A response to *Brisas del Caribe*," Capetillo starts by thanking the editor for his interest in her writings and proceeds to clarify some of the issues he raised.[22] She argues that it was man and not nature who placed women in a subordinate role in society. Capetillo connects the ability of women to provide the gift of life as a sign of their physical, intellectual, emotional, and moral strength and one that men could not even aspire to. She quotes some passages from *Mi opinión* to document the important physical and intellectual roles females play in some species as a sign of nature's intention for equality for women. It was a very concise defense by Capetillo, but we have no way of knowing if the editorial staff made any changes or deleted sections of Capetillo's response, or if what was published was exactly what Capetillo submitted.

Capetillo moved back to New York City in 1919–20 where she ran a hostel, continued to serve as a reader in cigar factories, and kept writing for the local Spanish press. Bernardo Vega, one of the chroniclers of New York's Puerto Rican community at the start of the twentieth century, commented that Capetillo ran a boarding house located on Twenty-second street and Eighth Avenue and that the establishment was well known in the community due to Capetillo's generosity and superlative cooking skills (Vega 107). Running the boarding house did not prevent Capetillo from remaining active in advocating her anarchist and feminist ideals in local organizations and through the Spanish press.

Through her work and travels, Capetillo tried to remain close to her children. Contact with her daughter Manuela became increasingly complicated through time. After her father Manuel Ledesma interned her in a Catholic girl's school—Colegio de la Inmaculada Concepción, located in the town of Manatí—the nuns running the school destroyed or censored the correspondence between Manuela and her mother (Valle Ferrer, *Historia* 57). The nuns considered Capetillo's influence over her daughter undesirable and dangerous. Capetillo regretted having consented to her daughter entering the school (1911 97). After Manuela married, at a very young age, her husband prohibited Capetillo from visiting their house. Manuela's husband considered his mother-in-law to be a radical and suspicious person and a bad role model for Manuela (Valle Ferrer, *Historia* 57). Capetillo was able to have more contact with her son Gregorio, with whom she corresponded often. She also mailed him clothing and other gifts while traveling. Capetillo also bore a third child, Luis, out of a relationship she had with a pharmacist in Arecibo (Valle Ferrer, *Historia* 72–73). The pharmacist, who was already married, refused to recognize the child. Luis remained close to Capetillo during the later years of her life and was with her at the time of her death.

Luisa Capetillo returned to Puerto Rico in 1920 and moved to the new working-class barrio of Buen Consejo in Río Piedras. She had dreams of starting her "Granja" project in that neighborhood (Rivera de Álvarez 291). Capetillo was active in the 1920 campaign supporting the Socialist Party and the candidacy of her friend Santiago Iglesias Pantín (Valle Ferrer, *Historia* 95). By 1922, she had developed a bad case of tuberculosis, a disease she had contracted while in the United States. Ironically, tuberculosis was a disease that affected and killed many cigar workers and one of the many health hazards that labor leaders like Capetillo struggled to eliminate as they argued for better working conditions in cigar factories (Cooper 100–102). Capetillo died in the San

Juan municipal hospital, at the age of 43, on April 10, 1922. Capetillo
was buried in the Río Piedras municipal cemetery a day after her death.
Only a handful of family members, including her son Luis, and labor
leaders attended her burial (Valle Ferrer, *Historia* 95–96).

The Historiography of Luisa Capetillo.

Although one can find scattered printed references to Luisa
Capetillo's literary and political work prior to the 1960s, it is the
interest in labor and women's history of the 1970s that rescued her
figure from historical obscurity.[23] With the surge of the "Nueva Historia"—as the new paradigm in Puerto Rican history and the social
sciences was branded in the 1970s—some of the first references to
Capetillo appeared in the work of scholars exploring working class
history and culture such as Angel Quintero Rivera, Isabel Picó,
Ruben Dávila Santiago, and Marcia Quintero Rivera (Matos
Rodríguez, *Women* 12–19). These and other authors often prepared
conference papers for university symposiums or for events sponsored by the Centro de Estudios de la Realidad Puertorriqueña
(CEREP), one of the pioneering institutions in the analysis and dissemination of working-class history in Puerto Rico during the 1970s.
One of CEREP's earliest publications was an anthology document-
ing working class history and culture edited by Angel Quintero
Rivera in 1971. This anthology included several brief excerpts from
Mi opinión (Quintero Rivera 34–42). Many of the papers and bibli-
ographies prepared by CEREP members and others became anthologies and full-length monographs published in the late 1970s and
1980s. In 1973, another anthology of Puerto Rican women's writings included a significant excerpt from *Mi opinión*.[24]

In 1975, journalist Norma Valle Ferrer published a small biography of Capetillo. This was one of the first inquiries into the life of
the labor and feminist leader, and one that would culminate in Valle
Ferrer's lengthier biographical study published in 1990.[25] Valle Ferrer combined a close reading of Capetillo's texts with notes from an
unpublished journal, some letters she obtained from Capetillo's family, and research on ecclesiastical archives; in addition to relying on

the growing literature regarding Puerto Rico's turn-of-the-century labor movement. Valle Ferrer's biography remains the most authoritative study on Capetillo's life to date.

Other scholarly references to Capetillo's labor movement participation and her writings appeared in several essays published in the anthology edited by Edna Acosta-Belén, *The Puerto Rican Women: Perspectives on Culture, History, and Society* in 1979.[26] In this anthology, Isabel Picó, Blanca Silvestrini, and Valle Ferrer all include small references to Capetillo in their essays. Picó provides a historiographical account of women's political struggles to achieve equality and parity in Puerto Rican society.[27] Capetillo is presented as the best exponent of the working-class ideology that equated female emancipation with an end to their oppression as workers. In this essay, Picó also proclaims *Influencias*—Capetillo's last book— as "a collection of essays which could well be considered the first 'women's lib' manifesto in Puerto Rico" (Picó 1986 53). Silvestrini's essay analyzed the participation of women as workers and their role in politics during the turbulent 1930s decade. Discussing the antecedents of 1930's working-class feminism, Silvestrini highlights the figure of Capetillo and the importance of her writings, particularly *Mi opinión*. The fact that Capetillo also called attention to the oppression that elite and middle class women brought on their working-class "sisters" was, according to Silvestrini, one of Capetillo's main contributions to the women's movement (64). Oddly enough, of the three authors mentioning Capetillo in the anthology, Valle Ferrer was the one who dedicated the least amount of time to Capetillo. She only makes a brief reference to the fact that it was Capetillo who pushed the FLT in 1908 to embrace support for universal female suffrage although she never received proper credit for it (78).

In 1979, Yamila Azize published *La mujer en la lucha,* a very important text in the development of Women Studies in Puerto Rico. The book tells the history of how Puerto Rican women became incorporated into the workforce from the nineteenth-century onwards with a particular emphasis on events occurring during the first three decades of the twentieth century. The author is concerned with what she considers is the erroneous portrayal of professional and middle-class feminists as being responsible for getting women the right to vote in Puerto Rico. To counter this perception, Azize documents the pioneering role of working-class feminists in the suffrage movement and the ties between these feminists and the labor movement (9–10). The author is also interested in recompiling some of the materials previously analyzed by those associated with CEREP regarding the incorporation of women into the labor force and the changes caused in Puerto Rico's economy as a result of the first decades of U.S. colonial rule and connecting that story with the one from the Puerto Rican feminist movement.[28]

Capetillo emerges in Azize's study as emblematic of working-class feminists in early twentieth-century Puerto Rico: eager to achieve universal suffrage, but also aware that her complete emancipation would only come with an overhaul of the social, economic, and cultural structures advocated by the labor movement (88, 166). The book chronicles Capetillo's positions as articulated in her four books: defense of anarchism; attack on the institution of marriage; profound anti-clericalism; advocacy of free love; accentuating the role of women as teachers both in the family and in schools; and emphasis on true social change (defined as the moment when the exploitation of women as both workers and women would end). Capetillo's story, believes Azize, had experienced a fate similar to that of history of the Puerto Rican working class. They both had been removed from the official and mainstream history books and their contributions to Puerto Rican society had been neglected (87–88). Azize's book is an attempt to set the record straight and to advance the history of those so-called "without history" which, in the context of Puerto Rican historiography in the 1970s, included workers and women.

Except for the publication of Valle Ferrer's expanded biography (1990) and the anthology edited by Julio Ramos (1992), there were no more significant interpretations of Capetillo's writings and politics published until the late 1990s.

In this decade, interest in the history of the Puerto Rican working class had subsided, and the traditional scholarship in Women's

Studies had shifted emphasis into areas like gender analysis and sexuality, for example (Matos Rodríguez, *Puerto Rican* 23–24, 27–32). A combination of these topics can be found in the path-breaking study by Eileen Suárez Findlay, *Imposing Decency: The Politics of Sexuality and Race in Puerto Rico, 1870–1920.* Capetillo's writings and political activity are used in this study as way to comment on the boundaries between labor discourse and politics on the one hand, and gender and sexuality on the other in turn-of-the-century Puerto Rico. Suárez Findlay accentuates Capetillo's importance in the formulation of sexual politics in Puerto Rico, arguing that even among the progressive circles of the early twentieth-century Puerto Rican labor movement no writer, except Capetillo, made radical sexual ethics a central political priority (160–61). Even Capetillo's own first book focuses more on restructuring production as the mechanism to advance female emancipation and freedom than on other issues more closely associated with feminism. In *Mi opinión,* and subsequently in *Influencias,* we find a shift in her anarchist thinking in which sexuality, particularly women's sexuality, becomes a political priority for the labor movement and central to any true radical agenda. So central was this topic to Capetillo that it eclipsed one of the more debated issues of her time: women's suffrage. Although Capetillo advocated for universal woman's suffrage within the FLT, she barely included any references to the issue in her writings.

One innovative aspect of Suárez Findlay's discussion of Capetillo's thinking is its attempt at measuring the responses of different groups to Capetillo's ideas on sexuality, politics, family, nation, religion, and health. Although there are very few archival sources that document the reception that Capetillo's speeches, newspaper articles, and books generated, Suárez Findlay suggests three possible scenarios, none of them being a very positive one for Capetillo (164–66). First, bourgeois feminists probably ignored her ideas, in part because of her call to reject their material goods and join the working-class to help advance the socialist revolution. Second, working-class women, particularly mothers, might have not been receptive to the idea of "free love" if it meant that their partners could leave at any time and disregard providing financial support to the family left behind. Third, men probably found Capetillo's calls for ending male dominance and her emphasis on sexual politics ridiculous. Capetillo did make a few references in her writings to facing cold receptions from men or having her work sabotaged intellectually, politically or financially (Suárez Findlay 164–65). The previously mentioned exchange with the publishers of *Brisas del Caribe* serves as an example of the type of reactions Capetillo faced throughout her life.

Suárez Findlay's work also demonstrates how the leadership of the labor movement during the early decades of the twentieth century used gendered discourse to maintain a patriarchal relationship over plebeian women. She argues that "in the end, the early labor movement activists retained solely the elements of the working-class discourse on sexuality that did not challenge workingmen's power over women" (204). Findlay thus breaks with the more traditional interpretations of the "Nueva Historia," which presented the labor movement and male workers not only as sympathetic and supportive of feminists claims made by fellow female workers, but also as part of a political and intellectual vanguard in Puerto Rico with respect to gender relations. Suárez Findlay's critique of previous interpretations of the convergence of labor and feminist discourse in early twentieth-century Puerto Rico has also been echoed by scholars such as Janer (1998) and Baerga Santini (1999). For them, Capetillo was an exception rather than the rule in terms of the labor movement's willingness to articulate and defend women's emancipation and equality.

One more recent work that analyzes Capetillo's political ideology is Ivette M. Rivera-Giusti's doctoral dissertation.[29] The larger context of her work analyzes and brings attention to working-class feminist writings from the first three decades of the twentieth century. Rivera-Giusti argues that it is fundamental to look at the experiences of women workers in the factories and in political events such as strikes and rallies to understand the development of a class identity expressed in a gendered language which was the core of working-class feminism (2003). Among the writers included in Rivera-

Giusti's study are Franca de Armiño, Josefa Maldonado, Antonia Lefebre, Carmen Puente and Genara Pagán. Most of these women have remained mostly invisible, perhaps included on some list of the most vocal early twentieth-century labor feminists, but never having their scant and difficult-to-locate writings seriously studied. In Capetillo's case, Rivera-Giusti sees her as representative of other working-class feminists who connected their maternal roles with their labor activism. These women argued that it was precisely their role as mothers in the domestic sphere that led to their activism in the labor movement as a way to strive for justice in the public sphere. Rivera-Giusti shows that Capetillo, like many of the feminists in her study, used articles in labor newspapers and journals and didactic short stories and plays to get her message across. One of the main features which unified Capetillo with other working-class feminists was their belief in the need for the true emancipation of women as indispensable for the disappearance of economic exploitation.

Although the history of Latin American feminism has received substantial attention in the last two decades, there are scant references to Luisa Capetillo in this literature.[30] This, despite the fact that Capetillo was included in feminist anthologies as early as the 1920s—such as the previously mentioned *Voces de Liberación* (1921)—and that Capetillo's writings were reprinted in labor and feminist newspapers in countries as far away as Argentina. A column commenting on the limitations imposed on women's sexuality by traditional marriages was published in the Argentine anarchist newspaper *Nuestra Tribuna* in June 1924 (Lavrin 133, 393).[31] Although there are several other earlier examples of feminist books published in Latin America during the late nineteenth century, Capetillo seems to be the first or among the very first in the Caribbean to have produced a book length treatise articulating feminist ideas (Miller, Stoner, *House;* Lavrin). This alone should have brought her more attention among those studying Latin American women and feminism.

Historians, of course, have not been the only ones interested in the study of Luisa Capetillo. Literary critics Josefina Rivera de Álvarez, for example, included Capetillo in her extensive *Dic-*

cionario de Literatura Puertorriqueña (1974).[32] Not many other serious inquiries into Capetillo's writings were available until 1992 when the study of Capetillo and her literary and political legacy received an important boost with the publication of Julio Ramos' *Amor y anarquía: Los escritos de Luisa Capetillo*.[33] The book is an anthology of selections from Capetillo's writing accompanied by a provoking introductory essay prepared by Ramos. Until Ramos' compilation of significant sections of Capetillo's works, her four books had never been re-issued since the late 1910s.

One of Ramos' main arguments is that Capetillo's works, and *Mi opinión* in particular, are among the best early examples of "hybrid and alternative discourse" in the Americas (58). Since Capetillo was not a trained academic, she was lacking in some of the literary tools available to learned scholars of the time. Her status as a woman, worker, and unwed mother further marginalized her. Like many other early Latin American feminists, Capetillo had to publish initially in the proletariat press partly because she did not have access to more traditional or established publication venues. Yet, writing for labor newspapers and in hastily produced pamphlets, was one of the many ways Capetillo displayed her political and class solidarity, even after she became well known in literary and political circles. Ramos believes that Capetillo's trajectory is an example of marginalized subaltern writing in the early twentieth century and is thus worthy of study and analysis (12–13).

According to Ramos, Capetillo was a woman who always challenged existing frontiers and often did so by engaging quotidian practices, such as the practice of wearing trousers (Ramos 11). She appropriated and manipulated the discourses and practices of others to cause instability and force change. As an author, Capetillo disputes the authority coming from universities and professional schools and postulates one emerging from lived experienced and intuition (Ramos 18). She also challenged unitary rules of purity within literary genres and accepted an extensive bibliography of works from different and divergent traditions as appropriate for the task of writing on behalf of the working-class and laboring women.

Capetillo's books show a willingness to use whatever literary genre connected best with the slice of everyday life she was depicting—women being abused by their husbands, factory owners limiting the rights of workers, or people attending a religious gathering—and thus her books are a collage of essays, plays, short stories, news clippings, translations, autobiographical notes, journal entries, letters, and essays. (Ramos 139). Her written work is very antinationalistic; she is not concerned with defining who is Puerto Rican and what is Puerto Rican (Ramos 49). Capetillo is more concerned with local problems or larger structural issues of class and gender oppression. Her prose has a marked oral syntax combined with non-essentialist writing that is always looking for alliances and for zones of contact (Ramos 43, 53). Following Ramos' lead, other authors such as Cristina Guzzo have presented Capetillo's work as a precursor of several postmodernist and poststructuralist positions. For Guzzo, the roots of Capetillo's avant-garde position come from what she describes as Capetillo's "anarchofeminism."

Another literary scholar, Zilkia Janer, has also studied Capetillo from the perspective of a subaltern writer. In her study regarding the role of subaltern intellectuals in the development of the national debate in Puerto Rico, Janer portrays Capetillo as emblematic of attempts to dismantle patriarchal structures within working-class intellectuals and writers, and also of replicating gender and other hierarchies in her works. Janer applauds Capetillo for providing some of the few female leading roles in working-class fiction and essays (145–47). In *Influencias*, a play inspired by Tolstoy, for example, the main character is Angelina, the daughter of a rich cigar factory owner. Janer, however, is critical of the play's message in which the workers advance to a perfect society as a result of the efforts of the factory owner and Angelina. "Like her male counterparts," writes Janer, "Capetillo gave herself a messianic role as an intellectual" (149). Janer also comments on Capetillo's writing on prostitution—a theme further developed in Suárez Findlay's study—as a mode of depicting class aggression. She praises Capetillo for "her careful attention to the discontinuities that class determined in women's struggles, and because she insisted on all women's right to control their life, freedom, and sexuality" (151).

The most recent scholarly interpretation of Capetillo's work has been done by literary critic Lisa Sánchez González. Sánchez González, in presenting a case and providing a history of what she describes as a distinct "Boricua" literary tradition among Puerto Rican writers in the U.S., argues that Capetillo, along with Arturo Schomburg, are the initial cornerstones of that literary tradition (*Boricua* 22–24). There are several important characteristics of this diasporic Boricua literary tradition according to Sánchez González. First, the author writes within a context of "forced exile and dual national identities and nationalist intellectual tradition" (*Boricua* 20). Also, writers need to be in a dialogue with their communities, often taking adversarial or controversial positions and not merely engaging in the practice of describing that community to outsiders or serving as their representative. This tension or "elaborate or elaborated threat from below to sacrosanct narratives of national and nationalist signification—not only to Puerto Rico's, but to the United States' as well" is one of the fundamental elements distinguishing early Boricua literature (*Boricua* 21). For Sánchez González, Capetillo's writings fit perfectly into her definition. Capetillo's feminism and anti-nationalism made her a pariah among the more traditional labor leaders in Puerto Rico. This led to Capetillo's disenchantment with the political and labor movement in Puerto Rico and caused her to pursue a more diasporic life among working-class folks in Cuba, Santo Domingo, New York and Tampa. Her writings reflect her frustrations with deeply entrenched nationalist and patriarchal paradigms within the communities she engaged: workers and migrants.

Although Sánchez González analyzes all four of Capetillo's publications, she concentrates on the last one, *Influencias de las ideas modernas,* published in 1916. For Sánchez González this book is not only the best example of Capetillo's mature thinking as a feminist, theorist, and fiction writer, but it also represents the perspective of exile as it was mostly composed during Capetillo's diasporic years (1912–1917) when she moved between Puerto Rico, Cuba,

New York City, and Tampa.[24] Sánchez González argues that in *Influencias* Capetillo had developed her feminist thinking past some of the more binary paradigms found in previous works. Also, Capetillo ended up relying more on works of fiction—particularly plays—to present her ideas because fiction allowed her the maximum range of creative expression at the time. Capetillo's fictional characters could behave, speak, and live in a way that was not possible for Capetillo to reproduce in either essays or letters that were the literary genres she had used in her previous publications. The complex logic of Capetillo's revolutionary ideas could be best expressed through fiction, according to Sánchez González (*Boricua* 37–39).

Capetillo is an ideal example of the literature produced by the "pionero" generation who migrated to the U.S. in the early decades of the twentieth century, according to Sánchez Gonzalez. She describes Capetillo's later writing as showing an "intransigent rejection of geopolitical, gendered, erotic, philosophical, and generic borders as obsolete concepts which suggests the kind of socially, ethically, sensually, and aesthetically engaged hermeneutics relevant to a community barred wealth and socio-symbolic status, in transit, from one stifling national context to another" (*Boricua* 40). It remains to be seen whether future scholars of Puerto Rican literary production in the U.S. will take Sánchez González's lead and embrace Capetillo as a pioneering figure in the formation of a Boricua literary corpus or whether they will continue to see her as mainly belonging to the "Island's" literary tradition. It is still not clear if statements from scholars such as historian Altagracia Ortiz—who argues in reference to Capetillo that "the biographies of these temporary residents are important, but those of women settled permanently in New York City during these years truly are historical prisms through which the cultural, social, and political development of the Puerto Rican people on this area can be traced"—are indicative of potential reactions to Sánchez Gonzalez's arguments rejecting the use of Capetillo as embodying the Puerto Rican diasporic experience (43).[35] The contradictions in Capetillo's works and political activism, also leave room for challenges to Sánchez González's reading of Capetillo's writings. Capetillo's unwavering support for Santiago Iglesias could be interpreted as running counter to her critique of nationalism and patriarchy, for example. Also, Capetillo did not spend a significant part of her life in the United States and her connections and quotidian involvement in communities in New York City and Tampa still need to be explored further. These reservations notwithstanding, Sánchez González must be credited with advancing the scholarship on Capetillo by providing a fresh and challenging perspective on her life and her writings.

"Mi opinión": Significance and Contribution to the Humanities.

Capetillo's *Mi opinión* provides a crossroads for the study of feminism, literature, labor history, immigration, intellectual history, and US-Caribbean relations at the turn of the twentieth century. The book is a collection of many heterogeneous materials—essays, translations, letters, pamphlets, newspaper articles, memoirs, and speeches—all woven into a single text. The book's central theme is the need for the liberation of women emphasizing the need for divorce legislation and the acceptance of "free love" as the guiding principle in heterosexual relationships. Women's oppression is part of the systematic subjugation enforced by the State and by unscrupulous businessmen. In *Mi opinión*, Capetillo makes a case for the need to change radically all structures of social and economic domination so women could be truly liberated. *Mi opinión* is also a comprehensive exposition that argues for a holistic approach to women's liberation by delving into areas such as sexuality, mental and physical health, hygiene, spirituality, nutrition, and political and economic rights. Although some of Capetillo's ideas on marriage and sexuality were clearly influenced by anarchism, her writing has a distinct local and quotidian focus. Like many of its contemporary feminist writings in the Americas, *Mi opinión* is a call for change and action in areas such as labor laws, education, marriage, and religion.

Capetillo stresses several key themes and ideals throughout *Mi opinión*: (1) her belief in anarchism; (2) the need to grant women more liberty and rights as a way to bring true equality in society; (3) the crucial role of women as mothers; (4) the need for women to achieve autonomy economically, intellectually and sexually; (5) the need for free love and an end to the institution of marriage as practiced at the time; (6) her belief in natural laws and wholesome life-practices like good nutrition, exercise, and hygiene; (7) her repudiation of churches, hypocritical political leaders, and capitalists; and, (8) her belief in spiritualism.

The book's preface clearly lays out its central message: that women should acquire more rights and freedom in order for society to advance to a more perfect and just state (1911 viii). The author makes a clear connection between what she calls the "ignorance" of the present system and its insistence on keeping women in a subordinate position and on the exploitation of workers. For Capetillo the "current social system, with all its errors, is sustained by the ignorance and slavery of women" (1911 viii).[26] The preface also provides Capetillo an immediate avenue to present her credentials. She states the sources of her knowledge and authority to speak publicly: her lived experience as a worker, woman, and mother. Her familiarity with the writings from international writers and activists; and her knowledge of international news regarding the debates on the changing status of women worldwide. As Julio Ramos has argued, Capetillo was aware that her lack of academic or "learned" credentials would have some challenge her authority. Still, she dismisses "the criticism of more experienced writers" and warns the audience about potential contradictions and inconsistencies in her positions (Capetillo, 1911 v).[37] These contradictions might result, according to Capetillo, from her struggle to reconcile theoretical paradigms with her lived experience in a hostile and volatile environment (1911 xi). The preface also introduces the importance of motherhood as a position of utmost consequence in society and as one of the vantage points that allows women to make more claims for justice and equality in society. It is from their position as mothers that women had a truly revolutionary opportunity to help reshape Puerto Rican society.

Immediately after setting some of her key themes in the preface, Capetillo provides one of the most important sections of the book entitled "Women in the home, the family and in government." Motherhood is at the center of the autonomy that Capetillo hopes women acquire so that they can elevate their personal and societal standing. In this section the author argues that the State should invest in the education of women because women, as mothers, provide the first and probably the most far-reaching schooling that children receive in their homes prior to starting in the school system (1911 11–14). Capetillo's argument at the time was not a new one in Puerto Rican society, as many had been demanding educational reforms, precisely on similar grounds, since the second half of the nineteenth century (Barceló Miller, *La lucha;* Matos Rodríguez, *Women*). But what was innovative in Capetillo's discourse was that the education for which she was advocating could not be just any type of education. Capetillo wanted an education that focused on "natural laws" and wisdom and thus ingrained in women the values of exercise, hygiene, nutrition, sexuality, health, honesty, and true love (3, 10, 29). She also wanted an education for women of all social classes, not just for the privileged elite. In this section, Capetillo also launches a critique of marriage as a loveless ritual based on starchy rules and social customs perpetuated by dominant groups, such as capitalists and priests, in order to be able to control and exploit women. "For me, marriage as currently practiced is an error" stated Capetillo boldly (28).[38] Men and women should be together and stay together only if they both truly love each other. Relationships based on love also entailed reciprocity and equality. For Capetillo, women had a special responsibility to enact changes on social customs that kept women in bondage, such as marriage (33). Capetillo discusses the need to distinguish between love, marriage and desire in a later section of the book by including a translation of a book on free love written by French feminist Magdalena Vernet (Capetillo, 1911 38–56). Capetillo believes, like the French author, that women have sexual needs just like men and that male-female relationships needed to take these needs seriously. Free love must be practiced within contexts of dignity, respect, and purity. From Vernet and other writers, Capetillo would get her ideals to propose what Suárez Findlay has called a "radical sexual ethics" at a time when virtually no one else was making these claims in Puerto Rico. Finally, in this section Capetillo also makes an appeal to bourgeois women to join female workers and all workers to end the exploitation of the proletariat. Although this might have seem as a contradictory request at first, Capetillo was convinced that even if rich women did enjoy a certain degree of more freedom compared to male and female workers, their structural subordination under patriarchy could only be abolished by a socialist revolution. Thus, for Capetillo it was in women's self-interest, even for affluent women, to support the "redemption of the Puerto Rican proletariat" (25).

Some of the sections that follow in *Mi opinión*—"On Free Love"; "Varieties"; and "On Honesty"—provide translations and clippings from important books or events which substantiate some of Capetillo's feminist and socialist positions. These sections provide Capetillo with the opportunity to demonstrate her vast culture and extensive knowledge of European, US, and Latin American authors and events as a way to counter critics who might challenge her intellectual credentials. It also provided the book an international flare that showed readers that Puerto Rico was not isolated and that change was occurring all throughout the world. This collection is an example of that hybrid and subaltern literary style suggested by Julio Ramos. In these sections, for example, Capetillo quotes reports and articles from Paris, Boston, and Barcelona in order to show the international dimensions of anarchist and feminist ideology and also to show the changes in the access of women to positions of power and prestige in other parts of the world. Capetillo wanted the same kind of modern change to occur in Puerto Rico.

Following the sections which focus on transcripts and reports from other authors in Europe and the Americas, Capetillo's writing in *Mi opinión* begins to take a more intimate turn. In the section titled "Natural Forces" Capetillo shares her awe for the sea and its mysteries. "What powerful admiration we have for the sea," she writes (Capetillo, 1911 80).[39] Capetillo also reveals her admiration for the concentrated power of the sun's rays. This fascination with the sun and light will also be echoed in a subsequent section of *Mi opinión*, where the author makes repeated references to the contrasts between light and shadows in her discussion of contradictory forces in nature (Capetillo, 1911 141, 142). She argues that these contrasts often create harmony in nature (Capetillo, 1911 141). This is Capetillo's lyrical side echoing mythological and classic literary references to the sea as a symbol of female power and sexuality and the sun as a symbol of maleness. It is also interesting that Capetillo would make so many references to "luz y sombra," (light and shadows) perhaps to signal her familiarity with the epistolary novel *Luz y sombra* published by feminist and suffragist Ana Roqué in 1903.[40] Roque's novel was also an indictment against the oppression women face in loveless and sexually unsatisfying marriages. In Roque's novel there are two lead female characters: Matilde, who lives in the world of light because she married her husband because of love, and Julia, who lives in the world of shadows because she is in a loveless and sexually unfulfilling marriage that ultimately leads her to consider committing adultery. Capetillo wanted to show she was familiar with Roque's writings and also with her political work on behalf of getting literate women the right to vote.

Following this section featuring her admiration for the sea and the sun, we find a segment dedicated to Capetillo's first-born: Manuela Ledesma Capetillo. In this section Capetillo states her hopes that her daughter, the result of "her only and sad love," be a "good human being," (Capetillo, 1911 83). The author also reinstates several of the already known components of her political philosophy—the belief in anarchism and natural laws, her disdain for churches and empty religious practices—while presenting some new topics. First, Capetillo affirms that she does not believe in violence and rejects the militaristic rhetoric of governments (89). Her non-violence convictions also lead her to oppose the death penalty. Capetillo also discusses her belief in spiritualism for the first time in *Mi opinión*, explaining that she believes in multiples lives and the immortality of the soul. Capetillo defends her position that spiritualism and anarchism are compatible as belief systems that promote progress and scientific reasoning.[41] She argues that those who criticize the incompatibility of spiritualism and anarchism are only familiar with the vulgar forms of spiritualism and with "fraudulent spiritists" who trick the poor, and support causes like the death penalty and anti-labor laws (105). As studies like Herzig Shannon's have shown, spiritists were among the most progressive political forces in Puerto Rico in the early twentieth century and women were very active among its leaders. Capetillo's spiritism must be understood within this framework of the progressive political action, scientific inquiry (even when dealing with religion), and a reaction against the dogmatic control of the Catholic Church.

Towards the middle of the book, Capetillo turns to sections praising and thanking women and men that have been helpful to her or have served as examples to her. She compliments her friend, the famous pianist and music teacher, Elisa Tavarez de Storer (156).[42] Tavarez de Storer came from a musically-gifted family, as she was the daughter of pianist and composer Manuel G. Tavarez (Hostos 466). Jurist and novelist Jacinto Texidor is praised for his novel *Los culpables*. In this novel the author argues against men that take advantage of women and thus soil the woman's virtue and honor. Capetillo takes advantage of this comment to ask rhetorically when the day will come that such abuse against women will cease. Tomás Carrión, a labor leader, is thanked for accompanying Capetillo in several rallies in Juana Díaz and Cabo Rojo and for helping her sell subscriptions for her magazine *La Mujer*. In all these brief sections Capetillo blurs the boundaries between the more private epistolary genre and the more formal essay form used to comment on literary and cultural events. She uses these sections to encourage those active in the labor struggle with her and to show her knowledge of current literary and artistic happenings in Puerto Rico.

The last three sections of the book—"My Profession of Faith—To Manuel Ugarte"; "Remembering the Free Federation—Impressions of a Trip July 1909"; and "For M.L.—Arecibo—Thinking of You"— serve as a way to reinforce several of the key motifs of the book.[43] "My Profession of Faith" serves as Capetillo's opportunity to reiterate her socialist and anarchist beliefs. She proclaims herself a socialist because she strives for a society where the advances of modernity and new technologies can benefit all and can be shared by all (163). Capetillo also reinstates her dislike of government and her anarchist belief in the need of little or no government. She also stresses that her beliefs are not utopian, as she considers socialism a "tangible and real truth" (164). Capetillo concludes the section accentuating the role played by universal fraternity as centerpiece of socialism.

"Remembering the Free Federation" combines an exposition of her political ideology with reflections and reminiscences of her participation in the FLT's "Cruzada del Ideal" in 1909. Throughout the section, Capetillo reinforces the need for embracing socialist and feminist ideals as the only way for the advancement of the proletariat. She documents some of the people she met while participating in the crusade and some of the criticisms she received for her socialist and anarchist ideas (173). In this section she also tells how she took time from her travel schedule to write the children's story "Verdad y Justicia" (Truth and justice) for her children (179). In addition, we get a glimpse in this section of how Capetillo tried to balance her duties as a mother with her work as a labor organizer.

The book closes on a profound personal note with the chapter entitled "For M.L" which presumably was written for Manuel Ledesma, Capetillo's first love. Here we find a personal account of how she experienced and understood "free love"—she tells her daughter that she was the product of "my spontaneous love without fetters, evasions, hypocrisies, and self-interest" (186).[44] This is not Capetillo telling others how to practice "free love" or providing her intellectual ponderings on the matter. This is Capetillo's lived experience and she is showing that, although her life has had its fair share of political and intellectual inconsistencies, she has tried hard to reconcile her beliefs and her life. She sets a final fatalistic tone in terms of her capacity to be able to love again with the same intensity she loved Ledesma—she has tried, and she has not been successful. It is ironic that an author who has been telling readers that socialism and that her program of beliefs are attainable and non-utopian, ends the book by saying that since no love has been able to measure up to what she experienced with Ledesma, she would wait for true love until her next existence (187). Perhaps the words describing her state as she gets ready to wait exemplify what Capetillo wants to convey to her readers: ". . . with a smile on my lips, entrenched in a supreme struggle, and with supreme calm" (187).[45] Capetillo's ideology is firmly grounded on continuous struggle and perseverance, on trial and error.

One of the most formidable elements of *Mi opinión* is that it documents the universal appeal of humanistic thinking in early twentieth century Puerto Rico. In this text Capetillo quotes freely from an eclectic set of sources including European feminist thinkers, Russian philosophers, US physicians, and Italian and Spanish anarchists. Capetillo's writing, a precursor to current forms of interdisciplinary scholarship, is a truly comprehensive treatise that analyzes the situation of Puerto Rican women by incorporating findings in ethics, philosophy, recreation and health, religion, nutrition, history, and politics to substantiate her arguments. Even while one might disagree with her beliefs and interpretations, *Mi opinión* shows that Capetillo as an author was convinced of the power of humanistic thought—in her case based on anarchism and feminism—as an effective tool to bring about change in the world. This belief in the transformative power of knowledge and of education is a constant theme in Capetillo's writing.

Mi opinión, which was reissued in Tampa in 1913, should be of interest to US labor, immigration, and intellectual historians and to literary critics. Capetillo was part of a mobile Hispanic-Caribbean, working-class, political culture that included several northern cities, such as New York and Philadelphia, as well as maritime-commercial enclaves like Tampa and New Orleans. Capetillo's participation in the working-class Hispanic press during the first two decades of the twentieth century mark her as one of the first Hispanic women to be active in this literary and activist enterprise. Her pioneering work, particularly *Mi opinión,* is illustrative of the hemispheric connections among feminists, intellectuals, and political activists in both the United States and in Latin America.

Midway through *Mi opinión*, Capetillo writes, "a final summing up: women are capable of everything and anything"(152).[xlvi]

Capetillo clearly showed her competency, originality, and force as a writer and thinker throughout the books she wrote and the life she lived. She wanted to open up an autonomous space for women and to make labor politicians focus on women's issues and on sexuality as central tenets of the revolutionary struggle that would help to end the exploitation of all, men and women alike. This is one of the most important aspects of Capetillo's legacy. *Mi opinión* is part of that legacy and it should be read by all those interested in the early twentieth century history of Puerto Rico and the Caribbean and in the history of feminism and labor in the Americas.

Notes

[1] Quote from the preface of the 1913 edition of Capetillo's, *Mi opinión; disertación sobre las libertades de la mujer. "Amor libre;" la mujer como compañera, madre y ser independiente en el hogar, la familia y en el gobierno.* 2nd edition. (Tampa: Imprenta de Joaquín Mascuñana, 1913).

[2] In 1992, literary critic Julio Ramos published the important anthology *Amor y anarquía: Los escritos de Luisa Capetillo* which included excerpts from the four books published by Capetillo. This was an invaluable contribution to the study of early twentieth-century Puerto Rican literature and history.

[3] An original copy of the 1911 edition is available at the Colección Puertorriqueña at the University of Puerto Rico's main library. The Centro de Estudios Puertorriqueños Library at Hunter College (CUNY) has a bound photocopy from the 1911 original at the University of Puerto Rico. The Recovering the U.S. Hispanic Literary Heritage Project has a bound photocopy of the 1911 edition. The New York Public Library has a microfilmed copy of the 1913 edition, which has a slightly modified title: *Mi opinión disertación sobre las libertades de la mujer. "Amor libre." La mujer como compañera, madre y ser independiente en el hogar, la familia y el gobierno.* Nancy Hewitt also notes that a copy of the 1913 edition is at the El Centro Asturiano library in Tampa (2001: 322). I was unable to verify this information.

[4] The translated selections in Quintero Rivera's 1976 anthology, for example, come from this edition.

[5] *Mi opinión* (1913) 7.

[6] *Mi opinión* (1913) 37–43, 150–161.

[7] Her references to what a "persona educada" is appears in *Mi opinión* (1913) 19–21. Her comments about academic writing are found in page 166.

[8] *Mi opinión* (1913) 1–4.

[9] According to Valle Ferrer (*Historia* 83), the book was published as *Voces de Liberación* by the Editorial Lux in Buenos Aires in 1921. Capetillo's essay was originally published in the labor newspaper *Cultura Obrera* in New York City.

[10]An English version of Valle Ferrer's biography is currently in press. See, *The Story of Luisa Capetillo, a Pioneer Puerto Rican Feminist* (New York: Peter Lang Publishers, 2003).

[11]Josefina Rivera de Alvarado incorrectly gives her year of birth as 1883. See, her *Diccionario de Literatura Puertorriqueña*; vol. 1 (San Juan: Instituto de Cultura Puertorriqueña, 1974) 292. Ramos dates her birth both in 1879 and 1876 (17, 65). I assume 1876 was a typographical error.

[12]Luis Capetillo had two siblings: a brother (Antonio) and a sister (Rafaela). Their family claimed that the Capetillo last name was originally French. They were related to the businessman and conservative leader Pablo Ubarri Capetillo, Count of Santurce and executor of Rafaela's will and estate (Valle Ferrer, *Historia* 40).

[13]For some scholars such as Sánchez Gonzales and Isabel Picó, Capetillo's most influential and important book is *Influencias de las ideas modernas* (1916). They believe that this is a more seasoned and mature text and that it provides the best example of how Capetillo's thinking had evolved around issues of feminism, anarchism, socialism, religion, and family-life. Although I also agree that *Influencias* is the most mature example of Capetillo's writing, the fact that *Mi opinión* was the first published feminist treatise in Puerto Rico makes it Capetillo's most important work. It is also the one quoted and analyzed the most often by those who have studied Capetillo.

[14]See *Mi Opinión* (1913) 163. On the issue of women's suffrage, Capetillo supported universal female suffrage while Roqué favored limiting the right to vote to literate and educated women.

[15]See *Mi opinión* (1913) 157, 163. Interestingly, the New York Public Library copy is dedicated by Capetillo to "the cultured and intelligent ladies of the brave Association to the Right of Suffrage, in their presentation to the distinguished Ms. Mary Wame Demeth."

[16]Capetillo still supported the Partido Socialista and Iglesisas Pantín throughout her life.

[17]Jaime Vidal, Preface, *Mi opinión* (1913) 1.

[18]*Mi opinión* (1913) 162, 179.

[19]*Brisas del Caribe* 17 feb. 1917, Year 2, #XIV: 1. The newspaper is available in microfilm at the Centro de Investigaciones Históricas, University of Puerto Rico-Río Piedras. The translation is mine. I want to thank Humberto García-Muñiz for alerting me to the content of this newspaper and the references to Capetillo.

[20]We were not able to find the first article of the series "Por el Fondo: La libertad de la mujer." The second article is found in *Brisas del Caribe*, 28 feb. 1917, Year 2, #XVII: 2.

[21]*Brisas del Caribe* 28 Feb. 1917, Year 2, # XVII: 2.

[22]*Brisas del Caribe* Apr. 1917, Year 2, # XXXIII: 1.

[23]It is interesting, for example, that a 1972 publication about influential women in Puerto Rico's history, targeted for a general audience, did not include a single reference to Capetillo even when it included dozens of other biographical sketches from other prominent women. See, Federico Ribes Tovar, *La mujer puertorriqueña: Su vida y evolución a través de la historia*.

[24]See Nancy Zayas and Juan Angel Silen, eds, *La mujer en la lucha hoy*. (Río Piedras: Ediciones Kikiriki, 1973) 19–36.

[25]Valle Ferrer had published a newspaper account of Capetillo's life in 1974. See "La primera en liberarse," *La Hora*, April 25–May 1, 1974: 12–13. The 1975 biography is a document that Valle Ferrer published herself. For the history of Valle Ferrer's biography, see the preface and bibliography of her book (Valle Ferrer, *Historia*, 13–15, 147–48).

[26]This anthology originated from a Women's Studies symposium at SUNY-Albany in 1976. The book was published in 1979—a slightly modified and expanded Spanish edition was published in 1980—and quickly became one of the standard reference works for Puerto Rican women's history and culture (Matos Rodríguez, *Puerto Rico*, 14–16).

[27]Picó's essay was previously published as "The History of Women's Struggle for Equality in Puerto Rico."

[28]Azize's work was a significant contribution to the historical literature on working-class women as it condensed in a single monograph the findings regarding the history of the labor movement and of the early feminist movement that had been scattered in book chapters, journals and unpublished papers.

[29]I want to thank Ivette M. Rivera-Giusti for sharing with me several chapters of her doctoral dissertation (SUNY-Binghamton History 2003), "Gender, Labor and Working Class Activism in the Tobacco Industry in Puerto Rico, 1898–1933."

[30]For overviews of recent works on gender and feminism in Latin American and Caribbean Studies see the articles by Sueann Caulfield, Meri Knaster, and K. Lynn Stoner listed in the bibliography.

[31]Although it is not clear whether this was a reprint of an article Capetillo had written for local Puerto Rican newspapers or a direct contribution to the Argentine publication, given that Capetillo had died two years prior to the publication of the article in Argentina one can assume that the article in *Nuestra Tribuna* was a reprint.

[32]Rivera de Álvarez corresponded with Capetillo's daughter, Manuela, in 1963 in preparation for her entry in the *Diccionario*. See her bibliographical notes (292). If this is accurate, Rivera de Álvarez would be one of the first scholars who became interested in Capetillo before she was "re-discovered" in the 1970s.

[33]In Antonio García del Toro's *Mujer y Patria en la dramaturgia puertorriqueña*, for example, there is only a passing reference to one of Capetillo's plays (32). This is typical of the way most literary scholars have approached Capetillo's writings until very recently.

[34]Most of the sections included in *Influencias* were written while in New York City and/or Tampa, but the book's centerpiece—a play that shares the book's title—was originally written in Puerto Rico between 1907 and 1909 (Valle Ferrer, *Historia* 52–53).

[35]It is important to note that Ortiz's observation was written before Sánchez González made her case for Capetillo as an example of the "pionero" generation, but it could be indicative of potential resistance to Sánchez González's perspective.

[36]". . . actual sistema social, con todos sus errores, se sostiene por la ignorancia y la esclavitud de la mujer."

[37]". . . la crítica de los escritores de experiencia." It is interesting that this sentence was deleted from the 1913 edition, indicating perhaps that Capetillo had grown more comfortable with her distance from upper-class literary discourses either by learning to dismiss them or by feeling more secure about the reception of her ideas in literary circles.

[38]"Para mí el matrimonio es un error, tal como está establecido."

[39]"Que poderosa admiración sentimos por el mar."

[40]Capetillo dedicates a new section to Roque's *Luz y sombra* in the 1913 edition. See *Mi opinión* (1913) 163–164.

[41]Capetillo was even more forthcoming regarding her belief in the compatibility of anarchism and spiritualism in the 1913 edition of *Mi opinión*. She dedicates an entire new chapter to this issue and contends, "God is not an obstacle for the dissemination of anarchist socialism, nor does he oppose any of the methods employed by the anarchists. It is men who interrupt . . ." (1913 171).

[42]The sections dedicated to Tavarez de Storer and Texidor were eliminated in the 1913 edition.

[43]These three sections—among the ones most often quoted and reproduced in Capetillo's anthologies and feminist and labor studies—were deleted from the 1913 edition of *Mi opinión*.

[44]". . . mi amor espontáneo, sin trabas, sin rodeos, sin hipocresías, sin interés."

[45]"Y con la sonrisa en los labios, en una suprema lucha y con una suprema calma."

[46]". . . resumiendo finalmente, la mujer es apta para todo."

Selected Bibliography

Acosta-Belén, Edna. *The Puerto Rican Woman: Perspectives on Culture, History, and Society*. New York: Praeger, 1986.

Ayala, César J. *American Sugar Kingdom: The Plantation Economy of the Spanish Caribbean, 1898–1934*. Chapel Hill: University of North Carolina Press, 1999.

Azize, Yamila. *La mujer en la lucha*. Río Piedras: Editorial Cultural, 1985.

Azize-Vargas, Yamila. "The Roots of Puerto Rican Feminism: The Struggle for Universal Suffrage." *Radical America* 23: 1 (Jan–Feb 1989): 71–80.

Baerga, María del Carmen. "A la organización, a unirnos como un solo hombre . . . ! La Federación Libre de Trabajadores y el mundo masculino del trabajo." *Op. Cit.: Revista del Centro de Investigaciones Históricas* 11 (1999): 219–252.

Baldrich, Juan José. "Gender and the Decomposition of the Cigar-Making Craft in Puerto Rico, 1899–1934." *Puerto Rican Women's History: New Perspectives*. Eds. Félix V. Matos Rodríguez and Linda C. Delgado. NY: M.E. Sharpe Publishers, 1998. 105–125.

Barceló Miller, María de Fátima. "De la polilla a la virtud: Visión sobre la mujer de la Iglesia jerárquica de Puerto Rico." *La mujer en Puerto Rico: Ensayos de investigación*. Ed. Yamila Azize Vargas. Río Piedras: Ediciones Huracán, 1987. 49–88.

_____. *La lucha por el sufragio femenino en Puerto Rico, 1896-1935*. Río Piedras: Ediciones Huracán, 1997.

Bird Carmona, Arturo. *A lima y machete: La huelga cañera de 1915 y la fundación del Partido Socialista.* Río Piedras: Ediciones Huracán, 2001.

Cabán, Pedro. *Constructing a Colonial People: Puerto Rico and the United States, 1898–1932.* Boulder: Westview, 1999.

Capetillo, Luisa. *Ensayos libertarios: dedicado a los trabajadores de ambos sexos.* Arecibo: Imprenta Unión Obrera, 1907.

_____. *Influencias de las ideas modernas. Notas y apuntes. Escenas de la vida.* San Juan: Tipografía Negrón Flores, 1916.

_____. *La humanidad en el futuro.* San Juan: Tip. Real Hermanos, 1910.

_____. *Mi opinión; disertación sobre las libertades de la mujer. "Amor libre"; la mujer como compañera, madre y ser independiente en el hogar, en la familia y en el gobierno.* Tampa: Imprenta de J. Mascuñana, 1913.

_____. *Mi opinión sobre las libertades, derechos y deberes de la mujer: Como compañera, madre y ser independiente.* San Juan: Times Pub. Co., 1911.

Caulfield, Sueann. "The History of Gender in the Historiography of Latin America." *Hispanic American Historical Review* 81.3–4 (August–November 2001): 451–92.

Cooper, Patricia A. *Once a Cigar Maker: Men, Women and Work Culture in American Cigar Factories, 1900–1919.* Urbana: University of Illinois Press, 1987.

Cubano Iguina, Astrid. *El hilo en el laberinto: claves de la lucha política en Puerto Rico (siglo XIX).* Río Piedras: Ediciones Huracán, 1990.

Dávila Santiago, Rubén. *Teatro Obrero en Puerto Rico (1900–1920): Antología.* Río Piedras: Editorial Edil, 1985.

_____. *El derribo de las murallas. Orígenes intelectuales del socialismo en Puerto Rico.* Río Piedras: Editorial Cordillera, 1988.

De Hostos, Adolfo. *Tesauro de datos históricos.* Volume V (S-Z). Río Piedras: Editorial de la Universidad de Puerto Rico, 1995.

García, Gervasio and A. G. Quintero Rivera. *Desafío y solidaridad, breve historia del movimiento obrero puertorriqueño.* Río Piedras: Ediciones Huracán, 1982.

García del Toro, Antonio. *Mujer y patria en la dramaturgia puertorriqueña.* Madrid: Editorial Playor, 1987.

Guzzo, Cristina. "Amor, anarquía y feminismo: El texto de Luisa Capetillo como Anticipación del discurso posmoderno." *Fragmentos de Cultura.* 12-6. (November–December 2002): 1157–1163.

Herzig Shannon, Nancy. *El Iris de Paz: El espiritismo y la mujer en Puerto Rico, 1900-1905.* Río Piedras: Ediciones Huracán, 2001.

Hewitt, Nancy A. "The Voice of Virile Labor: Labor Militancy, Community Solidarity, and Gender Identity among Tampa's Latin Workers, 1880–1921." *Work Engendered: Towards a New History of American Labor.* Ed. Ava Baron, Ithaca: Cornell University Press, 1991. 142–67.

_____. *Southern Discomfort: Women's Activism in Tampa, Florida, 1880s–1920s.* Chicago: University of Illinois Press, 2001.

Janer, Zilkia. "Colonial Nationalism: The Nation-Building Literary Field and Subaltern Intellectuals in Puerto Rico (1849–1952)." Diss. Duke University, 1998.

Knaster, Meri. *Women in Spanish America: An Annotated Bibliography from Pre-Conquest to Contemporary Times.* Boston: G.K. Hall, 1977.

Lavrin, Asunción. *Women, Feminism, and Social Change in Argentina, Chile & Uruguay, 1890–1940*. Lincoln: University of Nebraska, 1995.

Matos Rodríguez, Félix V. *Women and Urban Change in San Juan, Puerto Rico, 1820–1868*. Gainesville: University Press of Florida, 1999.

_____ and Linda C. Delgado, eds. *Puerto Rican Women's History: New Perspectives*. Armonk, NY: M.E. Sharpe Publishers, 1998.

Miller, Francesca. *Latin American Women and the Search for Social Justice*. Hanover: University Press of New England, 1991.

Ostolaza Bey, Margarita. *Política Sexual en Puerto Rico*. Río Piedras: Ediciones Huracán, 1989.

Ortiz, Altagracia. "The Lives of Pioneras: Bibliographic and Research Sources on Puerto Rican Women in the United States." *Centro Journal* (Winter 1989–90) 41–47.

Pérez, Louis A. *Cuba: Between Reform and Revolution*. 2nd ed. New York: Oxford University Press, 1995.

Picó, Fernando. *Los gallos peleados*. Río Piedras: Ediciones Huracán, 1983.

_____. *1898: La guerra después de la guerra*. Río Piedras: Ediciones Huracán, 1987.

Picó, Isabel. "The History of Women's Struggle for Equality in Puerto Rico." *Sexual Change in Latin America*. Eds. June Nash and Helen I. Safa. New York: Praeger Publishers, 1976. 202–213.

Poyo, Gerald E. *"With All, and for the Good of All": The Emergence of Popular Nationalism in the Cuban Communities of the United States, 1848–1898*. Durham: Duke University Press, 1989.

Pozzetta, George E. *The Immigrant World of Ybor City: Italians and their Latin Neighbors in Tampa, 1885–1985*. Gainesville: University Press of Florida, 1998.

Quintero Rivera, Ángel. *Worker's Struggle in Puerto Rico: A Documentary History*. New York: Monthly Review Press, 1976.

Ramos, Julio, ed. *Amor y anarquía: Los escritos de Luisa Capetillo*. Río Piedras: Ediciones Huracán, 1992.

Ribes Tovar, Federico. *La mujer puertorriqueña: Su vida y evolución a través de la historia*. New York: Plus Ultra Educational Publishers, 1972.

Rivera de Álvarez, Josefina. *Diccionario de literatura puertorriqueña*. tomo II, vol. 1. San Juan: Instituto de Cultura Puertorriqueña, 1974. 290–92.

Rivera-Giusti, Ivette M. "Gender, Labor and Working Class Activism in the Tobacco Industry in Puerto Rico, 1898–1933." Diss. SUNY-Binghamton 2003.

Rodríguez, María Elena. "Oír leer: Tabaco y cultura popular en Cuba y Puerto Rico." *Caribbean Studies* 24. 3–4 (1991): 221–39.

Romero-Cesáreo, Ivette. "Whose Legacy?" *Callaloo* 17. 3 (Summer 1994): 770–790.

Roque, Ana. *Luz y sombra*. 1903. Río Piedras: Instituto de Cultura and Editorial de la Universidad de Puerto Rico, 1991.

Sánchez González, Lisa. "Luisa Capetillo: An Anarcho-Feminist *Pionera* in the Mainland Puerto Rican Narrative/Political Tradition." *Recovering the U.S. Hispanic Literary Heritage, Vol. II*. Eds. Erlinda González-Berry and Chuck Tatum, Houston: Arte Público Press, 1996. 148–67.

_____. *Boricua Literature. A Literary History of the Puerto Rican Diaspora.* New York: New York University Press, 2001.

Santiago-Valles, Kelvin A. *"Subject People" and Colonial Discourses. Economic Transformation and Social Disorder in Puerto Rico, 1898–1947.* Albany: State University of New York Press, 1994.

Stoner, K. Lynn. *Latinas of the Americas.* New York: Garland, 1989.

_____. *From the House to the Streets: The Cuban Woman's Movement for Legal Reform, 1898–1940.* Durham: Duke University Press, 1991.

Suárez Findlay, Eileen J. *Imposing Decency: The Politics of Sexuality and Race in Puerto Rico, 1870–1920.* Durham: Duke University Press, 1999.

Tirado Avilés, Amilcar. "Notas sobre el desarollo de la industria del tabaco en Puerto Rico y su impacto en la mujer puertorriqueña: 1898–1920." *Centro Journal* (Winter 1989–90): 19–29.

Valle Ferrer, Norma. "La primera en liberarse." *La Hora* (April 25–May 1 1974): 12–13.

_____. "Luisa Capetillo (1879–1922), una herejía en la sociedad puertorriqueña." *Caribe* IV–V. 5–6 (1983–84): 3–35.

_____. *Luisa Capetillo: Historia de una mujer proscrita.* Río Piedras: Editorial Cultural, 1990.

Vega, Bernardo. *Memoirs of Bernardo Vega: A Contribution to the History of the Puerto Rican Community in New York.* Ed. Cesar Andreu Iglesias, trans. Juan Flores. New York: Monthly Review Press, 1984.

Zayas, Nancy and Juan Ángel Silen, eds. *La mujer en la lucha hoy.* Río Piedras: Ediciones Kikirikí, 1973, pp. 19–36.

A Nation of Women
An Early Feminist Speaks Out

FIRST FRUITS

I dedicate this book to all my compatriots
And to all the workers of the universe

To my children

I Remember You

For whom I have sighed and continue to sigh . . .

To you, my mother, who never imposed or forced me to think
according to tradition, and let me freely delve into
things, reproaching me without violence only for
what you thought were exaggerations.

The Author
San Juan, October 1910

Preface

I publish these opinions without seeking praise, glory or applause, without worrying what the criticisms of more experienced writers will be.

The only motive behind making this book public is to tell the truth, which even those who are more qualified and in a better position to speak it do not. Why? Because of the possibility that public opinion may not support the concepts of an idea whose doctrine they consider to be utopian. This manner of judgment is not sufficient reason not to publish the truths that doctrine contains.

Anything that cannot be done immediately can be considered utopian. Success in business is utopian, because it is equally possible to make a profit or turn a loss.

Any future endeavor, no matter what kind, is utopian, since there is no complete guarantee that it will turn out as we hope.

You will say that this is a conceptual mistake, that it is not utopia. It is a matter of opinion. . . . However, I understand that what others consider utopian is for me something that can become reality.

The idea of a "Social and Beneficent Fraternity" was utopian for many.

And would you like an idea even easier to put into practice? It was not Anarchy, it was not called Socialism. However, many who saw that equality was its core feared and, opposed it, saying that it was utopian, that it was a form of exploitation.

It was Communism. It was true love. Those who accused its initiators of masking a new form of political exploitation, who were they?

Those who lived and continue to live off the ignorance of the working people. Did they tell the truth? No, they falsified the facts and slandered its apostles! What do we think of those who oppose all ideas of equality and human freedom? We consider them traitors, Judases who have betrayed the Teacher. Those who judge unrealized ideas to be utopian are obstacles, and obstacles must be pushed aside. They are those who hinder great initiatives, works for the common good.

And still, they call themselves patriots and fathers of the homeland.

What idea of the homeland can they have? One that is egotistical, which begins and ends with them. They are everything.

ଔ   ଔ   ଔ

There is nothing more harmful to the success of an endeavor than timidity, pusilanimity, and doubt. This type of cowardice that I believe only the lazy possess. I do not believe anything to be impossible; nor am I amazed by any invention or discovery, which is why I do not find any idea utopian. What is essential is that the idea be put into practice. Begin! The rest is weakness and an erroneous concept of human power.

Wanting is doing!

ଔ   ଔ   ଔ

It's been some time now that I have wanted to express my opinions on the life of woman in all its manifestations. After some light study, I found myself confronted with an arduous and difficult task, as I was faced with a social system so contrary to my ideals. Light study, I said. Yes, due to the fact that most of my study has been through my own experience. It is collected from events, incidents, and mistakes that for some years now I have observed in my own life. It is relatively short, to demonstrate in all its detail. But I will be able to offer a more complete picture later in another study.

For the moment, you must acknowledge these concepts that I have developed in the few years of scant freedom of women. It is a result of the analysis and study I have undertaken.

Woman, as an important factor in human civilization, is worthy to obtain complete liberty.

If we were to provide a detailed history of the powerful influence of women since the antiquity of primitive times, the list would be endless, and that is not my objective. These important details have been published in Emilio Castelar's *Mujeres Célebres* (Famous Women), in which he lays out in minute detail the general history of the slavery, sovereignty, and intellectual and emotional activity of women, from primitive times to the present.

Need we repeat or plagiarize him? No, read the work.

The only thing we want to put forth is that women must acquire greater freedom and rights.

The current social system, with all its errors, is sustained by the ignorance and slavery of women.

We will begin by narrating the slavery of woman in marriage, the inconveniences resulting from her lack of education, and the manner in which the consequences of her misfortune are reflected in her children.

Then we examine how women should understand education so that they may explain it to their children. Because woman must enlighten herself in order to free herself from a slavery that ruins her as a woman and a mother.

We also examine what method she should adopt to educate her children and her husband.

After finishing the part devoted to women's freedom and rights, we continue with some dedications and some explanations of important matters of interest to all.

I ask you, my esteemed readers, to forgive any defect that the following words may have.

You will find contradictions, given the conflict between my ideas and the environment in which I live, which tries to suffocate my ideals.

No matter. Analyze the goals to which I aspire, and I will be satisfied.

October 1, 1910, San Juan, Puerto Rico

The Author.

Woman in the home, in the family, and in government

The true mother of a family must know how to do it all, both intellectually and physically.

It is absolutely essential that she not only know how to make a dress and select the combination of colors and lace, if necessary. Indeed, she must also have talent and taste to prepare a meal from the most modest dish to the most exquisite and truffled. She should know how to prepare different desserts, from the most simple to the most refined; without getting dirty, without making a mess in the kitchen, and with the most utmost cleanliness. So your hands become rough or ugly? If you can, rely on some old gloves, or ones you do not need. Why, useful hands are preferable to ones that are merely beautiful.

If you are fortunate enough to be with a good and loyal husband, a pair of useful hands will help you to lay the foundation for your domestic happiness. Because if you have not had any practice with which to develop your abilities with ease, the peace of the home begins to totter; a clean, proper, affectionate, indulgent, and persuasive woman will delight her husband. If he is good, attentive, and affectionate, you will make an ideal couple. If, on the contrary, he is rough, uncaring, and egotistical, try to educate him; attempt to persuade him and have the utmost patience in order to keep the peace; do not answer back with the same harshness as he does. Be as gentle and harmonious as you can be. Do not demonstrate to him that you are more reasonable, wait for him to concede, in accord with the current social system which does not recognize that a woman can be right.

Try and be as agreeable as possible. These sacrifices can be made when the husband is home-loving, but if the suffering is too great: then seek divorce.

Likewise, I tell husbands: be patient, sweet-tempered, loving, and spend time at home, or go out, but do so with her. Otherwise, marriage is useless.[1]

So if a companion is affectionate, all the efforts that are made to please him are not useless, such sacrifices like showing moderation and patience.

This is not true of other sacrifices that are against nature. Sacrifices should be made only when he reciprocates your affection loyally because love is not by formulas.

These should be commitments of love, not for the sake of etiquette or acquired customs by family or social traditions

It is hard to imagine a woman who does not know how to keep up the house, and the clothes, to maintain the house in order. Yet there are indeed women who do not have these skills, who do not even know how to wash a dish, nor remove a stain from the floor, nor mend, nor cook.

What awaits them should their status change? Unpleasant experiences, grief and disillusionment.

As a general rule, women nowadays dedicate all their energy, all their attention to their appearance; they are not concerned with anything except wearing the latest fashion; they squander all their intelligence in trying to become more beautiful, and not even in any practical way, by some beneficial and hygienic method, like practicing gymnastics, exercising in the fresh air, or swimming every morning.

But no, it must be done with ribbons and lace, by cutting their breath short from the excessive use of tight-fitting corsets. And this translates to a waste of time, health, and money.[2]

Women must strive by all natural methods to become more beautiful, but it must be a true beauty, real and lasting, achieved by a healthy diet, without eating meat or drinking alcoholic beverages,

---

[1]As I understand it, two people simply together, without bowing to convention.
[2]Here I express my agreement with the actual social system.

by practicing gymnastics and taking walks in the open air, not a fictitious beauty such as that of the adornment, without which, she is no longer herself.

A woman should be naturally beautiful, without ridiculous adornments, beautiful because of her strong constitution, neither too heavy nor too thin; because of her sweetness of character, patience, her innocence, her honesty.[3] All these gathered together form a precious bouquet, which every woman must preserve, without letting any one flower wilt.

In my grandparents' time the following virtues were believed to be the most excellent and appreciable adornments for a woman:

"Silence, modesty, a retiring nature, her endless hard work, her ability to sew, and other labors that befitted her sex, her constant dedication to governing the household, her disdain for fineries and elegance. The forgetfulness or even ignorance she should show of her own beauty and skills. She should be admired by others, and should seem that she alone is unaware of this admiration. She must be gentle, natural, amiable, and prudent. Her hands must not disdain or avoid work; she must anticipate tasks and complete them on time; and her greatest source of pride is a well-ordered home. She must not compensate for her spirit and body with vain adornments."

All of this is magnificent for the woman and mother, since it is with these qualities she will never leave her husband and children waiting while she is off perusing trinkets in a store. I agree with all of this, but now we need husbands to support their wives and aid in helping them fulfill their duties.

But if his actions cause her not to act virtuously, then there is no reason to accuse the woman only.

He must be at home with her, sharing in the difficult task of raising their children.

---

[3] I do not confuse this with the so-called honesty imposed by society, which is hypocrisy. True honesty is in accord with natural law. Anything against this natural law is dishonest and harmful to one's organism.

[4] I do not mean that this is sanctioned by judges or priests. Marriage need not be sanctioned by law nor follow an established custom. The will of two human beings of both sexes [to be together] is sufficient to form a marriage and constitute a home.

CR   CR   CR

Could there exist true happiness in a marriage[4] when the man is the only one who can regularly exercise his free will and satisfy his desires, without caring whether or not his wife agrees? Accustomed to the passive obedience of women, he does not bother to find out whether or not she is satisfied with his conduct. And if she is not, he does not attempt to please her, nor to adapt his conduct to a new way of life.

How can the holy priestess of the hearth preserve the sacred fire of love in the home when she has to officiate alone? Where is the principal object of her devotion? Look for him outside the home at those times when he should be at the side of his companion. Will a solid foundation for domestic happiness be established by this behavior? No. Men have the right to do or undo, without his companion. He goes to a masked ball or not, to the casino, to gamble, or chases other women . . . . and meanwhile, poor woman! A sad scenario for domestic bliss! She is subjected to a sad solitude for days and nights on end, orphaned of love, of sweet attentions and joys while the above-mentioned companion gambles, dances . . . or falls in love.

How sad and bitter are love's deceptions, and how long are the hours spent waiting, endless nights of waiting, always waiting . . .

Oh! how awful it is to wait . . . hours . . . and more hours . . . Days and more days. . . Those of you who have suffered these bitter travails that bring on such fatal consequences; when a woman lacks experience, when she does not know how to fight, alone and without friends . . . without diversions . . .

Poor woman! Poor happiness!

That loneliness either breeds deceit, perfidy, hypocrisy . . . or the ill-created union is broken.

Why do men keep a woman by their side at dances, at the theater, before they are married, and later when she is his companion, he leaves her alone at home and goes off with other women? Is it out of novelty? Or for the sake of variety in women? I don't know.

True love does not proceed in this fashion; if a man does not feel true love for a woman, he must not sacrifice her the firestorm of his desire, use her as a mere instrument of pleasure, that is unjust. What attraction can it offer?

Can a woman remain faithful like this, in those conditions? Apparently she can maintain her formulas and marital identity through convention, but the state of her heart, her illusions, where have they gone? Poor heart, poor illusions.

If this woman should feel attracted to another man, who during her solitude has shown her some affection, and should she end up forgetting her husband and children, who is to blame?

Could it possibly be just, that this man can be unfaithful to his companion, without anyone finding him morally culpable, and that he still believes he has the right to demand fidelity of her?

As I understand it, if a man has a wife, and, to satisfy certain vices, he turns to other women and leaves the one who loves him and has been faithful to him, thereby creating a situation which moves this slave to break the chains of her slavery. If this woman, because of temperament or education, is not unwilling to age prematurely, accepting a morality she does not comprehend because it contradicts the natural law and is virtue in name only, well then, he has no right to accuse her.

Is this morality? And they have the audacity to demand this of women!

If this woman does not understand why her husband or lover always leaves her alone, because of society's mandates, or because her pride will not allow her to understand, or because of her mother's opinion; if she neither understands why this man, who wants his woman to be faithful, goes off with women who belong to many, lacking a faithfulness he needs to practice if he insists on demanding it from her; and if this woman in these conditions and flattered by the affection of another man, whom in her solitude she finds pleasing and who conquers her with his diligence; finding in him more affection; and following her natural impulses, she gives in to his affection and embraces this assiduous and admirer, thereby exhibiting infidelity, that is an imposed morality and a violent, virtue established by tyrants over woman, who for centuries have oppressed her. Does her partner, who never passes up an opportunity to be unfaithful, in the most stupid manner, have a right to punish her?

No, only in separating; (did I say in separating? But they never lived together), in never returning to her. But that is not reasonable either, why does it make him angry if his lover gives herself to another man, if he himself prefers to be with other women who give themselves to men of all classes, even ones who carry disease? This kind of morality is incomprehensible! It repulses him that his lover gives herself to a distinguished, cultured and hygienic person, but he has no scruples about going to women when the brutality of tyrants have forced into belonging to many, and who pick up diseases; and even in becoming sick he snubs her, she who continuously waits for him, seeing him be unfaithful yet again.

What is this about? What is the type of morality that this society demands?

What right does the man have in these conditions to demand fidelity? Has he perchance bought this woman like a slave, so that she cannot manage her own affairs? If this man does not know how to fulfill his duties as a husband, or is incapable of it, why does he demand that his wife do so?

What kind of morality is this?

He has no right to accuse her. He has not separated from her in order to be unfaithful, and she fears leaving him or separating from him. To conclude, the man who is unfaithful to his wife does not love her, and if she ends up not loving him and she still does not dare to leave his side, she is stupid.

A woman has a right to separate from an unfaithful husband and in order to do so she must know how to work if she desires to maintain her freedom. But, if before separating she has used this freedom to accept another man, her husband will be the one to trumpet that he was cheated on and he will want to portray his wife as a vice-ridden woman. If they should have children, the father is obliged to support and raise them until they are of age. The woman in this case must demand her rights and not accept any pretext that would allow her children to be taken from her.

The father has the obligation to support his children until there is a new system. But for now, there is no other.

All of us must contribute with our energies and will to substitute the obsolete traditional customs that are an obstacle to progress. All of us must be tenacious and persevering in educating ourselves properly. The woman mother is the first who educates, guides the future monarch, just as she does the president or minister, the useful laborer or the intelligent teacher. She carefully shapes and models future legislators and revolutionaries, but at times wrongly, and almost always because of a lack of education.

If women were appropriately enlightened, educated and emancipated from routine formulism, the political life of most nations would be different.

But she, enervated by the fanaticisms of religion, creates chains that will imprison her children and grandchildren, without measuring either their breadth or power. Notice that the mother, from the early years on, filters in ideas, thinking they are good and suitable, but without analyzing or selecting them, only because they were received from her parents as a spiritual legacy. And she continues numbing the brain of her children with political and religious ideas that atrophy their mind, thereby making it impossible to analyze the truth of natural laws. This maternal influence is powerful when the children can be constantly at her side, until they form (or not) a new family of their own. The child who has been able to emancipate herself from domestic tutelage will surely change; if, at an early age a child loses its mother or is forced to separate from her, there is no reason to think that the child can retain the ideas instilled during infancy. There have been exceptional cases, but the circumstances surrounding these cases influenced some or another idea.

No doubt, the first and best school is the home. The best and most superior teacher for a child is an educated mother. The mother has the lofty duty of instilling in her children feelings of goodness, of enlightening them in the rudimentary precepts of primary education. As long as she is given the means and she does not find it necessary to seek work outside the home, in which case the child loses his best and most superior guide. An educated and enlightened woman makes a good mother and a good wife. Of course, she must find in her husband the perfect complement to her character and nature so both can raise their offspring.

Harmony within a marriage greatly influences the education of children, our future citizens. How many times have a mother's tears, cried in moments of pain and contradiction, powerfully influenced her children! I remember an incident recounted by Guy de Maupassant about a child who was playing in the garden of his house, and running in its little alleys, he heard a noise and observed, between the branches, his father pressing down on his mother's arm, violently trying to make her sign a document. She resisted and didn't sign, and he, in a fit of rage, held down both her arms and slapped her face in a cruel and villainous way. Such was the impression this scene made on the child that he let out a cry and fled far away, very far. . . .

It was nighttime and the child did not appear, and finally the next day they found him in the forest, and when he arrived and saw his mother he knelt down, crying. The child became a man, and he always had that scene present in his mind, it was like his eternal shadow, and to chase it away he would spend time in the café saying "Waiter, a drink. Waiter, another drink." And when he saw some old acquaintance he would retell the story that had made him retire from the world and live by himself, his only company being the memory of that scene.

The document that his mother did not want to sign was the endowment intended for her son. She was reluctant to sign because the father wanted to use it.

How many domestic scenes have influenced or still powerfully influence children and have made them good or evil?

How many fathers, due to their incorrect behavior cause disturbances and provide the means to separate theses children from their mothers. The mother who has sacrificed herself, who has given them their health and beauty, painfully sees that she has to be separate from her children and entrust their education to people with mistaken opinions and concepts, because of the stubbornness of a father who wants to impose his will over what is right for his children, children who must not leave their mother's side until they are twelve or fourteen years old. And so fathers shouldn't look for pretexts to deprive their children of such a beneficent influence.

Should this father deprive this mother of her right to educate their children? No. He should give her the means to do so and not force her, in misery, to leave them. His obligation is to provide the means for her to care for them, and not have separate from them so that others handle what truly pertains to a mother, forming and educating the soul, the heart of her children according to the preachings of Jesus and human freedom, only then can the children educate themselves without fear.

That is why women must become enlightened or educated, because being enlightened encompasses all the fields of human science: Physiology, Geology, Geography, Chemistry, Physics, Astronomy, Engineering, Agriculture, Geometry, History, Music, and Painting. But Education is different, since a person can be learned but not be educated. Education is a beautiful and necessary thing. The harmony of family and nations rests on it. Education is very important in the woman mother. Let us delve into some notions about culture. A child at the dining room table, in a moment of clumsiness, spills water or breaks a dish. A mother who is educated, who has cultivated a sense of patience, calms the child down because he or she is scared and sweetly helps the child pick up the broken pieces or dries the water. A mother who is not educated, takes the child down from the chair in one fell swoop, beats him, pushes him, and mistreats him, spanks him and keeps talking about economizing and a thousand other things until the husband is so bothered that he gets up and leaves without having lunch. And this woman who gets so fired up and mistreats the child because of a glass, a cup, or a plate, who gave her lecture on economics, misspends her money on useless items, and is so loaded with bracelets and lace that she looks like a bazaar. Education means cultivating patience, tolerance, a sweet disposition, harmony, abnegation, and temperateness. Anyone who cultivates these virtues is truly educated.

If a woman is not instructed and educated will she be able to educate, counsel, and guide her children suitably? No. And this is an important matter that should interest women, the home being the first and most necessary of schools. Whatever the child sees the mother do or say is what the child will observe and learn.

If the mother is violent and full of rage in her manners, the child imitates her. We tell the child, "children don't lie," and at that moment someone calls at the door and the mother says "tell them I'm not here," and so the child moves towards the door, opens it and says: "Mommy is not home." Or in a different vein, to offer something after it has been denied without reason, out of whim, out of a need to rule over the child, or make good (or not) on the promise. She says "I'm going to take you for a stroll" and then the mother hides and goes by herself. Why does an affectionate mother do that? I think it is ignorance of her responsibility.

There are many women who think that being a mother means contradicting a child, and later they beat them, and order them about for the sake of giving orders, to see herself obeyed, ordering the child not to run, not to jump, not to yell, in sum, a whole bunch of ignorant things, the truth is, to prohibit a child from doing all this is to prohibit them from being healthy. They act like this with girls precisely because they are girls, as if a girl's organism did not have to develop, so that they can grow up beautiful and strong, and not scrawny and pale, nor become mothers full of pains and ailments.

They think that being a mother authorizes them to mistreat and order the children at whim, and oblige them to do things against their will, that is an error.

Many mothers say I am poor and my child has to help me, and therefore, the child should abstain from playing, so that every time the mother needs the child she says: "Look, you don't think of anything else other than playing." What are they supposed to think about? That their mother is poor? A child does not understand that, and if it is a girl she is forced at a tender age, without having fully enjoyed the games of childhood, to do the wash, to toast the coffee, to clean the floors, and the mother, she goes to a neighbor's house to chat. Or she doesn't leave, but the situation is still serious when if the coffee burns, the girl is in danger of being burned, knocked, hit with the broom, or shoved onto the ground. This humiliated girl, after performing work beyond her age, feels the need to flee when she is so mistreated. How many girls pay for the tantrums, jealousies or vexations of their mothers, who act without any justifying motive, only because they need to blow off steam and they can't do it in front of their husbands.

By no means should a mother do this, it is heresy, an act of cruelty that does not resolve anything nor alleviate their vexations.

So, if the boy or girl breaks something this shows the mother is the one to be doing such things, and if the husband spends too much time out of the house or falls in love with another, it is the mother's fault and not that of her daughter. In this case she must seek to make the home and herself more agreeable and cheerful and not be spoiled or a spendthrift and be educated and tolerant of her husband's defects (because she has them too). Or if the problem is that she is bothered by her husband or tired of him, then she should be separated, and otherwise not make up pretexts. If women were enlightened and knew their rights, these things would not happen. Men would not dare to deceive them.

For example, no woman should accept a man who is in a committed relationship, without demanding that he either give up his wife or lover if he no longer loves her. And if this wife or lover does not want to leave him, she will have to admit to the fact that her husband has another woman, because she cannot force him to love her if she has not had the charm or persuasiveness to keep him herself, or she has not found a way to appreciate him. This man should have the freedom to choose another woman and live with her. And this woman must search for another to be her husband. And if it is the woman who is tired and bored of her husband, and despite knowing and understanding that he is a bother and a nuisance; persists in the idea of keeping her because he loves her, but he has not known or has not wanted to accept her sympathies or affection, or he hasn't loved, or he has been indifferent; and thinking that because she is married to him she is obliged to accept him without having won her over, then he is an uncouth lout, and this woman has a right and a natural duty to make amends of her situation by any means, and not fool herself or others. The man who takes a wife and thinks it is her duty to wait up for him every night until midnight or one in the morning is an egotist. If she waits for him for her own pleasure, fine, then she does not have a right to complain. But the woman who sheds tears and wants to free herself from that inequality, let her do it and show the courage of her feelings, without a bit of fear. A woman who accepts this type of slavery because she does not know how to work is an idiot. Women must penetrate all the pathways of human knowledge, and be in full possession of their own freedom and rights. A woman who wants to be easily supported in leisure and luxuriously attired, consents to or allows herself to marry an old man and to deceive him, is a stupid woman and he a ridiculous old man. Or, if a woman suffers and grows old because she does not dare to complain nor reclaim her rights out of fear of bettering her lot or because of the opinion of others, then she is a slave.

The woman who feels wounded in her rights, liberties, and her womanhood, has to recompose and reclaim herself, change her situation, no matter how high the cost. The established morality, or what is called moral, is not what it claims to be; one cannot accept a morality that is against the freedom and rights of each and every human. There is no need to fear a morality that is morality in name only. Let us establish a true morality that does not coerce or is contrary to the rights established by nature. The rest is make believe, deceitful, and false and we should not continue to permit it. Every person has the right to be happy, and one cannot be happy if the person who is supposed to be the one to help form or to round out our own self, is not that one. And if one does not look for the way to please one's loved one, and to put the beloved at ease, one should not oblige him or her to live in a manner contrary to his or her aspirations and desires, but instead leave them to freely choose their own path.

Another pretext is that of the children, that because of the children a couple who no longer please each other and cannot tolerate each other without great violence—cannot separate. Yes sir, they can separate, and the father, who can find work or is already employed, has the duty to appropriately support the children, and the mother, since she cannot work outside the house. And when the children are older, then they can take care of themselves. But in any event, this type of separation is preferable to living with constant quarrelling.

ભ   ભ   ભ

Nowadays, all this talk about the "silence and seclusion of woman" is unacceptable because today the European woman aspires to public office, to government, to administering towns, without losing her feminine personality, nor her motherly and wifely duties.

The author[5] of "Modern Women in the Family" believes "that it is good that the modern woman prove that she knows how to study on par with men in order to acquire an academic degree, that she knows how to handle the surgeon's scalpel, the naturalist's microscope, and the engraver's burin, all of which demonstrates how erroneous is the theory of female mental inferiority. It is good that a woman demonstrates that she knows how to carry out the duties of public office with as much skill as a man; that one's capacity, consciousness, and loyalty in fulfilling obligations are not the sole privilege of the stronger sex, and that she knows how to support herself and also her husband."

It is has been said countless times, that women in the public sphere and workplace would lose ground, jeopardizing their home, their family and their children!

But those who think in this way forget that the lady of high and well-off position goes to the stores, visits friends, museums and theaters, and dressmakers and the home is left alone, her children, with the servants or their nannies only. The mothers see their children for only a moment, they give them a kiss, and go out again, and this is their daily routine.

There is never enough time for their boudoir, or for courtesy calls, For the dressmaker, and for strolls along the Pardo or the Prado, the Bois de Boulogne, or the Champs Elysées. All those strolls are done at just the right time so that the woman can be seen there and satisfy their vanity and follow the fashion. How is it that the husbands of these elegant ladies neither care nor bother to find out if their home

---

[5]We do not know the author's name: she hides behind the letter A . . . just like that.

and children are jeopardized left in this continual solitude? The children don't see the mother at any moment. In these cases it would be more useful if she would devote herself to studying or choose a job that would give her the means to be more useful. Women possess a high degree of sagacious insight, promptness, and good administrative sense. Why not perform some administrative positions?

Why should one think that home life will be in jeopardy by women working?

Is home life not jeopardized when a woman does not want to breast feed her child, or when she doesn't want to accompany her husband to the theater, because she went to church to confess? And isn't the family jeopardized when she occupies her day in church, social visits, and strolls? But the home is not jeopardized when the woman contributes with her talent and activities to the development of nations.

And the working class woman who leaves her children at home in order to tend those of the rich, and who works in factories and workshops, doesn't she jeopardize her home?

The working-class home, the peasant and his wife, who abandons her home and has no one to leave behind to care for the children, and who returns home to find her child burned in an accident, this home is not in jeopardy?

So they say it endangers the household! It endangers the family!. Women are confused, mistaken for men! But this is the home of the wealthy, the family of the aristocrat! It is the highborn lady!

But what about the poor home, the working class family, does it not harm itself? The unhappy servant or peasant woman who rents herself out to breastfeed the son of the wealthy and who must abandon her own children, doesn't she suffer? Doesn't she have natural feelings? The poor woman who must push a cart in the mines, mixed in with male workers, who goes and comes back alone, does not become a man. And neither do the women who go off to work the land. No way! These people are made of bronze, and are tempered by adversity! The poor wife of a sugar mill or road worker, who only makes 50 or 60 cents a day and who does not make enough to look after four or six children whom she has to dress and cannot, so to help out she washes others' clothes and does odd jobs, and thus leaves her children unattended, doesn't she bring harm on herself?

A household protected by law and wealth receives more benefits and is more protected while the poor home is forgotten. People forget that the poor family instead of sending their child to school uses them instead to sell fruit or has to hire them out or force them to perform work beyond their age. Does that not harm them? Why not? The parents cannot manage to care for these children, who cannot go to school for lack of clothing and their parents cannot feed them and for this reason they are sent to sell candy or fruit in the street. Both the wealthy families and the State together should supply them with food and education.

My ideals remind me that these things should not be asked for but that people should be educated so that they take what they need without recourse to false and incomplete measures. Why ask that the wealthy and the State provide alms to the children of those who have provided the wealthy with their capital, and who sustain the State. It is ridiculous! Because there are those who—despite the fact that they know that without working people there would be no wealth, nor municipalities, nor employees—still think it is just to go begging to those who live from usurping the sweat and labor of the working classes.

We should not continue with our indifference, continue rattling the mean-spirited and degrading chains of wage slavery, which is the lot of the common worker. The work performed by every citizen should cover all their needs, tastes, and diversions according to current sanitation standards and the gains of progress. We should not continue saying "that the peasant should remain uneducated because it is not necessary for his work," nor should we forget that those who express themselves that way are those who claim to want progress for their homeland. Do you know who they are? The political patriots!

So much for those cardboard patriots!

CRZ CRZ CRZ

A woman whose husband owns a sugar mill or hacienda and calls herself a Spiritist or Christian should not seek to load herself down with jewelry, nor make useless purchases. She should visit the families of her peons, who produce the wealth she and her husband possess and who continue increasing it, and observe how they live, if they lack items that are useful or necessary, like chairs, beds, and other utensils. And she should notice if their roof doesn't leak, and if the inhabitants can live in the the house in sanitary conditions, that it is sufficiently clean so that she would want to live there herself.

After visiting their peons, she should explain to her husband the state and conditions of these unfortunate souls that produce her familty's capital and obtain a salary increase for them, and she should do so discretely and frugally instead of using fancy garments and other useless adornments on her body or in her home. She should go to them consoling and healing the sad homes of those victims of exploitation. Take them clothes, footwear, books and attempt to instruct them by reading to them and by making sure that there are schools in the neighborhood to educate the children of these employees.

How beautiful and comely she would be, woman sowing goodness, fulfilling her obligation to humanity!

What brilliant flashes of light would illuminate her soul!

How sweet and free of vexation would be her life!

The woman who begins to practice these actions and establish a modicum of fraternity and social equality, would elevate herself to a level so far above human mean-spiritedness and egotism, that her name would be inscribed in everyone's consciousness and she would occupy a sacred place in every heart that worshipped her. And in her future, what would await her? Her deeds of love and justice would blaze a shining path would lead her to enjoy the fruits of the good she had sown.

Woman, you are able to sow justice and are willing to do so; do not be upset, nor get upset, do not become restless, do not flee; move forward! And for the good of future generations place the first stone of the edifice for social equality serenely and resolutely, with all the rights that pertain to you, without bowing your head, since you are no longer the material and intellectual slave you once were. Your initiative will be crowned by success, being achieved by your own efforts, and your soul will be luminous and beautiful like a sun of truth and justice.

Woman of wealth! You can redeem your exploited brothers. Redeem them and the glory of heaven will be yours!

And if you find opposition from your husband, if he is cruel and egotistical and becomes an obstacle to your great and just aspirations, do not blame him and do not fear him; because in him, you will see the symbol of ignorance, trying to hold on to its power.

Do not fear him and continue marching forward because, like Isabel of Hungary, your contributions will become beautiful and perfumed roses that will lighten your step and will save you the displeasure of contradicting your tyrant.

Oh woman! you will set a great and dignified example by breaking all traditional customs, which are unjust and tyrannical, the symbols of ignorance, in order to establish the realm of Freedom, Equality, and Fraternity, symbols of truth and justice!

Do not fear criticism, nor mockery and scorn, they are the howls of impotence, rise up, rise up, higher, higher! Like Jesus at Calvary and seek the redemption of the Puerto Rican proletariat, which will be the preface to universal redemption!

ଓ   ଓ   ଓ

How are women going to become truly educated if they do not see or observe things as they really are?

For her everything is hidden behind a mysterious veil, which does not allow her to see things realistically; if she is at a dance, at the theater, in the home, everything and everyone will deceive her without her realizing it.

She is the eternal blind person who as a general rule is being taken along by a libertine who continually tells her: "Do as I say, not as I do"; and the woman keeps on believing this treacherous person without knowing she is being deceived. And she lives deceived, and with such deceits she is educated and perverted, and she is unaware. As a girl she is told: "girls shouldn't do this or that, because girls should believe in what is done at home and not in what goes on outside of it." Thus, she begins to be a victim of her parents' routines, and then of social whims, and later, or simultaneously, of her boyfriend's extravagances, and later of her husband's tyranny and in this way the woman must stay pure and not lie.

How deceived they are!

And when a woman realizes the vile and infamous comedy that she has been made to play out without knowing it, also perverting her; and when she takes liberties on her own, then there are no pretexts, nor admonitions, nor reasoning, nor any way she can be held back. In this case, why has she been deceived? In order to enslave her, because of stupid and carnal selfishness.

And after so much precaution taken by her parents so that she be unaware of what she really needs to know (which is the usual procedure of the way men deal with women since time immemorial, the way she has been considered and used and the vices she has been taught), then she goes to a new home to be a victim of her own ignorance. A woman educated in what concerns her sex, both before and after she joins with her husband, natural or not, has to know how to defend herself. And if she cannot do so because she is blind, knowing all this is still beneficial, because even if she were an accomplice to her husband, she would always have the opportunity to think about the inconveniences of her actions and she will end up finding loathing them. It is convenient for a woman to become scientifically learned. "The Hygiene of Marriage," should be read by single women and married ones as well. I cannot recommend this without thinking of the enemies of women, or those opposed to women finding out or leaving without men knowing it that these obscene practices exist, practices taught to them by those disciples of these enemies who always and on every occasion criticize women. But I think that—just as there are men who dare to be witness and facilitate a difficult childbirth with their doctor's degree—I also think that women should study the vices and diseases of men in order to preserve themselves from acquiring impure, obscene, and indecent customs. And those who dare to think this is immoral, are really guilty and fear being discovered by their wives. And these men must be given a strong corrective, without fear. Women of all walks of life, defend yourselves because the enemy is formidable, but do not fear him, because his cowardice matches his size!

Those who believe that the freedom of woman has special limits are mistaken. The parents who contribute to their daughters' not marrying at the appropriate time are the cause of what happens later. For whatever stupid reason they oppose a marriage bond, without noticing the damage their actions inflict.

And those who do not instruct their daughters in the practices of married life are committing an error that later they will lament and will not be able to avoid.

The current way of proceeding is against morality. I think that a man should not belong to a woman before he has fully developed as a person, and once having attained this maturity, then choose the woman he loves with all of his soul, and make her his wife, and create a family. And if they are not compatible and feel obligated to separate, then they can each choose again in the future.

This is what is natural and correct. For me, marriage as currently practiced is an error. In our current society, women get married only to follow the custom.

And men do so to have a helper or a slave. And in this manner they dare to speak of morality, in a society that finds it immoral that a woman runs away with her lover and lives with him, creating a family, and is not scandalized by the fact that both sexes commit unnatural acts, atrophying their brains and beauty and perverting the most beautiful of human acts: procreation. And by this they demonstrate that such criminal madness is committed because of ignorance and their parents' imprudence. And young men do not protest that, instead of going straight into their arms as the natural law commands; these women surrender to masturbation or the crime against nature of being with the same sex. And the ladies who know about it do not protest when it happens with the opposite sex, either.

But how can they protest, if that is called morality! . . . Morality! . . . What is essential is the appearance of "virtue" and "honesty," as if virtue and honesty were outside of the laws of nature.

There can be no virtue or morality nor honesty that is not included within the laws of nature. Herein lies the compendium of all virtues.

Nature indicates to us the true path toward goodness, but we want to be wiser than nature, and herein lies the origin of all our errors, in wanting to modify the natural laws, which is where beauty, health, harmony, and truth are to be found.

And where will these erroneous paths lead us? To crime, to prostitution, adultery, to the death of our spirit.

An Important Issue for Mothers

It is a general custom for mothers to complain that they have daughters and be happy if they have sons. Why this lament? "I'd like all our children to be boys and not to have any girls." Why? Because the boys don't give as much trouble and women have to be watched over, one has to be responsible for what they do. But there is no such thing and here is where most mothers are mistaken, because it is the boys who must be educated since they are never scolded, only the girls are found guilty. Those who could have educated the boys and have not done so, those who have said a thousand times that men always turn out all right, those who have allowed their sons to indulge this mockery (at least that is what they believe) and have shown little concern for the suffering of women, those are the true guilty ones. The best thing is to destroy the empty formulas and to create healthy and natural customs. Do not indispose women against men, let them be free and they will naturally love or repel each other, without giving in to ridiculous fear. One supposes, that with current customs, there are women who are despised and jeopardized, but these unfortunate souls are not at fault. This is the result of an egotistical system of masculine education; the young man has a sister and fears that she will fall be seduced, but at the same time he is wooing a young woman who has brothers, and he does not wish any other young man to court his own sister.

That is the way we are, but I really am removed from these customs and stupid formulas. The U.S. law that prohibits houses of prostitution is magnificent. Why should there be a certain number of women devoted to this? This is cruel and unjust, since all women must be properly considered and esteemed. In the same way that there are no men with this occupation, there should be no women with it, either; all should have the same rights and freedoms and this would make the world better. But wealthy young women are not educated to work, instead they are taught to find a rich man to marry. Herein lies the evil: here is where we see the woman's turmoil when her lover or husband abandons her. She does not feel the separation so deeply, what disturbs her is the financial support, the payment on the house; the necessities that are not covered because they were paid for by the lover or the husband, and because she does not know what it costs to obtain these things, she becomes wasteful and superfluous in her purchases. Shall we continue to educate women in this manner? Shall we not prepare them so that they can carry on with their lives freely and comfortably, and not be a victim of a mockery, of an illusory and mendacious dishonor.

But there is no such mockery or dishonor, only natural laws to carry out. And it is a crime to violate these laws and impose on them laws invented by egotistical men. Egotistic and cruel, why simply liking a woman is enough for him to want, without even knowing if the woman likes him, to possess her and later, if they feel like it, impose himself on her out of fear that she might fall in love with another. That is to say, that it is not a matter of whether or not she likes him, of being good and pleasing so that she will be moved and love him. No, it's not that. His desire and will is enough for him to want to be gratified, without trying to please her and to make himself necessary for that woman, which would be the natural and correct thing to do.

First, he should see if she likes him, and later continue to interest her in him and make himself needed. Now, I understand that all men and women have the right to approach each other and accept each other without dallying around, without any kind of privilege, but these freedoms must be attained, because now they are not established. We are going to struggle for them, which means struggling for truth and justice. In order to enjoy these freedoms, you must work to attain them. Let us emancipate women from the enervating routine called religion that makes them see a natural law as a dishonest and shameful act. If it is pleasurable to go for a stroll, to hear delicious music, or to eat a tasty morsel, why deny it and be ashamed in doing so? These are necessary things established by natural law.

Man and Woman

I cannot explain why a man always feels he has rights over a woman. For example, a young man, regardless of age, always aspires to form a bond with a young virgin without life experience. Although he has tasted and enjoyed all types of pleasures and knows of all types of vices, he thinks it perfectly natural to form a bond with a young woman who is temperate and honest.

This is what has been allowed by social formulas. Rather, this is what we women have tolerated, because of our supposed weakness that we have always been accused of.

When I have time to contemplate a young man wooing a young woman, and I focus on their respective physiognomies, I marvel and protest that this man dare do to court her when he is not of the same moral stature as she. He is all withered and worn, she is beautiful, enticing, and chaste, and even so, he finds that he bestows a great favor on the woman in marrying her.

We women have to change this system, we have to transform these customs. No woman should accept a man who is not up to her moral stature; and if men do not want give up these practices, they will have to agree in bestowing upon us the same liberties.

It is ridiculous, stupid that a couple in love with each other cannot belong to each other physically because, decrepit formulisms call it immoral, or that when they separate, the man goes off to satiate his pent-up passion with another woman, and the girl masturbates or has sexual "relations" with another woman, thereby atrophying her mind and jeopardizing her beauty. This is criminal, odious, and shameful, against nature, and the parents are responsible. What is natural is that this man and this woman fulfill their love by making use of the rights that nature has given them, without stupid fears.

What would be natural is that when the man develops fully and feels the need to search for a companion, he choose someone pleasing to him and, if she accepts him, the two make their nest and create a family, without preambles or silliness. This would be ideal, the sublime and correct thing, what nature ordains. Man and woman belong to each other as virgins, and in this manner there would be no fears of prostitution or adultery.

A man should not make use of his sexual urges until he has reached full development, and then he searches for a beloved, takes her home and creates a family.

With this kind of practice we would have a healthy, strong, robust, and happy generation.

No man should be with a woman other than she whom he will choose to create a family. Then we could speak of good manners, of morality, but in the shape we are in, all of us prostituted, speaking of morality is ironic, idiotic, and useless.

Let us put into practice this system and then we will take love to its true state. This is free love, which we are criticized for, which they try to profane and defame, saying that it is immoral, when immorality, emotional disorders, and vice are what currently reign. The man of today thinks it correct and decent to go and have sex with a woman who does not belong to him only, and that he has the right later to go and woo a young chaste woman, or one who seems to be chaste, at least to him. What I'm underlining is that he does not seek a woman who is in the same conditions as he is. No, he has to seek a virgin, and in this kind of inequality, he dares to speak about goodness. And the woman of today who has the same rights as men, has to deprive herself of being with her beloved because of a supposed honesty, making a martyr out of herself becoming sick as she destroys her baby, atrophying her brain, aging prematurely, suffering a thousand ailments, and dizzy spells; she becomes hysterical, laughing and crying without knowing why. All of this because she does not know her rights nor what would truly make her happy, which is to belong to the man she loves[6] without fears, taking from

---

[6]Understanding, of course, that this man really loves her, and will set up a home with her, and create a family, without the permission of a judge or a priest.

This man must be a healthy man, one who does not have bad habits, and has not belonged to another woman.

In order to establish these pure customs, we need pure individuals.

him the right to enjoy the first fruits of her love. And the man, in many cases, in order to avoid contagion, so as not to surrender himself to the arms of a woman he does not love, commits acts against nature. Who are the ones responsible for these aberrations?

The moralists have the floor . . . !

Who has contributed to the fact that the most beautiful and sublime act in which two people who love each other can engage, has become nothing more than a pleasurable pastime, without reproducing the species.

The "religious" celibates and other partisans have the floor . . . !

Who are the ones responsible when a man and a woman, because they live in misery, do not want to have children because they do not have the means to support them, and so resort to conjugal fraud?

And yet there is enough in nature to feed the mass of humanity that currently exists, without exploitation, fraud, or misery.

The egoists and exploiters have the floor . . . !

Answer, hypocrites, who has deformed humanity this way? Filling it with vice and misery when nature is so bountiful? Speak, so you do not dare to respond "brothers" . . .

All those who support and continue exploiting others, are the ones who sustain the state of misery of the people and therefore are the ones who maintain jails, penitentiaries, or better yet, the ones who create thieves, murderers, the insane, religious and political fanatics. Because if it were not for the fear of misery, there would be no political or religious fanatics,

The fear of misery, or misery itself makes one commit crude acts that degenerate into crimes, injustices, and madness, which is why we have jails and mental institutions, inequalities and injustices.

The Social Revolution will make these iniquities disappear.

And the revolution will rise up through propaganda and study and scientific research. And we anarchists are the ones who propagandize and an education is within the reach of all.

Let us study and prepare our generation for the future struggles that draw closer.

Free Love[1]
by Magadalena Vernet

It is necessary to investigate and to prove that for love to be just and healthy it cannot be other than free, given that painters show us love on the canvas as a beautiful winged child, and the poets in their happy, fantastic, or sad songs, show us love as capricious, volatile, changing, always seeking new horizons and sensations.

"Love is the child of the Bohemian spirit!"

And this is the truth: none of us can vouch for the stability of love. More so than any other human feeling, love is the most varied and fleeting, because it not only represents the emotions of the heart, but a desire of the senses and a physical need.

Love should not be confused with marriage. Marriage is a social convenience; love is a natural law. Marriage is a contract; love a kiss. Marriage is a prison, love a passion. Marriage is the prostitution of love.

For he who conserves his purity and dignity, love will be lived out freely; and he cannot love in any way other than freely if he is governed by its one and only law. There can be no moral or material consideration above this whim, of two beings who love each other, desire each other, and say it to each other. They have the right to give themselves to each other without any stranger intervening in their desires, and likewise, they should have the absolute right to separate the day one of them stops desiring the other.

I do not say "the day they stop loving each other," but the day

---

[1]Translated and edited by "Nueva Vida" (New Life) of Barcelona

they stop desiring each other, because these are two different things. One can stop desiring a woman and still love her; one can not love her lover more and remain faithful to her friend.

This is a well-known psychological state, because there are many similar cases. But what I want to focus on is the aspect of this case that concerns the woman.

For women it is generally admitted that her sexual life is null or subordinate to that of the companion—legal or otherwise—that she has chosen. She should live and feel for him; be passionate if he is, and maintain herself neutral if he is cold. Until now a man has considered sensual desire as something that pertains to him, not recognizing in women a moral and physical self organized like him.

I want to speak extensively on this matter as much as possible within this study on free love.

ଔ   ଔ   ଔ

Previously I said that to study the great natural laws it has been necessary to go back to the primitive eras, and study Nature in the context of animal life.

Fine, in the animal realm the females carry on a sexual life that is curious; she has sexual needs, desires she satisfies with the same freedom and regularity as the males.

No one will contest that the physiological laws that function for animals are not the same ones that function for humans. So then, why not admit, in this case, the same physical similitude for women and female animals, which one readily admits between males of both species? Why reproach women a natural life? Why make love an exclusive need of men?

Until now, acting as the master of this and other questions, men have responded: "because women do not have needs, because they do not desire anything; because she does not suffer from the privations of carnal satisfaction."

But what is it that men know about whether women have needs or not? Who better than women themselves to judge and decide?

I still have present in my mind a statement by a doctor: "The celibacy of a woman is more monstrous than that of a priest. To condemn a woman to abstinence is an iniquity, because to do this is to deprive her of the integral development of her feminine self."

According to what this doctor said, an overly prolonged virginity in women provokes a tyranny over their intellectual and physical evolution.

If there are really frigid women, without desires, what does that prove? There are also men who are this way, devoid of sensuality. But it is never the majority that find themselves like this, and allow me to say this: never have the majority of women been inimical to love.

Currently, with the defective education that women receive, she is seen as bad, judged from the point of view of sensation and desire. She does not analyze her interior life and frequently suffers without knowing why.

The virgin of exuberant health, whose ardent blood sears her temples and reddens the lips, perhaps does not know that it is virginity that makes her nervous, restless. She does not know that it is the need for love that makes her cry or laugh without reason; nonetheless, even though she does not know how to define it, it is still true that the natural law of love is what moves her.

Marriage will make women understand what they are unaware of, a marriage to which she will be taken blindly, because she will have conjured up two triumphant arms where she might find a refuge. Then when she is initiated into sexual life, her flesh will be vibrant and she will realize that she is linked to a man who perhaps she cannot love. And, depending on her temperament, she will go to the arms of a lover or resign herself to conjugal duty.

And if she resigns herself and accepts her duty without love, then she will see the same in herself as in other women, that she has no desires; if she does not approve of any carnal necessity, she will fool other women and herself. Nonetheless, carnal needs will have existed in her, but not having found the appropriate milieu for her passion, it will have become atrophied and dormant. If this same woman had followed a free life, if leaving the companion who did not respond to her desires had she been channeled towards a man who would have made her amorous life completely vibrant, she probably would not have become a cold woman.

Within our current state of love relationships, it is much easier for a man to judge whether he is "cold" or not. As he is free to give rein to his desires, he will simply be able—after passing through the embraces of various women—to declare whether he is in favor of or against sensuality. But the woman—condemned to know only one man—cannot really know if what she has not found in the arms of this man she would have found it in the arms of another.

Consequently, it is impossible to say exactly what women are from the perspective of sensuality. Nonetheless, if one would closely observe animal life, one would conclude that females rarely show the anomaly of lacking sensuality. It does not ever happen in wild species and if it presents itself in domesticated animals, that is because domestication has deformed them. Then we can say that the female goes about deprived of sexual satisfaction, ruins herself, and is robbed of a quarter of her existence.

There is no doubt that if a woman were to live normally, that if she were not deformed by the physical and moral contract, the number of "frigid" women would be significantly reduced. But I suppose even with fifty percent truly sensual beings, these fifty percent have a right to an integral life and it would be iniquitous to condemn them to a mutilation of a part of themselves, for the simple reason that there are fifty percent who are perfectly satisfied with their lot.

Freedom in love for women the same as for men is nothing other than a great act of justice. This will never force the "frigid ones" to become passionate, but it will allow the passionate ones no longer to suffer the oppression of social and conventional laws.

ଔ   ଔ   ଔ

I said at the beginning that love and marriage should never be confused. Fine, before leaving the physiological terrain I will go further and say that love should not be confused with desire.

Love is the complete communion of two minds, of two hearts, of two sensualities. Desire is nothing more than the whims of two beings brought together in one voluptuousness. Nothing is so fleeting or unstable as desire; nonetheless, none of us can escape it. If all women wanted to be real honest with themselves, they would see that there have been times in which they have given themselves virtually to a man they have only known for a few hours—or a short instant—and of whose name and feelings they are unaware. But a squeeze of the hand will have been enough, an exchange of glances, the sound of a voice, to spark desire, and whether she wanted to or not, that woman who has felt this desire will have belonged to that unknown man, who will never be able to possess her, because she might perhaps forget him tomorrow.

We cannot be masters of our carnal desire, just like we cannot control the stomach's tyranny. Both are inherent to our physical being; they are the result of two natural processes and both are equally legitimate. If hunger is not satisfied, weakness ensues, and later death.

I still insist on the difference between love and desire because they are often confused, and that confusion often leads to displeasure and sad outcomes.

"Spirit is fleet; the flesh is weak!" the Scriptures tell us. Yes, it is true that the flesh is weak. And what does it mean that there are times when desire impels us to act? And is this action, is it always fulfilled voluntarily and consciously? There are hours of time in which the notion of what is real vanishes, and nothing dominates us so much as the sensations of the moment.

One of the best things that we have seen in Nature is the following:

When in springtime the trees flower, covering the branches with leaves; when the flowering of life is born everywhere—from the Earth, from the Sun, the forest and all the plants—the desire born beneath the breast also moves hearts, making them frenetic. And in the summer evenings, hot and perfumed nights, who could deny that the needs of voluptousness is not more intense? Ask those who are passionate for each other, who on some nights have found themselves alone. They know something about this, and they will tell you what they have suffered in the solitude of those nights.

Well then, if there are days and hours in which sensuality can exasperate an individual, then there is no mystery in saying "the flesh is weak." If proof is needed, suffice it to put two persons of the opposite sex face to face.

But really, this is not love, this is nothing more than desire, desire that sometimes seems to be draped in the accoutrements of love, but once satisfied, it leaves the two lovers as two strangers. The same happens with the hungry person, who once satiated, gets up, and leaves the table without anguish.

But let it not be surmised that from this that I condemn feeling desire. Why would I want to condemn it, if I have been showing that it is naturally bound to our sexual life? What I want to make clear is the difference between desire and love.

II

Marriage, love, and desire are three different things.

Marriage is the chain that has men and women as mutual prisoners of each other.

Love is the integral union of the two.

Desire is the whim of two sensualities.

I will leave aside marriage, of which I am an adversary, and get to the issue of free love.

I say love must be absolutely free, as much as for women as it is for men; and furthermore, I add: love can never truly exist except under the condition of being free. Without absolute freedom, love becomes prostituted.

Selling one's body for a higher or lower price to numerous clients is not the only type of prostitution. Prostitution is not only a woman's tradition; men also prostitute themselves when they unfeelingly dole out caresses for any material interest.

Not only is legal marriage a form of prostitution, but it is also a form of speculation of one spouse upon the other, and it is always prostitution when a virgin is unaware of what she is doing by getting married.

And as far as conjugal duty is concerned, this is no more and no less than prostitution.

Prostitution is submission to a husband; prostitution is resignation and passivity.

And it is still prostitution when a free union passes from a bond of love to one of mere custom.

In the end, prostitution is anything reproached by both sexes that falls outside of desire and love.

ଭ   ଭ   ଭ

One of the reasons love should be absolutely free is precisely the similarity between love and desire that I have spoken of, asking that the two terms not be confused.

Rationally speaking, two human beings can come together in a bond, but is it possible for them to know if it can continue? Does one have the right to unite two elements when unaware of the affinity that exists between the two? Within a legal marriage there is always a doubt; women are at times deceived. The husband has not found in his wife what he thought he was getting. And there you have them, each attacking the other.

Marriage tends to have as its base reciprocal love and in a short time there can be an obstacle that impedes the harmony between the conjugal pair. This happens because said love was nothing more than a desire born of passion; and if the two spouses would have given themselves to each other freely before the law, experience would have taught them that they were not born for each other; and with all of this one clearly sees that laws for the union of two individuals have always been unnecessary, and at the same time it is proof in favor of the need for free love.

Love can be born of desire, but it is never possible to affirm it only through desire. When love arrives without first having passed through the heart and the mind, its duration will be precarious; but when it is based only on sexual desire it is quite probable that it will die out if it has not first gone through the head and the heart.

Lastly, because I am doing a detailed analysis of this study, and must go to the heart of the truth—I would say that sexual desire can unite two persons for a more or less long period of time without giving way to true love.

A man and a woman can have intimate relations without ever being attracted to each other by anything other than sexual desire. Their feelings and thoughts could be in total disagreement at the moment when they satisfy their carnal desires.

This—and I must make sure that this is keenly appreciated—can in no way be compared to prostitution, because the feelings that attract these two individuals—without it being exclusively sensual—is mutually sincere. There can only be prostitution where there is sale, contract, ignorance, or passivity. This is not the case with mutual physical attraction because the two lovers are drawn to each other by the same sensation within a bond freely made by both of them.

The truth of all that has been heretofore exposed is a condemnation of monogamy.

In effect, a diversity of desires is born of a diversity of feelings, and if admitted as a law that is essentially natural, monogamy can in no way be supported. Monogamy is still a form of prostitution: prostitution of men toward women, and of women toward men.

On the issue of the sexual life of individuals there can only exist one law and one sole morality for both sexes: the absolute freedom of love.

CR   CR   CR

The union of flesh cannot be governed by one rule only, identical for all individuals: it cannot be subjected to any definite and immutable law. Consequently, there should be no duties, nor rights constituted if one wants to conserve the absolute freedom of love.

Is it not illogical that such a word as duty be linked to the word love? One can easily see the irony at the root of these words, inscribed in books of infant morality: "The first duty of a child is to love his parents."

Within current morality it is also said that: "The mother must love her children; a wife must love her husband."

These words are ridiculous. No matter at what level, can love ever be a duty? Isn't it natural that a child love his mother out of gratitude for all the care given the child during infancy, and that the mother love the child who has caused her many troubles, a love born of the memory of sweet caresses? Is it not also natural that a woman love the companion she has chosen, the friend that has helped her develop her life as a woman? If a child does not love its mother, if a woman does not love her children, if she does not love her companion, what can be done about that? Nothing. All of the pronouncements written in the legal codes, all of the religious and moral exhortations can never make love flower if love has not bloomed naturally.

In the same way that love cannot create duties, it cannot create rights, either. The right of husband over wife and that of a woman over her husband is oppression, and oppression destroys love. The slave can never love the master.

The fact that a woman loves a man and gives herself to him should not be construed as the man exercising his privilege over the woman. And simply because she gives herself to her companion doesn't mean she has authority over him. Free before they lived together, they loved each other freely; and having joined together freely, the man and woman should be autonomous in all their manifestations after they have sealed their union.

In short, I'd like to conclude this study by saying the following:

Love has to be completely free; no law, no morality can rule over it, nor subject it any sense.

There should be no difference between the two sexes with regard to love.

In a word: sexual mutuality between two people should not create obligations, duties, or rights between individuals.

III

I am aware that at first glance my theory on love will seem immoral to many. Some will see or want to see in my words a consecration of libertinism.

If one wants to reason or dig deeper into the matter, you will agree with me in saying that free love, far from being a cesspool of immorality, will be the natural regulator of happiness and of a perfect morality.

And what is immorality? To define it you must remove yourself from the atavistic notion that makes us consider as natural law all that is nothing more than social convention.

For me, immorality is everything that is contrary to Nature, everything that makes an individual enter into a contract, making him or her abandon the natural rules of life so as to be subjected to purely conventional rules; immorality is all the things that put obstacles in the way of human passions in the name of notions without any value for the person who wants to understand deeply life and love.

Immorality is prostitution, legal or otherwise. Immorality is the forced celibacy of women, it is the sale of women's bodies, it is a wife's submission, it is the lies of a husband who no longer loves his wife. But free love cannot be a source of immorality because it is a natural law: nor can sexual desire be immoral, since it is a natural desire of our physical life.

If sexual need were immoral, then there would be no other option than to condemn to immorality hunger, sleep, and all other physiological phenomena related to the body.

If we were to observe well the current state of love around us, what a cesspool of immorality we would find in them! Marriages without a trace of affection, in which the man buys a dowry and the woman a situation, adultery of both husband and wife, violence of all kinds, the sale of the flesh, emotional mendacity, diverse contracts that lead the ignorant ones to licentiousness and poverty into the hands of the exploiter, who always speculates on the hunger of the poor.

Even if free love were a common practice, there could be no more immorality in it than already exists today. Even admitting that the situation would not truly change, at least under free love you would have openness in the way things were done.

I am completely convinced that free love will mean the moral liberation of all persons, because it will free both sexes of contracts and physical servitude.

Why do we believe that a free person will be immoral? With free animals there is no immorality. They know no physical disorders which beset humans, and that is because they obey no other law than the natural law. What creates immorality are the lies men force upon themselves and others; and free love, freeing man from falsehood, will put an end to disorders and libertinism.

When humans are completely free, when they are regenerated by an improved education, they will find within themselves a natural balance of their physical and moral faculties, and at the same time they will become a normal and healthy being.

We all have an instinctual sense that looks over our being: the sense of self-preservation. When we are no longer hungry we stop eating, because we know the problems it can cause; when we have walked to exhaustion, we are careful to rest, when fatigue weighs down our eyelids, we know that we need sleep. In the same way, we will find the natural regulator to our sex life in the course of our sexuality.

Animals obey this sense of self-preservation. Why should a free man be inferior? I wouldn't want to insult humanity in attacking that hypothesis.

No, the true and integral development of free persons will not be immoral. What is truly immoral is to falsify consciousness by falsifying the truths of Nature; immoral is to deny individuals the ability to live healthy and strong lives in the name of dogmas, laws, and conventionalisms contrary to the harmony and purity of life.

Varieties
Feminism
(from *L'Avenir Médical* of Paris)

The legislative elections, which have just been held, have not been favorable to feminism. One or another female candidate has run, but none has been able to sustain a true struggle until the end. But this doesn't mean despair for those apostles of women's causes. All countries will continue to heed their aspirations, either under a timid veneer as in France, or in tumultuous abundance, as in England or in the Americas.

In fact, the feminist cause has had many important partisans among the strong sex. In 1877, Victor Hugo heatedly defended feminism in a letter to Leon Richer: "Women", wrote the poet, "are seen as lesser beings civically and as slaves, morally. Her upbringing suffers from this double sense of inferiority; and from this all the suffering that man inflicts on her, which is unjust. Men have tipped the scales of the law, in whose equilibrium human consciousness is invested, putting all of the rights on their own little plates, and all the duties on the woman's. From this the profound upheaval, from this, the slavery of woman. We need reform and this reform will be achieved for the benefit of civilization, of society, of light."

The eminent philosopher, John Stuart Mill has written: "All of the egotistical inclinations, the cult of oneself, the injustice of self-preference that dominates humanity, has its origin and roots in the way that current relations between men and women take place, and it is from these relations that such egotisms derive their principal force. Consider the vanity of the young man who when he becomes a man, is convinced that, without merit, without having done a thing on his own, and even if he is among the most frivolous and incapable of men, just by having been born a man, feels that he is superior to half of humanity without exception, when in that half one can find people whose superiority is capable of weighing over him every day and at every moment. By giving women the freedom to use their faculties, letting them freely choose the manner in which they want to exercise those faculties, by opening up the same work opportunities, and offering the same stimuli as those available to men, one of the principle benefits of such an endeavor would be to duplicate the total of intellectual faculties that humanity would have at its service."

But perhaps we should not follow these authors so far along this road, and instead, to return to what concerns our profession we can agree that various women have undertaken this profession with great success.

Even in remote times we have seen woman become interested in our art. In France, Diana of Poitiers and Marguerite of Valois are known for having practiced the art of medicine from antiquity.

Madame Necker, wife of the renowned minister of Louis XVI, was responsible for the reorganization of French hospitals.

In Germany, women doctors were numerous, during the Middle ages, and even more so in the fourteenth and fifteenth centuries.

And in our times there are many women who have devoted themselves to medicine. Miss Elisabeth Blackwell, who had been a primary school teacher, is the first in the United States to become a doctor, at Boston University in 1847, also having studied in Geneva and Paris. Only eight years after Boston, the University of Philadelphia began to admit women to medical school, and this example was quickly imitated by other universities. In 1874, for the first time, Madame Putnam-Jacobi became a professor at Mount Sinai's teaching hospital. Later, there have been women doctors in the Army and one could cite the example of Madame MacGée, who was appointed military surgeon in Puerto Rico, with the rank of Lieutenant. Miss María Walcher had a similar position in the Union army during the Civil War.

Without trying to make this brief analysis something more extensive, and even if we didn't recognize that women have the same aptitude as men to undertake study as arduous as that of medicine, we can safely conclude from the previously cited examples, that women, by force of will and energy, are quite capable of doing certain jobs that they previously had been denied. This theory is constantly disputed by those who claim women's inferiority due to sexual difference, which, it is said, seems to be an immutable law of nature. But there is nothing more false than to attempt in this way to uphold the permanent superiority of men. There are numerous animal species for whom this rule has been broken. Elephants, for example, when they migrate and are about to cross into rough terrain, send the females ahead, because they are considered more apt to find the safest road.

Among birds it is often the female that is dominant in the couple. The female sparrow is not bashful about harshly reprimanding the male; and the female tosses the male sparrow out of the nest when there isn't sufficient food for the both of them. The female pigeon makes the male sit on the eggs and guard the nest from ten to four every day, while she goes off and gets some fresh air.

Among birds of prey, the female is more ferocious than the male, a fact that well known to falconers, who prefer the females. She is so unaffectionate that, when made prisoner, she will kill her male companion.

Even among insects a husband's fate is frequently of a most humiliating nature. The queen bee has many suitors. Forced to dash after her, the most agile male catches up with her and is accepted; but the joy of this husband is ephemeral because of course he dies. The destiny of the rivals he overcame is more enticing. These well-fed and non-working bees take on the leisurely pace of a lord, but then one fine morning, the female worker bees realize that they are feeding lazy and useless beings, and massacre the males.

But the true epitome of female triumph in the animal realm is reached in the spider. In this species, the female is much heavier and much stronger than the male, which is why the male is reduced to slavery, immediately and until the moment of fertilization. Once mating is finished and there is no more need for his services, he is simply devoured.

An elegant solution to conjugal problems! But we trust that the amiable members of the female sex have yet tended toward such a solution, in spite of overwhelming us everywhere with their vindications, and in spite of the fact that they already greet in the figure of a liberated Eve—according to the phrase coined by Miss Odette Laguerre—the engenderer of a more worthy humanity.

Doctor Paul Vigne
Paris, 1910

Important!

To all women, teachers, and mothers

It is impossible not to quote some of the paragraphs of "The Human Comedy," a lecture given by Doctor Luis Gámbara. In it he says:

"The human comedy is the comedy of honesty, divided into three evils: the hypocrisy of education, the hypocrisy in women, and social hypocrisy. I will make some observations, enough to make evident the hypocrisy of current education, which seems to have no other purpose than to awaken feelings of kindness and egotism in children.

I say hypocrisy because education is based on lies and nourished on appearances. What we have are well-trained parrots who admirably recite their lesson, but their hearts are bereft of feeling, their minds are blank, their backbone is corrupted.

The systems that are imposed on secondary instruction, do they not represent the daily triumph of appearances, underwritten by encyclopedic programs? Books, books, and books, voluminous programs and everything devoted to passing the exam. But what happens after the exam? A great emptiness, a multitude of laureates in the science of being moles, falsely condemned to burn incense to what is above ground."

Here is another quotation:

"Always and everywhere superficiality reigns. In well-off families, with the help of young, inexperienced governesses, young women are prepared, who know a little of everything, but nothing really well, without their own ideas and convictions, who think like everyone else, and who are taught not virtue, but a conventional modesty.

The noble mission of motherhood, I speak in general, is an ordeal. Nothing is felt of the importance or duty of that duty, and it is handed over to the governesses, who comprehend this gravitas even less.

The rich bourgeoisie imitates, copies, by way of blind idolatry that one feels for all that appears to be distinguished.

The somewhat wealthy bourgeoisie imitates as well and as often as they can, but it always imitates: they manufacture young women, who as they stroll about or go to the theater, can be confused one with the other. Among the poorer classes, there is a lack of time and resources to educate, and so they sleep peacefully thinking that school is the answer to everything. Good God! It is really a sacrifice to send these children to school!

Gentlemen!

What are these children like?

What tendencies do they have?

What kind of psychic and physical organism?

Who will be cured of their upbringing?

Spencer wrote with a sociologist's love, and let us hope that others will be concerned with future generations as much as he was. "You know how to produce an ox for work and woolen lambs for the scaffold, the horse for racing, the cocks for fighting, and bulls for the bull ring. You know how to produce animals of all kinds, but behold the strange case, you accept your children as they come, without knowing ahead of time if they will be healthy or sick, weak or strong, miserly or generous, resolved and energetic or pusillanimous and lazy." That's the way Spencer spoke.

Here are the words of Gámbara: "Let us tear away the veils, those that hide false modesty, and here you will find a double-edged moral, like the smuggler's trunk, especially used by young women, the future mothers." Poor young women! condemned to blush according to the occasion.

"Parents need to study their children at the age in which a girl becomes a woman, and a boy suitable for procreation. This is the most critical period for the young girl, who suddenly finds herself on the road that leads to maternity."

"No to hypocrisy, no to puerile lies, no to dangerous illusions; let the girl know from the chaste lips of her mother—before she learns it from others—that she is becoming a woman, that a new life opens up before her, and that the sacred mysteries of nature not be contaminated by vulgar stories, which sooner or later, if heard from other sources, will create malice, perversions, vices, that otherwise would not have flowered if truth had not been manifested in order to guide the young woman on the path to virtue, on which the mother is guide, consoling force, and advisor. Do not shun nature, which speaks a language of sincerity; don't draw a curtain over things in the name of a false morality, which is the mother of all immorality. Mothers, be the friends, the confidants of your daughters! Let them learn from your lips what life is, and that way they will not ask the maid, the governess, their first boyfriend, who will tell more lies than you—if you have lied—you, masters of the sorts of vices which would never remotely have entered into the fantasies of your daughters'. That is the way I speak, gentlemen, and I'm aware that I am speaking the truth. I agree that is the oriental despotism of men in great measure that forms the way women are now, false."

In sum, I should refrain from quoting anymore and briefly synthesize.

For Gámbara, women's vanity is due to a false education, which is remarkable and frenetic to the extreme. And I concur with him that this is due to the fact that as a rule men take women as an instrument of pleasure and not as a future mother; and, of course, if she happens to give birth, it is by accident and not because she really wants to reproduce herself. And so I echo Gámbara's words: "It is corruption that undermines the family, because people want to love without procreating, perverting the woman, and increasing the number of courtesans and crimes."

"It is the fever of perversions that is consuming man's organism in this unfortunate century."

If we examine fashion, we see that it creates many victims. The desire to be or to appear pretty makes women want to dress fashionably, generating social hypocrisy, because all the women that do not have the means to follow fashion in all its whims, sacrifice appearance and with their outward demeanor affirm what in substance they are not. How many young women sell their honor for an elegant and fashionable dress? How many go without bread in order to have gloves? How many say: "We all have our pride."

There is a need to protect decorum. One cannot be less than others. I do not want to look bad; I do not want to be taken for someone in rags.

All of this constitutes defense of hypocrisy, sung in homage to fashion, that creates bitterness, disillusions, rivalries, immorality, offenses; and all because of that fascinating, all-conquering fashion, because in the elegant life it has a profound cult, that, out of vanity, servility, and irritation, recruits high priests from all social classes. Fashion creates luxury, so that which is a source of pleasure and taste for those who have more than they need, becomes a hundred times more damaging for those who have only the basics. From this there follows an increase in more abandonment, in unhappiness, and a more vigorous development of social hypocrisy. Tell me, gentlemen, is it not the school of hypocrisy this that sings the praises of our current civilization, of progress, of advancement, and leaves in the dust all the miseries that stand in our way? Oh, all of you, you who; with a smile on your lips, with joy in your heart, sit down at life's happy banquet and enjoy its pleasures! Have you never thought of the sad plight of an abandoned child?

Have you never heard his laments, nor have you never listened tell his story, nor seen his tears, have you never entered into the depths of his heart in order to understand his pain, his torture, his tears? Have you never done so? For humanity's sake read Gámbara's *Criminal Sociology* and *The Human Comedy*.

These books should be a part of any library. In them, the printed word contains the expression of human pain, and it rips away the mask of hypocrisy of a society that calls itself Christian and that allows, tolerates, and approves of injustices, crimes, and bestial disorders.

All this when Christianity in its essence is communist anarchy, that tolerates no privilege, nor impositions, nor masters nor servants, nor class distinctions of any kind. Christianity is a belief that practices and organizes brotherhood, that does not allow for the accumulation of goods, nor the hoarding of wealth. Where is that primitive Christianity, that true love of one's neighbor? It is hidden by the Vatican, under the priest's robe that puts forth its brutalizing dogma before the maxims of the self-sacrificing and just man who preached the truth. Should we be complicit with these crimes that are currently committed, instead of protesting and looking for a way of living in accord with what is just and natural?

On Honesty

The false concept of honesty that is in currency obliges me to write of this matter.

Individuals of both sexes have fallen into the error of believing that it is only men that have the right to use their freedom as they please.

A woman has the duty to conserve her beauty, but she cannot with the prejudices that bind this duty to the whipping post of social hypocrisy's convention. "The Human Comedy" as Gámbara has said, is the comedy of honesty. One wants to appear "honest" with a fictitious honesty, one that is criminal, against health and life, against natural laws.

Let us hear the words of Dr. Drysdall, who writes in "Health and Strength" from Barcelona: "Lately, many are deceived about the sexual desires of women. To experience strong sexual passions is considered shameful for a woman, and these passions are denigrated as if they were purely animalistic, sensual, vulgar, and worthy of revilement. The moral emotions of love by women are looked upon positively, but physical emotions are viewed as degrading and unfeminine. This is a grave mistake. In women, as in men, the vigor of sexual appetites is a great virtue; it is the sign of a robust constitution, with healthy organs and a naturally-developed sexual disposition.

The venereal appetite is similar to normal appetites. If a woman enjoys perfect health and her body is strengthened by exercise, and by a life led according to human nature, she will eat with a hearty appetite and with pleasure. The same can be said of sexual desires. The two are the great regulators of health as long as they are exercized neither excessively nor insufficiently. Instead of despising a young woman who has strong sexual passions, one must understand that she has one of the most beautiful virtues, whereas weak or morbid desires are, on the contrary, a sign of an imperfect or sickly constitution. Frequently I have been consulted in cases in which, according to reports facilitated by the family, I expected to find a non-threatening illness, and then found out that the ailment was a desperate one.

Unfortunately, there is nothing truer than a delicate weakness, and irregular menstruations are, now at least, more the rule than the exception among the young women of the cities.

This type *of health* among women is seriously inadequate. If we make the rounds through any city, we see that, in general, the women are pale, skinny, and deteriorated. When vital faculties are in such a lowly state, it is almost a sickness, and in all cases this produces innumerable effects.

Chlorosis (*) and hysteria in women are analogous to spermatorrhea (**) in men. Both ailments are a weakness, a state of exhaustion, indicative of the breakdown of a person's constitution, and both are related to genital weakness.

We have seen that the only true and natural remedy against spermatorrhea is the healthy and frequent exercise of the sexual organs, a field of action for the emotions and for amorous passions. The same is true for a woman. Her nature languishes in the absence of the natural stimulation that only her organs can provide. Her spirit and feelings turn morbid for the same reason and the only true and permanent remedy is sexual exercise. This exercise would stimulate her constitution, it would satisfy the natural passions that consume her strength and would imbue her spirit with natural and healthy feelings instead of the sexual shame and morbid timidity that crush her. Sexual commerce is necessary above all when chlorosis is the result of masturbation, since in that case it is not only a question of establishing a natural practice of sexual exercise, but also of uprooting one that is not natural: masturbation, something at times difficult for both sexes. In fact, there is only one means with which to combat venereal masturbation in both sexes and that is the normal satisfaction of sexual appetites. If that satisfaction were achieved, rarely would the solitary vice be recurred to, and thus one of the most frequent causes of bodily and mental illnesses would be uprooted.

I well know how many prejudicial opinions will be opposed to recognizing sexual intercourse as a great remedy for genital debility in women, but I am deeply convinced it will come to be recognized despite the attempts to keep the matter steeped in mystery. As much as we want to condemn poets, philosophers, and doctors that seek a new path to free themselves of the labyrinth of sexual ailments, all are struck dumb in recognizing the merits of free, normal and sufficient sexual intercourse, since it is precluded to most people by the enormous baggage of religious prejudice. To prevent the occurrence of this important malady we must do as much as possible to increase the physical strength of women, starting in early childhood. It is necessary to completely change the education of young women and renounce enervating ideas about female comfort. We have to fortify the body her same as we do with boys and adults using expansive games and gymnastics. It is equally necessary to teach them to be proud of their intellectual capabilities. It is not just for their own benefit that women should strengthen their bodily potential, but also for their future children, since pale mothers will engender equally pale and sickly offspring. Solid and real knowledge must be communicated to them at all costs. Above all, one has to teach both men and women something essential to their formation to believe in their body and their spirit. In a word, if we don't study anatomy and physiology, if we don't study human nature, education does not deserve to be called education. Ignorance and false delicacy of women bring on the same defects in men, because they cannot freely discuss any sexual matters as long as women do not find themselves able to reason on this subject.

What Men Do

We have very unique habits that are different in men and women.

A man of any position, educational level or race can frankly say, without beating around the bush: "Oh yeah, I fell for this dancer, a really nice girl, but above all, a real dish!"

Others, in diverse situations, say the following: "Lilia and I had a thing, she is so young and beautiful, a little dumb, and full of herself, very flirtatious . . . and a liar, I quickly tired of her and I courted Margot, a stunning girl, very smart and educated, she knows French and speaks perfect English, plays piano and dances like a charm! . . . But wouldn't you know, the dad spoke to me (a day she was out for a stroll) he was quite mysterious and what not about my visits, and ended up setting a date for our wedding and quickly I left and did not return. Then I went nuts over Carolina, a scrumptious doll, about 16 to 18, refined; and excessively beautiful, sensitive and affectionate, an angel . . . but she would not let me lay a hand on her, I was courting her for a few weeks, she paid attention to me and wouldn't go out with anyone else except me and a close girlfriend of hers. I grew weary of the monotony of her pleasing but cold character, and after two months I dumped her for a haughty dark-haired beauty with black fiery eyes, with a deep and daring look, a graceful body and a majestic walk. She had me overboard, she would allow me short visits, for up to five minutes, and after three months, desperate, I told her I couldn't continue to see her like that, and I left and never returned."

Countless men proceed in such manner. They play with and laugh at many, many women.

Women do not have the right to do the same in our society, which must be changed as soon as possible.

It is time that "equality" stop being a vain phrase, and that the rights of both men and women be equal. If some woman falls in love and says, "Well, I fell in love with this tenor or such-and-such an artist, and saw him on several occasions, but he was very busy and didn't pay me any attention.

And after, I fell in love with a young man, a business agent, but he was a skeptic and so I left him."

But a woman doesn't find the same sincerity in a man that he does in a woman. When a young woman is wooed by a young man, if she likes him, she is sincere, affectionate, attentive, and faithful, when wooed by the woman, a man is pedantic, unjust, vulgar, troublesome, and ends up scorning her.

All of this is because of established customs, but after both men and women are accustomed to freedom this will change. I do not blame men because when they address a woman, accustomed as they are to these rights, they forget that she can arouse interest in a man, that she can hurt, and a woman figures that when a man attends to her it is because he loves her.

And he, when a woman woos him, or shows that she is in love with him, he thinks that she is flighty and loose, shameless, a nobody, and he starts to dress her down in his mind and believes she is not dignified enough to warrant attention.

And there's the rub, but let us women destroy this quandary with our persistence, and demonstrate that we have equal rights and then men will truly vary their demeanor.

When a man he woos a woman he wants to possess her, without great concern for the result; if he is accepted, he says the woman is too weak and not worthy, and does not dare continue as her lover because he mistrusts her. As, I understand it, this man, or all men in general, should become accustomed to refraining from courting a woman until he meets the one he really loves and with whom he is willing to form a family.

The fundamental point is this: that men have to control themselves and not go after women they don't love, and that they wait until they are eighteen or twenty to do so.

In a communist social system in which individuals have the right over everything produced by nature and the ingenuity of all, there could be greater liberty, and a man could form a family without economic and social worries. But we still have not arrived at such an era, it will not take long for this beautiful common process to be established among humans.

In spite of the opposition, from those who feel they will be adversely affected, these customs will arrive and will be established, bringing happiness to the human race.

It is natural that under the present system a woman would be jeopardized when having a child, and that the father not be with her.

If both sincerely and faithfully love each other, prepare to have a home and go off to live together to form a family, then this cannot jeopardize either of them, and if society believes it is jeopardized by this union, then society will have to become used to seeing no crime, where instead they should only see a natural law.

A man only used to seeing a woman as an object of pleasure forgets that she is destined to be the mother and teacher of a new generation.

The union of sexes is for procreation only. That man's invention has placed it at a lower level doesn't mean that this state of affairs should continue.

And it is because of this that I state that a man should approach a woman when he really loves her and feels the need to live with her and make her the mother of their children. Tolerance and indulgence are Christian virtues, they are part of a true education, but these values can suffer contagion in a social milieu where these values are absent.

But the thoughts that spurt forth from the spirit are its essence, and they will be set it free of that contagion.

Natural Forces

It is a little past midnight. I'm getting ready to retire. (At this hour I've returned from the theater where the excellent actors Paco Fuentes and Antonia Arévalo performed with taste, verve, and artistry.) Facing my bed is an open window that freely lets in a fresh and lively breeze. It is not cold even though it is our winter. I hear the sound of a thousand voices wafting through the window . . . I listen . . . it is the sea! The waves are in their strange and eternal conversation, so full of tenderness at times, at others full of curses, as if they wish to spill out of their inmense vessel, yet too small for their expansive reach; and at other moments it seems to weep as if it wants to draw something to its breast to console the waves, sweetly lulling them, or otherwise peacefully moving; its choppy waters with the oars of a boat, and then a sudden fury, to return these ships to the shore broken in a thousand pieces, ships that had entrusted themselves to its safety wrapping up in its white foam the remains that bob on her irritated surface, as if to caress that which it has destroyed.

As I write these lines I still hear the waves, crashing up against each other to get to the shore and kiss the sand. How beautiful, what an imposing presence the sea! Over its tranquil or stormy waters, the brave fisherman returns with his daily catch; on these waters, in moments of delicious calm, a poetic little boat glides along carrying two lovers, two souls who united by common aspirations, will weave together their destiny.

On these waters rest the great steamships that bring news and useful things for our needs.

On the immense surface of the sea thousands of vessels, ships, and small boats cross each other, and whether they are stopping over, or making a longer call, they enliven our ports and commerce.

What a powerful admiration we have for the sea, it is so suggestive to contemplate the ocean and how it exercises an enormous attraction on our being. When you contemplate the sea on moon lit nights, its luminous waters of a thousand colors combining with the cold rays of the moon, it seems to sleep under the clarity sent it by the eternal and solitary nocturnal orb. And at other times, in plain daylight, under the ardent rays of the Sun, which gilds its white foam as it splashes against the rocks, the sea proudly shows its powerful beauty, under the tutelage of our father the Sun, as if the sea knew of the Sun's great influential heat, that gives life to the thousands of fish that leap and play within its watery bosom. Yes, we find the sea beautiful! But why? Without the Sun, nothing would be beautiful, it is the Sun that causes the plants and fish to produce and multiply, the Sun that purifies our life, gives us joy and beautifies our existence. The sun is the true source which pours forth our riches, converted into beautiful and tasty fruits, in leafy and corpulent trees, which serve as the resource of one of the true great riches of the globe, wood, of all different types and with which we build furniture and an infinite amount of necessary utensils. And the multiple mines that are also one of our greatest treasures, which we use to build roads and railways, bridges and columns for buildings and subways, all made of iron transformed into steel and other metals. Tin, silver, gold, nickel, all of this is the work of solar heat. What are they if not immense coal mines? All of the other inventions of concentrated heat, steam, light, electricity, are the work of thousands of centuries of our sun, while each century becomes slightly colder, just a bit, also making our planet colder, with a visible reduction of the sun's diameter, affecting our planet, which will finally become colder as well. From this we can deduce the important and intimate link between the two in the immense concert of systems and suns that orbit in space. The sun is equally important in relation to the number of citizens being careful of its movements or its cooling (whether a human being in a city dies or shrivels). Later it will be such a natural thing that it won't be lamented. So our products and ways of life, our inventions and discoveries, we can say that they are solar light, accumulated and concentrated. Our enthusiasms, our energies, are all solar light that irradiate from our being. Thus, it is not strange that ancients adored the sun, even if they didn't fully understand its powerful influence on our planet and our life.

To My Daughter Manuela Ledesma Capetillo

"Of all the conceptions and revelations, both ancient
and modern, the plurality of lives is the only
one that fully satisfies logic and reason."
—Bouchet

How many times, my daughter, have I repeated these words to you, remembering these phrases by Lumen! Life eternal, without possible end!

If you could only understand those sentences, oh! daughter of my first illusions, angelic reproduction of my one and only, sorrowful love . . .

If only you understood the greatness of these words, which as you pronounce them, make you kneel, to worship the great, unknown force that one feels throughout all the obstacles and all the refusals.

I never taught you how to pray, you have to feel that need. You have not been baptized under any faith. I have sought for you the greatest of freedom in tastes and desires. I do not like violence.

The only thing that I desire and expect from you is that you be a good human being, not a routine Christian, no. To be an interpreter of Jesus's maxims, without going to mass, without confessing or taking communion, without accepting any type of errors or lies of the absurd religions that have materialized.

Instead of going to mass, go visit the poor and help them, because you can do so; instead of confessing and taking communion, go visit prisoners and console them, something to teach them. Don't forget that most of the people in jails and prisons are the poor and the ignorant, the victims who have always been subjected to exploitation.

When this indifferent and egoistic society is reformed by a future one that is fraternal, altruistic, when injustices are no longer committed, nor the innocent punished, when the judges, the supreme liars, stop demanding "the truth, the whole truth and nothing but the truth"; when no one steals a loaf of bread because they are hungry; when private property ceases to exist, and we all see each other as brothers, then and only then will jails, prisons and useless, harmful churches disappear. Misery, hate, and prostitution will no longer exist. There will be free exchange among peoples, because borders will be abolished and true freedom will reign on the planet.

Try and help put these ideas into practice so that people who have no home, nor wealth, who live in the doorways of carriage houses, mangers, or palaces, to not die of cold and hunger. What a mockery! What humanity! To perish from hunger and cold two steps away from a table laden with food, from rich and sumptuous coats. So close to abundance and waste we find hunger, pain . . . poor children victims of misery . . . It seems like a dream or a story, but it is a reality that astonishes . . . What horror! How false are the foundations of this so-called society, one that is based on crime, fallacy, and hypocrisy.

It is necessary for you to dismiss from your mind all thoughts that might tarnish your natural simplicity, for it is possible that our separation might open up the space in your mind for certain aristocratic lines of thought which might cause you to believe in the differences between classes. You won't forget that we are all susceptible to the environment in which we live, and if there are differences between humans, be it of character, behavior, or appearance, these are the result of life-style and education, of those habits acquired or forced upon them by society or by a system of exploitation.

Listen: Severine, in her book "On the March . . ." tells of countless suicides verified in Paris, detailed in myriad forms and in a variety of occasions and circumstances.

It is quite painful to read these stories, knowing of the wealth that is squandered in Paris of the splendid gifts made to artists (who deserve more) and forgetting the misery that consumes the lives of thousands. You'll say with what is squandered on champagne and thousands of orgiastic parties, the silk dresses and gems; can none of this be used for something? Yes, everything can be used to the point of exaggeration, to a breakdown, or all the way to insanity. But tell me, is all this needed in order to live according to healthy reason and sound judgment? No, you will say, and yet, how will commerce and industry progress? Perfectly well, for the millions of families in the world that lack clothing, shoes, furniture, kitchen utensils, dishes and silverware, and all other necessary objects that should be in the homes of those who grow old in the factories, and later, unable to work, turn to begging, then die in hospices or on the street.

Tell me, or better yet meditate upon, the thousands and thousands of sheets, tablecloths, tables, chairs, dressers, socks, shoes, and the countless number of necessary goods that rot in the stores and warehouses. If we were to provide these families with everything they needed, the manufacture of these goods would be much greater and there would be no need for them to be locked up collecting dust, when there are those in need of them.

How can we put these ideas into practice, if the exploiters do not accept such innovations, nor try to remedy these miseries by any means that might threaten their power, privilege, and distinction. Give alms and build hospitals. That is what they do.

The religious institutions have helped to foster these privileges and class divisions. If workers in general, by educating themselves, are not able to destroy the privileges of caste, race, hierarchy, and untold nonsense that harm us as human beings, then revolution will do it. Many fear revolution, but there is nothing like being part of revolution to get rid of that fear. Things seen from afar have a different effect on us. Up close, one can touch them and the effects of distance and of evaluation disappear.

Because one can imagine that social revolution will not be a riotous shoot-out that takes us by surprise.

I understand as does Labriola that, "The working class cannot emancipate itself if it does not determine to take over the means of production and 'absorb' public power." Not to make use of that power, but to destroy it. How will we begin to take control of the means of production? By way of cooperatives, and thus, when we have garnered the land and all its instruments and tools in general, then the government will be annulled.

Now everything is in the hands of capital. Capitalists do not cede their "rights" or privileges, misery is pitiless and perennial to the home of the worker. When the king leaves his residence with his entourage, all bedecked in luxury, either to take a stroll or to go to Congress, be it in Russia, Italy, or Spain, and on the way, he meets the unfortunate father of a family, who has left in his home tears, pain, and hunger, a man who can't find work and does not understand why he has to go hungry while the other squanders his luxury in leisure . . . and if a Mateo Morral or a Caserio steps forth, it shouldn't be surprising, it is the natural consequence of injustice. You should read "Impressions of a Chronicler" by M. Abril, which is a delightful book to read, interesting and pleasant, some pages about anarchism written by a distinguished literary figure and friend. I recall these paragraphs: "But in France you see the outbreak of strikes at Cremiex, and after the strikes the plots against Ravachol, and his execution. And Carnot, shortly after, is stabbed by Caserio." And further on: "The castle of Montjuich is filled with prisoners.

Some are shot and others submitted to such barbarous torments that those of the Inquisition paled in comparison."

These torments consisted of ripping their tongues out, castrating them, burning them, and executing them before a firing squad. Well, my daughter, despite having written this, Mr. Abril thinks that "Anarchism is a terrible cancer that must be extirpated," because he believes that, "this fanatical and criminal *sect* seems to be have been formed in order to exact vengeance."

Now, I would like to know, why did they lock up those workers in Montjuich, just for the thrill of it? Then anarchist action is more just. It is not vengeance, it is an act of justice. But, well, my daughter, take note: what right did Cánovas have to incarcerate, martyr, smash, and destroy the lives of those poor workers? Is it just because they declared themselves on strike to demand higher wages? (I think the mines belonged to the government).

How many poor innocent people have been jailed or executed from time immemorial, and because they were poor, without legal representation or money, they have been forgotten? And what about their wives and children? In a most cruel situation. In another paragraph I remember the following: "Don't fire and steel yield results?

"Let us appeal to human fraternity. With that fraternity Christianity was able to defeat the power of the Caesars." These words are addressed to the anarchists, but it is to the rulers and exploiters that they should be directed. My daughter, I am no advocate of violence. But we say[1] "Let those who are in power start by giving an example. Shouldn't we use the right of legitimate self-defense when we are exploited, oppressed, jailed, shot, or garroted, simply for reclaiming our rights and propagating ideas of justice and fraternity! The violent death of a man is lamentable, whether he be a beggar or a king, a bourgeois or a proletarian, but . . . who is doing the attacking? Who is the first to victimize, to play the executioner or the assassin? Are the lives of those in rags worth less than the powerful?" (from "¡Tierra!")

My daughter, if they had not tormented and butchered and shot those poor workers (who leave behind numerous families) in Montjuich, during the miners strike in Spain, Cánovas del Castillo would not have fallen to Angiolillo's dagger.

The government spends fabulous amounts of money on munitions, gunpowder, swords, and rifles, to use against the workers, that if the bourgeois exploits them, they can be threatened should the workers complain. And if they go on strike, they are shot. With what right? The right of force and ignorance.

In another paragraph Abril says the following: "Czolgostz, coldly and serenely assassinated (why?) the man he selected as a victim,

---

without hate, without malice, guided by a passion, by a malevolent hallucination, believing like every fanatic, that he is committing an act of redemption." (Do governments achieve some kind of redemptive act, with wars, jailing strikers, and making martyrs of them, leaving countless families in misery?) "And Czolgostz is killed little by little, he is tormented, they tear at his soul first, and then he is completely crushed. To his judges Czolgostz does not symbolize anything, he is not even a man, but a beast in a cage who is poked and flayed."

ʘʘʘ   ʘʘʘ   ʘʘʘ

Now then; here rises another issue of ideas, I am a believer in the diversity of existences, [reincarnation] and therefore in the immortality of the soul. But many say that spiritists and anarchists are different, and many do not want to accept that the ultimate goal of both is the same. But, fine, let us suppose they are not the same. Anarchists say that the fact of having been born gives them the right to enjoy all that exists and they are not content to want for the necessities of life, nor to spend a life-time in difficult labor only end up turning to the hospitals or begging for alms. Spiritists believe that there is no effect without a cause and that those who go hungry do so because they have made others go hungry; and that those who suffer injustice suffer because they have made others suffer. Very well, all that might be true, but the anarchists are not satisfied with that and they must bring bread to their children, and they have to go out and get it. Spiritists have no problem exploiting others in order to tend to their own needs and to enjoy creature comforts by any means possible. And even if those methods are not violent, are they not perverse and unnatural? Indeed they are! Anarchists prefer to make use of practical, just, and courageous methods before begging or exploiting by fraudulent or criminal means.

My daughter, choose, analyze, think, who are more reasonable? The spiritists dare tell a hungry person, a beggar: "you must have patience, we do not know what you did in another existence."

The anarchists say, fool, you are degrading yourself, you feel inferior to others, and after a lifetime of work you find yourself obligated to beg? Before arriving to that state, demand your rights. And the anarchists does not wish to give alms, not for lack of feeling, but because the anarchist become irritated with all the injustice, and says that the beggar is the product of the capitalist regime. It is natural that a full box weigh more than an empty box; if more and more money is accumulated without measure, on the one hand, then the other has to do without. If industrial and agricultural products go to waste in the storehouses, it is natural that there will be people who go hungry and destitute.

And so, the anarchists are not willing to console, as the friars still do, by saying, "Blessed are the meek for theirs will be the kingdom of heaven." They say that the kingdom of heaven is here on earth and that those responsible for this state of affairs are those who usurp the labor of others.

Now, if spiritists are willing to say to the workers that they should not demand their rights, that they should not asks for salary increases, that they be content with their own exploitation, that they not go on strike, that they patiently suffer through hunger and disposession, because in another existence they did the same to others.

Then I will not tell them these things! And certainly not in the name of spiritism, and now without ceasing to be a spiritist, I tell them that it is as criminal for them to let themselves die from hunger and lack of clothing, as it would be to kill for bread, and that before killing they should assault all of the cattle ranches and bakeries or food stores.

The spiritists don't dare tell the workers that they should attack the bakeries. Why? How did the owner acquire that bakery, if he only had one dollar and now has thousands? And how is it that those who work in the bakery don't have a dime? What a mystery! . . . This is it the silent and artificial mode of exploitation: it is violent, for it is in opposition to the will of the workers that these exploitative methods sustain the system. Spiritists say we must respect private property, but should we do so even if people die of hunger? Is the property of one or two individuals worth more than the health or life of thousands? What are the bases or principles of this property? Fraud and deception are violent and artificial.

The anarchists say property made in this fashion (and there is no other way to create property) is a crime; that to accumulate capital through the cautious deduction of a quarter a day from the daily wages of thousands of workers, is robbery. The law does not punish this hypocritical robbery, hiding behind the mask of virtue and honesty, and we will tear away that mask persuasively and will make them understand that they are in error; and if they don't want to understand, we will rip that mask off. It is not possible that this hypocrisy squander away without working for it the fruit of others labor. These anarchists who believe in their acts of justice cannot respect property gained by theft.

Spiritists call themselves rationalists, and so do anarchists, nonetheless, spiritists don't dare attack private property although they are away of it how it came about, but instead they allow people to die of hunger, and that is not rationalism.

Because even if it means depriving ourselves foods, an individual should not create capital while there are people who go naked and hungry.

Anarchists cannot respect private property, because they know it is made through exploitation, and if they were to respect it they would be as hypocritical as those who make it, and that would not be rationalism. That which is based on reason is openly analyzed, not hidden.

I accept all missions current and future, but if there are people who go naked and hungry, I protest. If someone has chosen the mission of coming to live here in order to go naked and hungry, knowing that the laws will punish him, jail him and that there he will be clothed and fed! In this manner, the mission is not realized. This business about missions is difficult to analyze. This is the only thing on which Anarchism and Spiritism differ. But when they come to the problem of poverty, everyone is mistaken. The most clear-headed about this, according to reason, are the Anarchists.

This is not a criticism but a comparison, my child, so that you can see on whose side reason lies.

They are the most elevated ideas, the ones most in agreement with the progress of the century.

On all other points we are in agreement, the transmigration of souls, different inhabitable worlds, the peace and harmony that should exist between enemies, through their mutual incarnation, that is to say universal harmony, through multiple lives.

You will accept what is most reasonable, without any kind of imposition.

We need to spread the word in order to destroy the fanaticism that weakens and destroys all kinds of initiatives. Ignorant souls believe their salvation lies in prayer, even though their lives might have been and may continue to be an accumulation of injustices and egotisms.

What kind of prayer is this and directed to whom, if it is created by a cruel heart? "Because what is within the heart is spoken through the mouth."

In my opinion, praying is unnecessary, but I do accept that thoughts of mental strength be sent out to contribute to the success or to the tranquility of all, or of one in particular. I also believe that one must never think that an action or a goal might not be achieved as one would wish. Never, upon conceiving of some project, have I thought that I will not be able to do it. This was and is natural in me: I understood this to be and acted accordingly, but I didn't know what it was called. Later, several letters that I received from "Club Success" Segno of Los Angeles, California, in which I receives some cards, one of which said: "Trust and constancy are the ultimate proofs of ability."

That is to say that I was practicing without knowing it, by innate instinct, a mental strength, mysterious and invisible desire in favor of my endeavors. I want something, and my tenacious desire alone, brings me the satisfaction of having it. These forces, educated and strengthened by some method, that of practice I suppose: can come to be very powerful.

I have never wanted to do something that ultimately I did not achieve. And when I think I could easily become a capitalist, I'm terrified, and I discipline myself and say "I don't want to," "I don't want to" with all my mental strength. And I prefer to be financially unstable before exploiting others. I don't want to become infected. All of the mental courage that I could muster would not be sufficient to destroy the notion of wealth. Wealth is so pernicious in the current state of the world that it destroys all human feelings. This does not mean that I would despise the comforts and abundance of a communist society. But as things are now, yes, because to have things means taking it away from others. I have always been in doubt, if it was that I sensed something, or that I desired it, but it is both, desire and premonition. If many I had tried to do many of the things I have considered, I would have been able to do them. But I stopped myself first, asking whether I was doing wrong or right, if my actions were not violent, or contrary to freedom as I understand it. And I have abstained from deciding upon any action contrary to my ideals, for fear of benefiting my own self-interest.

This is why when one thinks about a project it must immediately be put into practice, done without fear or hesitation, because decisiveness is lost and there is not the same level of firmness. Because of that indecision you are now in Catholic school. Had I been more resolute, and no human power would have prevented it.

One has to feel this! Yes, truly feel the vehement desire, to achieve, that which is already recognized in the wind, and that pushes us forward to carry it out.

So our mental strength, developed to a certain degree, makes us powerful. But in order to have this power, one needs to have good manners, so that the aura that irradiates from within or encircles without, has sufficient energy to attract all that is good, noble, and just. An individual who is impatient, choleric, a gambler, lazy, the aura that surrounds that person will attract what is in a similar state when they direct their will toward the preparation for undertaking of some project or search for employment. This aura reflects their true being, a being driven by their will to establish the energy flow of what they want to achieve. That person can only draw currents of energy that relate and attract elements and energies of similar conditions, so that he can be successful, but within the milieu in which he moves, lives, and develops.

This man or woman can obtain better conditions.

There are all types of people who smoke but don't drink, who drink but don't smoke, but I think it would be difficult to find a gambler who doesn't do all three at the same time, that is, smoke, drink, and gamble. It seems like all three are needed to round out the trilogy. He who has never gambled and acquires this "new hobby" will also acquire the habits of smoking and drinking to the same degree of the gamblers. They are habits of the trade. All of them pernicious. So smoking and drinking out of vice or habit should only be for gamblers or full-time indolents. There are those who learn how to drink and smoke without gambling, even hating or disdaining gambling and those who do it. But I would assure you that it will not be long before they join and befriend them, because that environment attracts them, and the aura of this smoker-drinker is already in almost the same conditions as that of those of the trilogy. We have young people of both sexes who, the majority of them, prefer to be gamblers and drinkers before having a steady job, which according to the majority them, only brings on scorn because there are many people who disdain those who do not live squandering money on booze and partying, even if it is at the price of crime, and to be sure, these individuals don't have the will power to overcome these stupidities and realize that they do not lose anything by taking a humble position. And the other women prefer to be pimps, lechers, and gossipers going from house to house, instead of heading to a factory or doing any sort of work to cover their basic needs.

You do not need glasses to see this. All right then: all these flaws and vices, do you know who provides for them, who supports and bolsters them? The current social regime, the pernicious custom of one man's exploitation of another.

Parents do not imbue their children with a love for work of any kind because they know that workers are paid poorly, and the fate of the manual worker is to end up in the hospital or begging.

Young people with the precepts of their parents, like "one must become a decent person," "what one should or should not do", and not knowing any sort of trade, but only a career learned for the sake of obligation, not for pleasure; they are not able to find a job that suits their ambitions, because they don't like people telling them what to do this is natural in all human beings, but some become so atrophied that they become indifferent not only to being ordered around, but also to being insulted and struck; and because they need a job to feed a family, they lose their freedom, their personality, their dignity, and become slaves of their pocketbook). Instead of having the courage to protest and struggle for reform and substitute this pernicious system which damages generation after generation, without hope or with only the most remote regeneration. That is because they fear revolution like the plague.

So the young women in such circumstances as these do not go to work in factories because they do not want to be exploited or become sick in an unhealthy environment, and in this manner they resort to any kind of deformity as long as they can maintain appearances, they prefer to get used to talk about the flaws of others, so as to lunch here or there and not have to think about it at all.

And this is how our society operates and they do not have the courage to protest.

With these kind of deformed customs the soul becomes perverted, as do the purest of feelings, even the notion of good goes astray, and all that is beautiful and noble in human nature is lost. Can the spirit progress? No way! Acquire bad habits, that it can do. And should we become accomplices to these calamities? The only wish guiding human conduct is to live whatever way one can, we desperately struggle to acquire the means for survival, even if it means turning to the most odious crimes and vices. It is not a question of perfecting one's home and making it more livable. No, it is about living in any possible way even if it be wallowing in mud. And this is called perfecting oneself and living again to purify oneself? No, this would be the same as saying that to bathe oneself it is necessary to jump into a pestilent pool. The same as if a person covered in sores were to wash himself with contaminated water, instead of using some antiseptic liquid.

In the same way, we are here to perfect ourselves and every day we learn more perversities. There can be no way of perfecting oneself with a system of life so contrary to natural laws.

So that if one wants to enter the path of perfection the methods used by our current society cannot be accepted. Any person avails themself of exploitation in order to make a fortune cannot come to perfection. He who truly wants to better himself should not conform to this environment without protesting. They will tell me that protest leads nowhere. But it does! How can we be silent and go with the flow? We need to expound some new system or doctrine, in order to get out of this labyrinth, in which we lose all noble sentiments and the most altruistic of aspirations. We have the duty to form groups or associations with the expressed purpose of emancipation. To accept things as they are, without proposing new forms of freedom is cowardice. We have ample means to emancipation offered to us by Radical Socialism. Why don't we use them?

Who is it that we fear? This is not a matter for just a few, no! But for all of us in general, all of us are victims of immense exploitation. Why do we not defend ourselves?

Those capitalists who think that they are exempt from these concerns because they have the means for an easier life. This concerns them to. Listen, up! You have children, and these become infected with the diseases caused by poverty. Suppose, that your children get together with others of bad habits. You know it, and you attempt to avoid contagion by prohibiting your children from associating with those others. But they encounter each other in the schools and there the contagion continues. And then you send your children to grade school. But the contagion remains, and do you think you have protected your children from it? No! We find leprosy everywhere, it is widespread, you are responsible, out of egoism! All right then, those children, who have the same right to go to primary school as your own do, are left out on the street; and others are exposed to infection. So, the ones you should have sent to school are not your children, who have the means to live comfortably. But the ones who had bad habits. Your children did not have these bad habits, so why did you send them to school? Out of egoism! Believing you were doing the right thing, because you only look out for yourselves!

You move along rolling the stone, instead of removing it from the path, so that the person walking at night does not stumble over it. But in leaving it there you suffer the consequences, since your son or daughter returns home from work and stumbles over the stone, the very stone the father saw and did not remove. If you see an obstacle on the path, remove it, because another may pass without seeing it and could fall. Avoid all possible evils. There are many types of obstacles in the path of life: bars are one, gambling establishments are another, and the courts another, tyrants, religious congregations, monarchies, jails, egotists, and usurers all attract an infinite number of obstacles the removal of which is the self-proclaimed task of revolution. Who are those that comprise these revolutions? Men and women who cannot pass the stone and leave in the road, because they know their fellow man and woman may stumble and fall. So, then, all those who contribute to maintaining a regime as pernicious as the present one are the ones that leave the stone in the path, looking at it as they go by, with no concern for those who come after them, who might not have the time to observe and avoid it, and so might come to harm.

And by doing so they become accomplices in the evils thereby created. Humans! Your indifference and egoism occasion many misfortunes, and even though you can live happily and bring good fortune to others, you do not do it, preferring to accumulate wealth at the expense of the work of others, without concern for pain and human misery.

ଔ   ଔ   ଔ

Some further comments on the power, or the influence of customs, on the fluid or invisible forces that we call mental strength, but that irradiates from our entire being. Our spiritual self can see, touch and even make itself visible, without the physical body; this is not religion. This is Science! Discover yourselves! . . . This is the methodical, persistent, analytical observation, of learned scientists.

Let me explain thoroughly, because you will not understand this as is, at first reading.

Understanding this does not make anybody more perfect. Claiming to be a spiritist because one knows and accepts its doctrine (sometimes without understanding the full range encompassed by its ideas) does not mean that this person is perfect, nor does it mean that they will become more perfect sooner than others; true, these spiritist ideas may help, but some, in trying to adapt them to their own circumstances, even come to Catholicize them, and the ideas become perverted for he who is not observant, this is the perverted individual who diminishes ideas, or remakes them according to his own whim under the same name. We see countless people who call themselves spiritists and form a union with their girlfriends through absurd rites, and they baptize their children, go to confession, join religious processions, trade in liquor, sell meat, water down milk, charge high rents, and sue those who don't pay. And they slander and insult, and respond to insult, and conduct bourgeois politics. And they call themselves spiritists, rationalists; well anarchists do nothing of the sort. So to call oneself a spiritist does not mean to be more perfect, not even remotely so, and these fraudulent spiritists who steal by weights and measures, who skim from a worker's daily wage, who uphold the death penalty, who help to repeal laws beneficial to the poor and the weak, who lie without shame, who are cowards (Jesus was brave), and who commit untold injustices (with few exceptions), meet together in a locale to invoke spirits . . . Tell me, what spirits or spiritual influences will be in contact with the fluid energy or the fluidic irradiation, or the aura that surrounds them? Spirits that are in a similar situation as theirs. For example, all those who drink alcohol, their breath is bothersome and repugnant, intolerable. The same happens to those who don't bathe frequently, or do not change their sweat-soaked clothes despite their bad odor, this same effect is created by one who is choleric and who expresses himself in rough tones or incorrect forms, these types of people cannot have their magnetic influences in good state and their fluids are in bad conditions in which to invoke slightly elevated spirits, because even if invoked these will not appear; the spirits that do are in the ones that are in similar conditions as those who invoke them.

"To deny that human misery is determined by divine influence, is not to deny that God is the creative force of the universe."

Antonio Otero

And, a poor group of altruistic and sober people, gather together and receive a communication, but the education and consciousness of this group does not permit them to interpret it, and they deform it with unpolished language, and those of the other group, when they discover this, make fun of it and express doubt that this humble group has received a better and more altruistic communication, because they themselves have never received such.

And some from the first group hear anarchist sermons filled with altruism and a beautiful selflessness and say: ah! we don't believe in throwing bombs, we take the peaceful path, we are spiritists! . . . and they really believe that they are. I would like for them to tell me what they understand by the word spiritist; (if they ask me I will say I don't know, because I understand spiritism to be so different from their notion of it . . . that they wouldn't accept it).

I don't understand spiritism to have remnants of mysticism, nor fanaticism of other so-called religious ideas. I can't accept a spiritism that observes criminal laws, nor, complies with any kind of authoritarian regime. I don't understand a spiritism that accepts customs, dogmas, and rites of obsolete, so-called religious institutions. Neither do I understand it to adapt itself to the exploitative practices of capitalism.

Nor do I understand spiritism as accepting an inheritance law, established by past generations, which is tantamount to privilege and injustice. Nor do I believe in the continuance of these odious distinctions and privileges. Nor I comprehend the egoism of some who preach spiritism and call themselves by its name. I repeat, there are extraordinary exceptions to this, like don Francisco Vicenty, father of a large family, modest, sober, humane, who does not spend his time accumulating wealth or setting aside inheritances for his family, very hard working, very intelligent, very selfless, and countless qualities of the highest caliber. And other qualities that would be valuable to present models of behavior, but this would take too long. And anyway, I don't want to exaggerate, or make a mistake in presenting them, because my ambition is to clarify the concept of the idea, and I don't want anyone telling me, "you are mistaken."

I forgot to say that don Francisco Vicenty is a professor of higher education, so no one should think he is some landlord or social parasite. He is man of worth.

Well, there are an infinite number of people of both sexes who call themselves spiritists and they get together to celebrate experimental sessions or to study, but during the day these persons are choleric, ill-intentioned, slanderous, ill-humored, gluttonous and lazy. Furthermore, it is proven that according to the conditions of those who gather to invoke spirits such will be the spirits, that appear or make contact with the energy flows: and if someone drinks, even if not at that moment. If they are choleric, even though they might not be in the moment of the invocation, it doesn't matter; their aura has already been formed, and even if they are not speaking badly of another at that moment, nor wishing ill upon their brethren, they have already done damage.

These persons can improve their conditions by taking control of their behavior, because natural laws are immutable and inviolable and even though you may pray a thousand times and appear to be a saint, at the moment of invoking spirits; it will yield no results, nor will you perfect yourself by that system.

I dare say that prayer is useless, concentrated thought is prayer, but if the individual does perfect himself, this prayer is useless.

And besides, what is the point of prayer, to ask for something? Then, everyone has the right to ask and to have their wishes be granted. And I have noticed that those who are always expecting miracles or divine intervention don't achieve anything of note. And scholars and scientists like Edison, do not owe their inventions and discoveries to prayer. Newton, Fulton, Galvani, and countless researchers didn't achieve their discoveries through prayer. Did these men have ugly habits, vices, pernicious behavior? Only a love for learning and for the natural laws.

Besides, if some guide or spirit occupied itself with rewarding those who devote themselves to prayer, how many are there who are continuously praying? The greater part of humanity is invoking, and offering fasts and sacrifices for a thousand causes! They even go without food in order to buy reliquaries, engravings, lamps and a plethora of useless objects for their sought-after objective.

And this spiritual power need such absurd things in order to grant something? To carry out a project beneficial to humanity, there is no need to ask for spiritual intervention, because, as I understand it, being in the material realm we need help from material sources. An intervention by some fellow man or woman who really wants to help us out with all their mental strength would be more beneficial.

Humankind's most beautiful and necessary progress and discoveries have come from that group of people who don't pray or invoke the spirits.

Those individuals who worship images and adorn them with silk and gold, and look indifferently upon the countless unfortunate men, women, and children living in degrading poverty. Which saint would approve of one who forgets human suffering and need, afflictions that are right beside us, in order to go search for something beyond us that is unnecessary? What criteria is used to say that a piece of wood or of plaster, well or poorly-crafted, should be adored and covered with gold, precious stones, and silk? It takes an atrophied brain and a high degree of indifference to take care of a statue, and leaves the people around us naked and hungry. Even accepting that such idiots might believe that certain saints could come closer to the image given to their name even though that image might not look like its namesake. But that would be supporting idolatry which does not belong to the realm of reason; because all of those apparitions and movement of images are the work of priests, who have placed them in a specific spot, and later through certain means the priests claim they have appeared, and by trickery the priest make them cry, and the people are moved.

Let us suppose that saints can receive messages and prayers. So why don't they respond to the petitions made to them? and that have been made to them since time immemorial by those who go off to war, and die or return without arms and legs, for the thousands of projects and business ventures that fail without the intervention of the saints? It is a miserable waste of time to dress up images, and these same people see a young girl begging a penny from a gentleman and they say: "Look at that lost soul, whose mother doesn't take care of her." But they do not call to her and instead of adorning their idols—clothe her and send her to school.

What a beautiful act, how many benefits would be provided to thousands of miserable souls!

If women, instead of going to church to show off their luxurious dresses, were to go to the houses of the poor to offer consolation. Instead of taking candles and oils to their images, if they were to take them to the poor who need them! the idols don't need it. Instead of sending money for masses or novenas and drapes and decorations for the corrupt and materialistic church. Take it to the poor who have nothing to eat and are starving. If you want a priest or friar to live without working, and you want to support them so they can spout words in Latin in front of an image. There when some poor woman asks for alms, or a poor peasant for help, you say "you are fat and tanned, go get to work " and it is the sun that has given them color on the road to see you. And so you say the unfortunate woman is a lost soul. And the reverend who is so happy and well taken care of, you don't tell him to go off and work.

What a bundle of contradictions, how you all correct one error and slide into another!

Women, how mistaken you are in thinking that novenas, masses and prayers are going to purify you! If you do not try and correct your defects, if you think you are superior to those who serve you, and you treat them as you would not like to be treated yourselves. You are superfluous spendthrifts and you are deceived when they make you feel that you will be forgiven with the prayers and the litanies of the priests. Wake up! And do not feel alarmed by reading what follows. There is no one who rewards or who punishes. That is blasphemy.

Our conscience will be our judge, our defects will adhere to our spirits if we do not try to correct them. Neither time nor prayer will be able to erase them, if you do not try to perfect your spirits. Therefore, educated woman, mother, unhappy worker, you can do much to benefit to your children. Awaken! Shake off the inertia, the fanaticism that subjugates you and help us destroy these social evils.

Observe the misery of the greater part of our brothers and come help us conquer, the triumph of suffering humanity. Of those who always work and whose statements are not deemed reasonable because they are never listened to.

This planet belongs to all of us and is not the privilege of only a few. Why are there so many injustices?

We must contribute to even out these inequalities.

ベ   ベ   ベ

We are heading toward an era of goodwill and peace among humans.

There are countless groups whose purpose is to initiate people in the ideas of general good, of universal concerns. In Sao Paolo we have the"Commission of Thought Circle", with the following objectives:

1) Promote the study of occult force among man and nature.
2) Promote the awakening of latent creative energies in the thoughts of each member according to the laws of invisible vibration.
3) To ensure that these energies converge so as to guarantee the physical, social, and moral well-being of its members, maintaining the health of their bodies and spirits.
4) To come together with the combined strenght of their forces so that harmony, love, truth, and justice may be realized among men.

The society will consist of an undetermined number of members of both sexes, without distinctions of color, nationality or belief.

For reports and information please contact the General Delegate, who will forward to you in the mail the Statutes and other information in Spanish, Italian, and German at the following address: "O Pensamento", Editorial Office, Senator Feijó Street, 19, Sao Paolo, Brazil.

This is not mentioned as a bit of news, it is a favorable comment on all institutions or societies established with this goal in mind. We have the Segno Club which is concerned with human progress led by Dr. Victor Segno. The Institute of Sciences in New York led by Dr. La Mote Sage and Charles Clark.

We have vegetarian societies and innumerable books and magazines that try to move people along the path of human, terrestrial, and spiritual happiness. "Our Mental Strengths" by Prentice Mulford; "The True Life" by Tolstoy. "Natura," a scientific magazine. "The Art of Being Happy" by J.W. Colville. "The Sentences of Judge Magnaud." "The Conquest of Bread" and many others that are causing humans to see the errors they have made, despite calling themselves Christians. All of them intolerant, vengeful, and exploitative. We are new in an era in which the protests and demands of the exploited are heard and given attention. Already we deserve that all these books, magazines, institutions, and clubs do not accept differences of color or race.

Well, you could have the case of a person of color writing to one of these clubs, showing magnificent aptitude for studying and its practical application, and the person who sends the explanations back to him has no idea that he is dark-skinned, or yellow, or red or olive-colored, and he attends to this applicant, whose intelligence responds to the established methods of study. And that after completing his education and fit now for his career, they were to ask him for a photograph. And upon sending it, by return mail, he were rejected because of his skin color. Wouldn't that be an injustice? We must advocate for abolishing the differences between one race and another, and for a brotherhood from one corner of the world to the other. We champion the abolition of the exploitation of man by man. It is true that not everyone can be initiated into these clubs or Societies because of a lack of resources, but still it represents a great progress that will provide magnificent results.

I understand it, the forces of nature are not hidden, but we humans do not understand them and we therefore do not see them.

Reflections

If today, in any part of the globe, an enlightened man were to take the strand expose the defects of and throw insults at a brother by father and mother, if he were to accuse this mand and insult him infamously. All those listening would say that this man is not the brother of the other, that he is a beast, and he would be seen as a being without feeling or tact. If a man were to speak ill of his mother, trying to defame and insult her, he would be seen as a bad son, like someone who forgets all the work and sacrifice that this woman went through to teach him and guide him in his first steps, and his first words and yet he pays her back with insults . . .

So we who preach and desire a fraternal world should not issue insults, nor attempt to dishonor our neighbor, if indeed we are brothers. Otherwise, we will never come to practice fraternity. This does not mean that we should hide the truth, no; abuse, hypocrisy, meanness, any kind of farce must be exposed, because, for the mere fact that, we are brothers, we must make others understand that we know our rights, and that if they trample on those rights, we have the right to remind them that we are incensed by the injustice of it. For example, if by mistake or neglect someone steps on our foot, and the person who steps on it does not realize that he is trampling on human flesh, the first impulse of the person who was stepped on is to push the other: because pain does not reflect, it cannot be courteous, because pain is anti-aesthetic. And courtesy is a form of beauty, and beauty is "the shape of truth," as Camile Flammarion aptly put it. So, the person who pushes the other looks badly upon the person who caused him pain, and says "you clumsy oaf" or "you must be blind," if they happen to be an uncultured person. If the other is courteous and cultured, then the offended tries to hide his pain, and to the other's "Pardon me" or "excuse me," he says "it's all right," "this is nothing" or other similar phrases. But this is said afterwards, in the moment being stepped on, the only thing he thinks about is getting the foot off of him. Then afterwards he makes his courteous statements.

Just as we do not mistreat or step on the person who stepped on us, but only remind the other that he has disturbed our human property so should we behave with other attacks made on our rights and liberties, make our needs worthy and inviolable; or will no one practice this when interests are involved and so then everyone will become enraged, difficult, and pay no attention to those demands?

But that is why we will preach, to persuade and convince and in this way came to a practice of brotherhood. It is not that we are not foolish and naïve in preaching forms of fraternizing, it is that centuries have gone by and still fraternity has not been realized, and this demonstrates the apathy with which the teachings of Christ have been observed, that brave and sincere brother who traced for us a luminous path so that humanity would not find pitfalls in its ascent toward the heights of progress. However, we have read and re-read his teachings indolently and always from generation to generation, we have interpreted the parables and statements made by Jesus abusively and erroneously. Are we going to continue to interpret them wrongly and without trying to correct ourselves, nor to practice the sublime human maxims of that courageous Jesus? No, the times are drawing nearer, the errors that have submerged humanity in the most abject ignorance must disappear once and for all. Let us propagate the Christian maxims, which are maxims of human freedom, let us spread and preach that people must educate themselves, so as not to need a government, nor ridiculous and anti-human laws, let us not forget that he said, "He who is without sin let him cast the first stone," and to this day no one has been able to cast that stone; therefore, a handful of men cannot govern or condemn others. The few who do not work cannot enjoy the fruits of all while those who always work lack the bare essentials.

Let us not forget what Jesus told a young man who had asked him how to attain life everlasting and Jesus said to him: "You shall not commit adultery" and "You shall not kill," "You shall not bear false witness against your neighbor", "You shall not steal." "Honor your father and your mother". And the young man says "I have assumed these teachings". Then Jesus "looking" at him, and this "looked" means that he was looking into his soul, reading his conscience, and said to him: You are missing one thing; go and sell all the things you have and give the money to the poor and you will have a treasure in heaven. Now we will explain how to understand this by way of reason. From the first, when Jesus says "You shall not commit adultery," I believe, it is my opinion, that adultery is committed when one does something without feeling; for example, pretending to love a spouse, a husband, while in reality loving someone else; and to have carnal relations with the other person and to have children with him while living with one's husband making believe that they are children of the husband when they are the fruit of the lover. So when two people who do not love each other get together, that is to adulterate one's feelings and to make legalized prostitution of the matrimonial bond.

This is adultery; the woman who breaks with these formulas and lives with the man she truly loves does not commit adultery. But in this stupid society, the woman who forms a union with a man by the law of the current institutions is obliged to live with, to please, and to love her husband. They will say, why then did she get married? But isn't the human heart capable of making a mistake? If she married him when she liked him, but no longer does for reasons not to be mentioned in this book, and which would mark it as scandalous and immoral. But there you have the "Encyclopedia of Private Life" like a code of passion written in letters of fire, severely accusing those who, without fear of tears, nor of the woman's resistance, want to convert her into a loathsome receptacle of vice, and take advantage of her apparent weakness, or rather, of her lack of knowledge.

So then the woman abstains from her freedom because one is not attended to, and she resigns herself to live against her will and against her desires, with her husband and this is adultery. And our present society is based on this; and so we have the duty to better ourselves.

"Chastity and freedom are inseparably united, there is no slavery more base, no chain more strong than that of unbridled sensual appetite."

"You shall not kill." In the legal codes in effect in our decadent society the death penalty is inscribed as a method of correction. Oh, accusing judges! "Oh violent soldiers and impatient policemen!" "Anyone who hates their brother is a murderer, and you all know that no murderer has within him eternal life." So then why does the death penalty continue to exist?

It is a beastly remnant that must yet be destroyed. Will we be able to regenerate by the death penalty those human beings who through ignorance have made mistakes? No, that's not the way, that is not the manner, the, method or system to succeed in correcting the ways of a poor wayward brother, we must educate him and make him see that crime leads to nothing of practical use, but because the law sets a bad example, that same law has no right to judge him, nor to correct him, because as men each has the same right to kill as the other. More practical is for the law not to authorize the crime by committing it; unless one thinks sending a man to the gallows is not a crime, but he who represents the law is a man, and this man is commending another man to be killed. In this manner we are on the road to the savage times of human beastliness. The just course would be that this representative of justice should make the perpetrator reflect, hesitate upon, and regenerate himself by generous and instructive means. This would be beautiful, humanly sublime, one man elevating another, his brother. This is Christianity in action. Oh judges, if you were to practice this, you would see that you would produce beautiful results.

The murder committed by so-called human justice is a monstrous mockery: if we find it horrible that a poor ignorant soul blinded by rage kills one of his fellow men, we should find it even more horrible that educated men without personal motive, with necessary calm, pass sentence and order the another unhappy soul to carry it out. With what right does the judge punish? And who will punish the judge for ordering such a death? Instead of one criminal now we have more criminals, since all those who have not protested this new crime are also accomplices. And this makes the situation more serious. If before there was one orphaned family, now there are two, and the latter one is worse off, given the degrading infamy reaped upon the family, created by this same society. And this society, after putting the family in such a situation, abandons them to contempt. Is this not a double crime? Is there justice in this barbaric procedure? Does the criminal instinct abate in this manner? No; on the contrary, it increases, we have the children and family of the executed who feel disgust and hatred toward society, and years go by and nobody remembers anymore the crime committed by the man nor the one committed by the courts. But someone lurks in the shadows, and when we feel the things are calmest, another crime erupts, they killed the judge, the secretary, who contributed with accusations or someone else; and who was the criminal? The son of the man who decapitated justice in combination with others. Ah! We forget that the spirit does not die, that in going to the hereafter in such a violent fashion, it is a disturbed spirit and certainly uses its influence so that the son who was provoked by the court's action will seek his father's revenge.

And we call these errors justice, true justice does not make mistakes: and this kind of justice is always mistaken, the Death Penalty is a mistake, one of many made daily by these men who believe themselves to possess the noble gift of justice, and yet they are only more of the many who are blind to humanity. The blind with a right to see more, because at times they carry the luminous torch of science in their hands. But I believe that this very fact has made them blind, their sight is too imperfect to be able to see things in all their clarity.

Oh judges! If instead of believing you are infallible as you issue sentences, you were to consider that, in addressing this man who made the mistake of killing his brother, you might do good, not contaminating yourselves by committing another mistake equal to the assassin's. And if you could turn to this misguided soul in compassion and mercy, with your illustrations talent, and if you helped to lift him up, and to see that he might transform himself into the protector of the family from which he took the father, the spouse or the brother. If you could do all this, then imaging how often he would remember his victim! and that same man would break into tears and repent his terrible deed. And instead of committing another crime, he would act out of love, out of brotherhood. You will argue that this is too lenient a punishment and that this would not bring back the life of the person murdered. The punishment is quite beautiful when carried out in this way, for neither does the criminal's execution bring his victim back to life. With the Death Penalty, you aggravate the consequences, you leave another family orphaned, to which you do not give a moment's thought, nor do you provide them with the means to live. By making the person responsible console and help the family; the spirit of the victim will have to feel the need for forgiveness, and will bathe everyone in beneficial fluids. In this manner there is greater justice, since we do not have the certainty of knowing whether in another existence the perpetrator was wronged by the victim. And because of this doubt the courts should abstain from imposing punishment that is superior to their knowledge or insight. You will argue that in this fashion all those who commit a crime will defend or excuse themselves by alluding to a previous existence. Far from it, for he who commits a crime is blinded by rage and is not responsible for this act, perhaps because the other person provoked or irritated him. This is certainly not sufficient reason to kill another human being, but when it does happen, it is the duty of the intelligent ones, the legislators, those who dare to propose and write laws for the people to ameliorate and soften the circumstances by educating, and one does not educate through punishment. The Death Penalty is too barbaric a procedure to be used by those called upon to rule the people, to educate generations. Those who undertake the noble mission of representing Justice must be men of self-control, impassive, calm, whose not easily frightened or agitated who do not form cliques like those who have no notion of what ignorance is. Judges and Courts that place themselves at the level of murderers, should not be given elevated positions like that of representing and practicing Justice. It has already been said that "Mercy is the highest expression of justice." And the duty of justice is to reduce violent and bloody acts, not to increase them by producing new acts of violence. If a man kills his brother, we should ensure that he repent and that he try to lessen the grief and hardship of his victim's family, and that, if the perpetrator has a family, they join with the other. This is the way that is most harmonious with human emotion, reason, and logic. And if reason and feeling do not come together? Maybe so, but then the reason is not genuine, nor is the emotion pure and good. Just because I might intensely feel the death of my brother or husband, it is not reasonable that I want the murderer to be killed. Just because he has been a criminal doesn't mean I should become one; the reasonable thing, the just thing is that I calmly accept the event, without a desire for vengeance. Should I cry? Sure. Lament what happened? Of course. But that does not justify me to seek vengeance. So if I do not feel the desire for vengeance, why do those who represent justice usurp that right that only belongs to the relatives of the victim? You will say that all of society is menaced by such a murder, and this society in the name of the victim needs to cleanse that outrage. These are reasons that do not merit attention. Why doesn't this blind society see other outrages that are more harmful, and see only this one? Why doesn't this society, when some man dies in the street, seek out the guilty party? Why doesn't this society feel wounded by a dishonest act carried out by high officials in houses that traffic in flesh? Why don't they feel outrage when a girl, some unfortunate peasant or the modest daughter of poor parents is taken to these houses to be prostitutes? Why, when a worker falls from a scaffold and is handicapped and forced to beg on the streets does this society not feel outraged? And this poor soul cannot even find a lawyer to defend him, and society doesn't feel offended or try to help? Because this society that is hypocritical and cowardly. On the other hand, we see trials of crimes committed by the well to do, sons of the rich, and society has compromised and not demanded the execution of these men, as they would have for others. Why these inequalities? If a rich person commits a crime he should be punished in the same way. If the rich person is not decepitated, why is the poor person garroted or executed?

Society does not see this, so why does it speak of justice if it does not know what justice is? If there is danger to society in letting a murderer free, why are rich people given complete freedom while those who are not rich are jailed or perpetually chained without even being offered the opportunity or the means to better themselves in humane fashion, but no, lock them up like beasts. And the rich person can continue without danger to society, frequenting casinos, public walkways, theaters and cafes where they can get drunk on champagne, and offer it to young people at dances, etc. So there is no danger in letting rich folk go free?

And so be it, but it should be equally true for the poor and the humble. If one is let free, the other should be also. This is what is just, what is humane. And one should proceed always according to human feeling.

Murder is terrible, (but the newspapers devote much ink to describing them), but can it be cleansed or corrected by committing another? No. Wouldn't it be more humane to reform or to regenerate the murderer? We should not forget Cain, from whom Abel did not seek vengeance. And where is Cain now? Is he not held up on high? Might he not now guide others, more perfect regions? Is it not likely that he is a guide and tender counselor for the wayward and the cruel? Surely, without the need to have killed Caín he ascended freely up the stairway to progress and to the love of one's fellow man. And this is the only kind of liberation one must search for and accept. Anything else is contrary to justice; who can judge one's brother? And how can one be so bold as to assumed the right to punish him?

These are errors that cost the human species dearly. And it is our duty to correct them, so that they will not be repeated. Punishment of this nature is erroneous, one must educate humanely and not violently.

"Do not steal." The truth; the absolute truth, is that the real thief is he who possesses more than he needs. These are the true thieves, who more and more every day are driven by the desire, stronger everyday, to accumulate and to fill their coffers with more and more gold and silver. They are the cause of all the deformities and diseases engendered by poverty that they create through their own exploitation of others. The one with no job and no money, those without a piece of bread, and who steals it to satisfy a need such as that of nourishing the organism.

How many have dared to take these unfortunate ones to court, because they have taken some significant trifle that the owner did not even need. Once a well-to-do man was robbed of a salt lick and rope by an unfortunate man, so he ascertains the man's identity, looks for witnesses and the bring him to trial and I heard that he was found guilty, because he was dying of starvation, and given six months in jail, sirs! . . . Of course, the gentleman left the proceedings proud that he had punished the bold wrongdoer who had stolen some worthless things of his. There are many cases like this one; on another occasion I observed a boy who yawned a lot and paced in front of a bread stand and when they weren't looking grabbed two loaves, and vanished in a flash, those who saw him said "Hey, a thief!" but the owner or the employee couldn't leave the stand unattended. There wasn't a policeman close by and there was no time to catch him. If they had caught him, to jail with the starving boy! he would have to degrade himself begging for a dime, which they would refuse him; and besides, one mustn't beg. If the law prohibits begging. Why should he get in trouble with the law! Better to take what one needs from wherever it is abundant! This is more beautiful than begging. A person who cannot find a job, and who sees that neither the government, nor the political parties, nor the religions will provide it for him, should not to beg. It is the duty of the authorities to be aware of those who not have work and there should be an eternal sign at city hall that says the following: "He who can not find work will find it here," and in this manner he will be provided with the means to bring a daily wage home to his family.

Otherwise, no one should beg, it is offensive to beg. Don't beg, you destitute workers, you victims of usury and exploitation; exploited by political parties, by religions, by commerce, you are the eternal mine, from which the bourgeoisie and the religions extract enormous treasures.

You are the immense building blocks on which the governments rest on your suffering backs, tyrants rise to power. You are the eternal steps on which perch the confident just of kings and emperors, ministers and priests, republics and monarchies.

And even though you are the powerful columns that sustain them through your ignorance. They still incarcerate you when you take a peace of bread to feed yourself. And even under these conditions they dare to impose upon you punishments in prisons and jails.

Workers! The true thieves are those who have more than they need, don't forget that, and even if they throw you in jail, do not beg. Make the governments you put into power with your votes commit to the task of providing you with work when there is none. Impose that demand, which is just and not favor, it is justice and not as splendid as you think.

You who adulterate goods of prime necessity, who exploit with these goods, charging more than what they are worth!

You who charge excessive prices for a miserable hovel, and you double the price of your property to three or four times its value and continue to be the owner of the house, even though you hold it up for four or five times its original worth. You are the thieves and I will show you for the world to see, and I accuse you of all the injustices committed against the poor!

You, after charging the value of the house, should give it over to those who paid for it before. And you should build another one in the same conditions.

You, who buy flour at a low price so as to sell bread in the market at prices that double your profits!

You are rogues and yet call yourself gentlemen and you despise those whom you have exploited who are worth more than you are.

You, all of you who live and accumulate great wealth at the expense of exploitation, you are the true thieves, the only thieves that a just analysis and critique reveal.

You, who raise offspring in luxury and wasteful extravagance so that they despise the dirty and broken children who roam the streets and for whose poverty and misery you are responsible for. You, who despise those who walk about dirty and shoeless, after having taken away their means of subsistence.

You, who dare to suppose that you are of better flesh and bood than those who have confected your wealth, I remind you that you are mistaken, that you are no better than anyone else. Actually, you are less worthy because you are useless, your only function is to accumulate the fruits of others' labor. You are egotistical and proud, and your conscience cannot feel the kingdom of Jesus when your hearts only issue bile towards your fellow men. The bile of disdain and cruelty is what you give to your brothers.

That is why you criticize those who make fun of your stupidities and ridiculous pretensions. But soon the day of redemption will arrive, because a century is nothing in the eternity of time.

        CR   CR   CR

"False testimony," do not give false testimony, do not lie, do not deceive, do not slander. All those who risk affirming something because they suppose it to be true, or because they are deceived by appearances, commits an atrocious crime, because it brings displeasures, serious consequences slander, and the loss of what little happiness that an individual or two might be able to have. What purpose can there be to affirm something not seen, only imagined? It is cruel and reckless to let oneself be deceived by appearances, aside from the damage created by these perverse criticisms. Moreover, what good does the slanderer gain for himself, what can be gained by one who confirms what has not been seen but only supposed. One does not gain neither time nor money, then what is the purpose? It must be to pass the time. Instead of studying and doing something useful.

        CR   CR   CR

Lying is almost a habit, a pernicious habit that should be stricken from our minds. We inflict great harm on ourselves by lying, our mental energies lose much strength. A good opinion, that we formulate that we of another person is always something positive. We should never give misinformation about others, even if there are reasons for doing so. It is very uncivilized, to speak ill of another person, nobody is perfect, and we should never say anything that could cause harm to others. We benefit greatly in always finding others to be good and acceptable.

CR   CR   CR

Disdain and gossip have a terrible effect; it is so pleasing always to speak well of others.

You should never lie, and therefore should never say anything you do not have the courage to back up. If you bought something cheap, say it, if it was expensive, say it also. Do not deceive. Deceit is a sign of backwardness and perversity.

CR   CR   CR

"Honor thy father and thy mother." One does not deserve more respect than the other. But how many times has the behavior of one or the other occasioned a child to make mistakes. A father who speaks ill of the mother to his child, or a mother who speaks worse about the father. Tell me what kind of conditions are these for educating their children.

CR   CR   CR

It seems that parents think they are owners of their children and oblige them to obey against their own will. A boy or a girl is a future citizen and should be respected and attended to. Parents have no right to mistreat their children nor to impose their will upon them.

CR   CR   CR

Some will say, but this right to "honor your father and your mother" is to reprimand the children, not the parents. That is how it seems, but how mistaken are those who believe that only the children will be held accountable to this.

CR   CR   CR

Are there parents who deserve to be honored by their children? No; just because they are parents does not authorize them to be respected, their conduct and austerity will be the primary judgement. Does a father have the right to arrive at the house drunk and smoking and demand that his child not do the same? Does a careless and sloppy mother have the right to ask her daughter to be clean and orderly? This cannot be. The saying from Jesus is an accusation against parents who tell their children to lie, who whip them cruelly, who lock them up in dark rooms, in order to satisfy their absurd rage.

ℭ   ℭ   ℭ

One does not instruct (by the lash) nor (through punishment), instead a sweet and persuasive tone should be used by mothers and fathers. But when parents need and want to deceive their children, then their authority turns against them. If you have to go out and you do not want to take the children with you, then send them on a walk with the maid before you leave, although it would be more proper to take them with you and not to deceive them by saying that you will take them with you and not fulfilling your promise. You have been untruthful and you want obedience and respect from your children. Can you possible think that by virtue of being children you will be able to fool them? You are wrong. The law is one and the same for all, regardless of age or size. Children, despite being small, if you are good and affectionate with them, will also be good and affectionate. If you are deceitful and fraudulent, your children will imitate you; don't believe that the label of parents absolves you of being true and loyal with them. They are human beings and their tender age grants them more right of respect and consideration than others.

ℭ   ℭ   ℭ

The whip is an accusation against you, against your lack of patience in educating your children. It shows selfishness to mistreat your children. You have no right to whip their, tender, little flesh. You must speak to them with all the patience possible and necessary, and answer all their questions even if they seem impertinent. Why, as is natural, they need an explanation for that which they do not understand, and who better than their parents to respond to them and to give explanation? No one can answer all of their questions, but none other can attend to them with the proper methods and the good will of their parents. We should not fool them telling them lies and things that are incomprehensible to their imagination.

ભ   ભ   ભ

We should explain material things to them just like they are, without adding or omitting a thing.

Truth must be the fundamental base of a child's upbringing. And the parents are obliged to refrain from deceiving their children and to teach them not to deceive others.

ભ   ભ   ભ

So this law addressed to the children is really an accusation against the parents. The child is naturally good at birth, and the direction he is given and the teachings he receives, will determine the resulting person.

ભ   ભ   ભ

The father has the right to punish him for a defect that, in spite of his age, his studies, and his experience, he has not been able to correct. Parents should guide and educate the child, but not punish him. It is a mistake to believe that mistreating and tormenting a child is a proper way to raise him.

Your Black Scarf
To María Luisa Rodríguez[1]

The way I remember your awarding it to me; I didn't deserve it. In this hypocritical environment, moments of disinterested feeling, of pure affection, drown, perish by suffocation. You don't understand it. I do not know why the emotions and affections that make their homes in mercantile venues are more pure, more sincere, more natural.

I keep it near my clothes, but way underneath, so you won't be too present, because it wounds my soul. I, who suffer from the ailment of compassion, without thinking that others can have compassion for me. I'm indifferent to that, but compassion for me I don't like. Those who make mistakes, do they deserve compassion? I don't think so. Well then, in me you have one who is mistaken about life. Worshipping sincerity, where everything betrays. To truth, where everything is a lie. To brotherhood, where everything is competition and egotism. To love, where everything is self-interest and hate, envy and resentment. What do you think, flower born in the slime of this society that takes pleasure in the misfortune of its brothers? Your fragrances have flown away, fleeing this infected atmosphere. But they have not vanished! No. There is a place for them in space, soon you will recover this place and you will perfume your soul. Do not be

---

[1]People will ask me, I'm sure, how can I dedicate this publicly? Public morality will be offended! Have you no modesty? Yes, those who degraded you (according to them), the ones who sought your caresses, your arms, and those who asked you for more refinement, more craziness, thinking that they were humiliating you . . . They want to despise you, well, laugh at them! They are crazy!

93

distressed, do not believe yourself to be humiliated. Lift up your white forehead, and don't be afraid to open your eyes, for those who would shame you are ashamed themselves and lower their heads. It is not you. They are the guilty ones.

I return to your scarf; only a few days ago I took it up and tied it around my neck, I looked at myself in the mirror . . . I became distressed thinking of you, victim sacrificed to the bestial lust of half-men. And I put it away fearing I would wrinkle it. The first time I took it in my hands, after having seen it in my house, it seemed prophetic, somber . . . and I tried to avoid looking at it! . . . Oh, the law of tradition, the power of custom! That scarfed seemed contagious to me. Forgive me, I'm not at fault: it is the environment we live in. The fountain we drink from it's muddied. There is no clear water, and the thirst burns, and so we must drink it. Soon it will be healthy, reform draws near. So then, your black scarf, it is a symbol for me. It is the black stain that society tosses into its own face, when it debases and degrades those reforms.

But don't worry, there are no victims without executioners, and in this case, resign yourself; they are the executioners. You, the victim. They despise you, you receive their disdain with a smile on your lips, they are cowards.

They hide their hand so as to not to lift you up. They deny help, so they can despise you all the more. Idiots! After they tasted your kisses, and laid out your divine-like body, they despise you. It is as if a child were to destroy the breast that created him, as if he were to beat upon the neat little dove with its red beak that nourishes him with its white liquid. Or like tossing on the floor the fine glass of exquisite crystal in which one has imbibed a delicious nectar . . . No, they will not do that in my presence! Anarchists do not behave like this, we are the reformers and practitioners of truth.

Don't be afraid, we will defend you, you are one of ours: you belong to those who suffer, you form part of our battalion, of these who suffer!

Until later.

Special Excerpts

I've heard it said often, "That one deserves a kick in the behind." As if this were the rudest, most dishonorable act. But feet are the pedestal of the brain, without them the brain would go nowhere. At the base of statues wreaths are placed to honor and glorify great men. They are not placed on the head. They are left hanging at the feet because many can be placed there. Who would have imagined that over mute stone rest all the honors of an entire generation?

So when I hear about being kicked I say to myself: what is it that they do to those on the receiving end? Being touched or struck by the most necessary part of the body. It is the same contempt shown to toilets, maids, and street sweepers.

Without the first, what good would a palace be? And cafes and kitchens, where would they be without the second? And what would happen to the streets without the third?

Sometimes a street sweeper is more useful to a country than a public official, the former light not reap glory for his country, but neither will he bring it dishonor. The latter's ambition can lead him to commit a crime. Although I believe that there are crimes that clear many consciences, sometimes of entire generations. As in sharp contrasts, like the shadow to its object. Nothing can be disdained, nor elevated completely. At times, a human deformity is necessary and it provokes great thought and produces beauty (Quasimodo). Just as a great beauty can lead to ruin, to disaster (Phoebe). While reading and writing I saw on the paper a luminous little shining spot, that made me hold my pen steady. I am observing it. It was a little wrinkle and I said to myself: that which is deformed does shine through. And I remembered Quasimodo, and that made me stop, and think a lot, and

analyze even more. At times the indescribable sinks into nothingness, the waves come and go without overflowing the ocean. Just
like the rainfall can make the earth fertile or leave it in shambles. The
waves that bathe and beat the sand of the beach just as they do the
rocks. However, the rocks fall from their base and roll about the
sand, and the sand is always in the same place and doesn't fall. The
sand plays with the waves, the rocks resist, they reveal themselves as
they move to the rhythm, to the ebb and flow of the waters. They are
rocks, and that is why they fall. They symbolize stubbornness,
roughness. In the sand [however] one's feet sink as if they were in
water. The sand symbolizes softness, tolerance. It is the eternal enigma of nature, in which the sun shines and gives life equally to the
sweet mallow as to the poisonous orchid, its rays reach the mountain
top as well as the plain; in its warmth sway both the most fragrant
flower as well as the insipid dahlia.

It is a terrifying volcano and perpetual snow, it seduces and over-
powers. It sings and it cries. It sobs and it smiles. The eternal contrast of life's sovereign power. A contrast that is harmony, light, and
shadow, fire and water, love and forgetting, heaven and hell. It rais-
es up the stupid and awkward and pushes down that which is great.
It soars into the infinite and sinks to the bottom of the abyss.

It is a blue dragonfly and a terrible monster. Shining light and
shadowy gloom. It climbs to the crystalline mountain peaks of the
North Pole and descends to the burning steppes of Arabia. It trills
and warbles in the little bird, roars and bellows in the lion or panther.

It is a hyena, and it is a lamb, it kisses and bites, and roars and
sings. Sweet honey and bitter aloe. It attracts and it repels. This is
human life, incomprehensible flashes of contrasts that produce harmony. They do not destroy they burn.

Both the criminal and the model citizen walk along the same
street and sidewalk, one going to jail, the other to the lecture hall.

The road, the route to achievement does not go beneath the feet
but through one's head. They march through the brain. That is why
it has been said that the kingdom of Christ, or justice, is within one's
soul. Both can live together, drink the same water, breath in the same

air. However, one lives in heaven, the other in hell, there is exasperation and tranquility, justice and desperation, the mother lode of vengeance.

Who has created the arrogant soul and the peaceful soul? Who has formed visible and invisible nature, made up of light and shadow? It plays on the surface of surging waters or tumbles deep into the abyss. And in this manner there are many human hearts submerged in sadness or joy, tears and laughter. Why? We can't explain it, but we guess. It is the creative muse of the aurora borealis and the luminous dawn, it does not need explanations since it creates the impossible. The sun and the moon, one illuminates softly, the other burns brilliantly.

It is the One.

In the appearance of nothingness is the One. It seethes in the pollen of flowers and shines on the insect. Which is more worthy the insect or the flower? From the flower we get fruit, they are equal, and the insect can damage them. Damage it? Why? Because the insect tries it, bites it, tastes it, and nourishes itself with that tiny part, because it does not need the whole flower. The insect has a right to nourish itself with these fruits since it lives among them. Men do not investigate, they think the insect is damaging the fruit, that the insects don't have a right to touch and eat these fruits, and wants to destroy insects and at times man destroys many of them. But who has more right to eat the fruit, man or insect? I think both have equal right: if the insect took its part, man should accept his part. An insect lives more in harmony with nature than does man. But man has fabricated absurd laws, has made them up. The insect accepts the natural laws already established, laws that cannot ever be changed.

Who is wiser, the man or the insect? (*in sectun*) If man, without varying or altering the natural order had studied and invented he would be a God. We would be gods. But even though he has made stupid laws we will always arrive to a so-called lauded civilization with primitive customs, with truth and reason.

And what man cannot build he cannot destroy. Can he stop the flow of the waters or the movement of the stars? He can alter the course of the waters and immobilize the stars and solar systems on a piece of paper, but he cannot guide them. Besides, nature has changed the course of the waters, this is nothing new. Nature has done it better and without human intervention. These are the great mistakes, sometimes they cast a light, sometimes they are frightening. It is the same mistake of the symbol of the cross, that in the hands of priests, friars, and men also, should not call themselves representatives of Jesus, nor educators of humanity. It is not a matter of destroying churches or casting out the cross, because they are the memory of a man who died because he preached justice and non-violence; what we need to do is to ensure that the priests, friars, and nuns flee from the convents and the churches and go live in places of devastation and sad homes . . . How so? By making sure that humanity does not accept them as representatives of a sublime idea that they have tried to substitute for by deforming it. But they are the deformed ones, and every day the idea is more beautiful, more human, closer to becoming a reality. What fault is it of the images, the walls, the churches, and the crucifixes? None. Let us behave in a manner so that others see what we see. The obstacle is not in the crucifixes or the laminated images, who has not lavished kisses on both? The unhappy orphan, sad and without a source of affection, needs those kisses given to an inert effigy, which is idolatry. And we need to persuade people that what creates obstacles and makes fanatics is the pernicious practice of false representatives who deceive, not in order to serve Jesus nor his ideas, but instead to acquire fabulous wealth and extensive dominions. So we need to ensure that there are no priests or friars.

Churches can become schools and libraries. And the worthy images in them will be consigned to museums. And how will that happen? Oh, the spoken and written word is the devastating pickax that will destroy all obstacles. Nothing else? As the ultimate and extreme action, we have to do it. Isn't the earth more fertile after a flood? After seismic shifts new islands appear from the ocean. Likewise for cleansing our homes and the world of fanaticism and ridiculous notions, and thus the environment will become healthy. That is all there is to the matter.

What is deformed is what shines through.

For kings, all the men who are obedient are good citizens. For the priests all those who accept their doctrines and dogmas are good Christians. In this manner, church and throne shake hands, sustain themselves, and help each other. When the king orders someone into war in the name of the fatherland, the priest affirms it in the name of God.

Neither one of them knows what they are saying, both are criminals before the laws of nature, both are taking humanity down the wrong path, teaching us pernicious customs. These two institutions maintain themselves because of the ignorance of the people, whom they dominate according to their whims.

Women During Primitive Times

In primitive times a woman was considered as object of little value until she was allowed to be a slave, and from that slavery arose her domestic dominion. Considering her so necessary that she could not be dispensed with under any circumstance, the community understood the value of this slave queen of the home, who was able to assume high roles and obtain privileges previously denied. Thus, women began to triumph within the heart of the family, and in positions of power. She was granted responsibility to educate her children and this is the basis of all education; and in having power she had great influence, keeping people from killing, both avoiding and provoking wars.

In a certain period in Rome women had more freedom that in many of the important countries now. Why did she lose those rights? A change in customs, a mixing of races and nations brought about a loss of freedom and rights that had been acquired.

Later, from the Christian era until the Middle Ages she began acquiring certain privileges that were beneficial and harmful. In that period she was considered by men to be queen and mistress of her thought, soul, and life. He was always willing to sacrifice his honor, his valor, and his life for his lady. He scaled the highest positions and put his life in constant danger in order to flatter his lady. Women in those times were idealized, but still slaves. This was true for countries like Spain, France, Italy and England, but not so in Russia, Turkey, China, and Japan. Later, women's progress had several stages and varied according to the country, the period, and local custom.

In the modern age she has been bestowed rights and privileges, but she is still a slave. A slave not because of her intelligence or her work capabilities, but because of her sex.

She rivals men in intelligence and in work she matches men in activity, initiative and perseverance; she has freedom in rights in all areas, except in being able to love with complete honesty and freedom. Men's egoism has not allowed this to happen. A few might be able to, but they will be seen as bad, licentious, and a host of other unjust and exaggerated adjectives.

But will we continue to spoil men by allowing them to impose themselves, to try and lessen the value of those who take the freedom they desire?

Women should not tolerate that others speak badly of women, and if it happens among a group of women, we should isolate that person if they persist; and we should do likewise to any young or old woman who criticizes another woman with regards to her sexual freedom, of which she alone is responsible. I said that men did not allow us freedom, but what right do men have to allow or restrict our freedom, or criticize our enjoyment of that freedom?

For centuries women have been considered inferior, and for even more centuries her inferiority has been discussed, sustained, affirmed or doubted. Today men recognize women and even allow for their superiority.

Marius de Zayas, in "America" referring to theatrical spectacles says: "impresarios always take special care to make their shows varied because women are more intensely emotional and they make up the majority of our audience. "This demonstrates, one more time, the superiority of women over men." I neither agree, nor doubt, nor disagree: I reserve my opinion, because women do not want to be superior to men, maybe they are, but it is not good to flaunt it, since it can be hurtful. And you cannot expect otherwise, of women being generous with those whom she must share the honors, the glory as well as love, which is the greatest glory and to which women vehemently aspire. We like to feel more satisfied in being the glory of our lovers than in being a glorious artist or scientist. And in this we are better than men, in wanting to be loved more than admired. If they admit that nowadays we are superior, then we have to suppose that they admit that we have always been so. This they cannot deny without confessing their guilt concerning our ignorance and slavery, taken advantage of by men without great benefits up until now. So now we sing of the freedom we have acquired as a natural right, because women are born just like men. And our old "masters" sing and desire this freedom without fear of losing their rights.

What Mr. De Zayas doesn't speak about were the culottes or the new ways women dress, since once you begin using pants, there is no turning back to wearing skirts. Skirts can be used in the theater and in dances of butterflies, or in dances with feather boas that use lots of color among the folds and pleated ruffles that one can't see the artist in her vertiginous waltz.

This custom of using pants is perfectly adaptable for the era of feminine progress. And this custom will mean that the coarsest or finest fabrics will vary and we will end up using a veil or gauze-like material to cover ourselves. And in this future epoch women will not put on weight, they will be thinner rather than heavier. And this will be both naturally and artistically beautiful, and the time is drawing closer, as quickly as sociological progress. Everything will tend towards communism in practice, so it won't be strange that communists take away a book, money clothes, and keep everything.

This is sociological progress, communist, anarchist, that is making its mark. We will create societies and have meetings without the blessings of the clergy or the permission of the judge or the mayor. Without realizing it, we have done without ecclesiastical, civil, and political authorities that are so highly acclaimed.

Women adapt admirably to this sociological progress. We expect from these ideas our complete emancipation and to have clearly established all our rights and duties.

Human beings are by nature anarchists and we are headed to anarchist communism, a surprising world without bombs or incendiary devices, nor useless terrorism.

I cannot disagree with these methods, given the repressiveness of some tyrants, what right do they have to execute Ferrer in Spain, Kotoku in Japan (Tokyo) and the others in Chicago and still others in many other parts? Monarchical, imperial or republican tyrants are the same all over. In [Latin] America we have a bumper crop of them, ask Mexico and Argentina, who are still in the 10th century in handling these issues. And still they do not want explosives or suppression. If these are necessary, let them be used. Are governments the only ones that have a right to kill? Let them start by giving the example, since they fancy themselves leaders and fathers of peoples, to be applauded as generous and "charitable". Let them show their charitableness by not maintaining standing armies of unfortunate souls ready to tear each other to pieces at the slightest order; or by not legislating foolish and contradictory laws. Let them uphold truth, not traffic in accusation, nor have prisons and jails for the hungry, but instead schools to teach a trade and warehouses of extra food. Let them not squander money on their vices and bestialities, while others go naked and shoeless, nor degrade women, and later despise her; and why put up with this contempt, and instead let's throw it back in their faces, and call it inferior behavior. Only in doing this will they have the right to call for the abolition of individual and collective attacks.

Do it rulers, otherwise do not complain, you will be always be threatened. I am not in favor of these attacks, either those by the government or by the people. So long as some exist, their counterparts will also. "That is the question." Sovereign rulers and presidents, resolve this problem!

A final summing up: women are capable of everything and anything.

To Jacinto Texidor
Memories

Dear friend, what an impression your novel *Los Culpables* ("The Guilty") made on me, an indescribable impression.

All these memories in my mind, wrapped in sighs and tears of a time long past, were like a scene from a movie.

You know well all the defects of this moralizing society without morals. You have said: "He who causes harm should repair it, he who is guilty of the fall of a woman, make her rise up; and raise her from the mud if it is in the mud you threw her."

How many would have to mend their errors! We women expect to arrive at an era where these abuses have stopped. It is not just when two people infringe the law and only one is punished for it.

Moreover, if a man wants to have a young virgin, he should be one himself.

What kind of law, what kind of morality is it that begins by not being fulfilled by those who legislate and proclaim it?

For me, all laws are useless, they do not serve the goals for which they were created. Natural laws are the only ones that should hold among humans.

If your book were truly valued for its worth, every citizen, male and female, would have an altar to it, the novel would have a place in every home.

There is no greater morality, so beautiful and real, than that of the sacred texts.

But those who think at an elevated plane are called "crazies" that have arrived a century before their time.

No matter, onward esteemed friend, onward in exposing those

truths that will govern in the future.

In this way you will help us —mostly women— tear down the obstacles and overcome difficulties in our path.

And we will be proud to count on you as one of the sincere defenders of our future freedoms.

I sincerely congratulate you for your timely book, because the truths that it encloses are timely for all periods of history. It will cease being so when men stop telling lies and stop cheating on women. And that moment, will it take some time or will it go on forever?

I hope that it will end when this unjust social system ends, which we are tearing down little by little, and by imposing new customs. And by counting on brave and enlightened souls like you, surely we will advance even further, and our long-cherished dream will draw closer, without scandal, without grandiose and useless political speeches made by superficial and clamoring know-it-alls who do nothing practical.

I hope you continue with your work since you seem to have the mettle for it. And this is the job of anarchists, who fear nothing and defy winds and tempests of whatever nature: political, religious, economic, social, no matter what the consequences.

You are one of those, and those are the people we need.

San Juan 1910

Elisa Tavarez de Storer

This genteel artist, excellent pianist and distinguished lady, is one of the most cultured and refined of our compatriots. She is the pride of our country.

Rare is the occasion when we can admire beauty, talent, and artistic distinction in such perfect harmony, not to mention her beautiful qualities as affectionate wife and lover, and tender, selfless mother.

With her mastery and elegance, she shares these traits between her home and her art.

As a delightful, varied and nuanced conversationalist, she makes the hours fly by without notice.

So these lines are by way of offering a humble but sincere tribute, to show my admiration and fondness for a distinguished friend.

Married to the young, hard-working, and cultured David Storer, also an esteemed friend and intellectual companion, since he his affiliated with the "Federación Libre" (Free Federation).

We appreciate the worth of such a dignified young man.

May they live in eternal happiness!

San Juan, January 1911

Postcards
To M. Martínez Rossello, Arecibo

The postcards are beautiful and suggestive, especially when they are engraved with some poetic landscape or with a bouquet of flowers, delicately colored, brought together harmoniously.

And they are useful and even necessary when friendly phrases or sentiments of sincere affection are written on their cardboard surface, and we keep them as mementos of dear friends.

And when we read them again and see what they express, we evoke the figure, the bearing, and the style of those who wrote them.

They are great auxiliaries in conserving the latent memory of those who we sincerely appreciate and stand out in our hearts. And it produces great satisfaction to be able to contemplate them, with their engraved proof of friendship and fondness.

I have felt great consolation one un-definably sad afternoon, by remembering the phrases of a distinguished and respected friend, from a postcard I still keep. It says the following:

"Oh! Blessed friendship, sublime passion
That redeems us from love
And dries away our tears.
When my soul weeps
Squeezing my frank right hand
I find in the friend's helping hand
A soothing saint."

A beautiful and suggestive postcard that brings back unforgettable memories of difficult situations.

They are beautiful, extremely beautiful when they have written on them phrases of sincere friendship. I have seen endless postcards and I'm moved by the expressions of affection in them: a message of friendship from across the seas to the beloved and esteemed person.

How wonderful to remember friends we esteem. And what an inexplicable and infinite sadness overcomes me, withdrawing my soul that cries out, and breathing an anguish sigh I say: Oh, my soul cries out . . . and then I remember:

"When my soul weeps
Squeezing my frank right hand
I find in the friend's helping hand
A soothing saint."

San Juan, October 1909

To Tomás Carrión

As I write your name I evoke our quick trip to Juana Díaz from Ponce, where we were, and another trip to Cabo Rojo when we were in Mayagüez. On this latter trip our dear friend Ramón Irizarry accompanied us, to whom I send my most loyal and affectionate greetings.

I was lucky to accompany you to these two towns and for your help in my efforts to garner more subscribers for the magazine "La Mujer" (Women). To see you so selfless, brave, noble, and loyal, in such an atmosphere of iniquity and injustice, and still you make your eloquent and vigorous words heard, filled with true concepts, free of all hypocrisy, and without fear of criticism. You launched your ideas that soared over conventional wisdom, formidable, loud, like Mirabeau (could you be him?).

My friend, in the struggle for human freedom I have rid myself of formulas and ridiculous exaggerations. And before public opinion we are considered crazy; yes, the sane type of crazy, the madness of telling the truth. You are not in our movement . . . I don't know why, but men like you that have a concept of morality and truth so beautifully formed should not be upholding political ideals that only benefit a few. You should be at our side in the anarchist ranks, defending the universal proletariat!

Come help us to free humanity from the exploitation of man by man.

Put your energies toward disseminating the anarchist message that will benefit all without distinction.

Good bye!!

My Profession of Faith
To Manuel Ugarte, Paris

I am a socialist because I want all the advances, discoveries, and inventions to belong to everyone, that their socialization be achieved without privilege. Some understand this to mean that the State regulate this socialization, I see it without government. That does not mean that I will oppose a government that regulates and controls wealth, as it needs to do, but I maintain my position in being decidedly against government per se. Socialist anarchism.

What I solemnly declare here is that to be a socialist it is necessary to have analyzed and understood psychology.

It is a mistake to think oneself as a socialist and accept the fanatical dogmas, rites and practices of religion because Socialism is truth and imposed religions are erroneous.

Equally wrong is to think oneself a socialist and be an atheist, a skeptic, and a materialist.

Socialism is not a negation, nor violence, nor a utopia. It is a real and tangible truth. Under socialism there isn't room for the cunning (no!) to live comfortably from the work of others. There is no deceit, nor the imposition or imperialism over the weak or ignorant. Socialism persuades with truth, it does not wound. In socialism we find pure reason, the harmony between all, sweetness of demeanor, equality in everything. It is truth not lies, sincerity not intrigue. Now I have said sweetness of demeanor, isn't that what religions preach? Let us analyze this further. Reason is a straight path, serene, peaceful, and impassive. Jesus was a rationalist. A person whose norms follow reason does not violate himself, does not run away, does not make fun off nor express joy at the evil of his enemy or adversary.

So a reasonable person does not have enemies, and should he have them he does not hate them. What are the results of this? If they are insulted or struck by a hand, or with hurtful remarks, and respond in kind, what do they get out of it? (I cannot accept that someone be struck or mistreated without motive). Well, you'll say, what about getting even, vengeance? But reason is serene, self-controlled, it is not vengeful or injurious, and a socialist, for the good and emancipation of humankind should be reasonable. Whoever has reason is in control of themselves, and is not the instrument of vengeance and its consequences: crime, violence, and all sorts of brutal passions.

Socialism is found within the luminous Christianity that shook the foundations of Roman power, because of its notion of fraternity. And universal brotherhood will be the implementation of socialism, which is selflessness, sweetness, modesty, temperance, "All for one and one for all." These are sure steps that lead us to human perfection, toward the freedom and the still undefined spiritual progress of a plurality of superior worlds.

Let us enlighten and purify ourselves, let us educate our wills to do good, and let us consume the fire of our passions under guiding reason, in an offering to human emancipation to achieve spiritual progress.

Impressions of a Trip, July 1909
Remembering the Federación Libre
(Free Federation)

I left Arecibo at ten in the morning going to Isabela: the train left and on the way the different tents were set up close to the city, and, among the plantations, with the soil ready to be planted I saw a girl who with one hand picked up her skirt and with the other was letting seeds drop into the earth. What a beautiful and poetic image!

A beautiful symbol of the constancy of work, which implacable egoism, that insatiable hydra of exploitation strangles in its monstrous arms, an egoism that annihilates the beauty and health of that poor creature, leaving her squalid and without means for her future. And after an entire life of privation and painful misery, she will resort to begging or wind up in a hospital, the only refuge of those who produce everything but enjoy nothing.

Ah! Winsome symbol of work and perseverance, I salute you in the name of universal fraternity! And you, monstrous exploiter, watch your step, lest you fall into the precipice of your ego, in the abyss of your errors.

Walk carefully, because Justice, in the name of Liberty, will straighten you out.

Tremble! Quiver with horror when faced with your final hour, since you were indifferent to your brothers, whom you have sacrificed in the most iniquitous and unjust fashion, sinking them into the most degrading misery. But every thing comes to an end and yours is near. Tremble tyrants of all ages and times because the Social Revolution draws nearer in order to place you at your true social level.

Beware!

CR   CR   CR

In Isabela I stayed a few hours because at night I set out for Aguadilla. In this city I had the opportunity to satisfyingly greet the carpentry workers who are organized into the only union that exists there. Politics in Aguadilla doesn't permit the workers to think about defending their wages. Wage slavery is the modern form of slavery, which oppresses and has made and will continue to make more hungry people and criminals, more than race slavery and bondage did under feudalism. It is more cruel and unjust. At other times the chattel slavery of buying and selling of human flesh was merciless, under the imposition of the feudal lord, owner of the castle, land, and with rights to all sorts of privileges to the point where a poor serf could not sell a piece of wood, or fruit without his master's permission, or give away his daughter in marriage without the first night belonging to the Master. Nor could he afford to buy some necessary good, pinched as he was between church and state taxes leaving the poor soul without a will to live. Slavery in those times cowardly crushed workers, and the usury of tyrants didn't let up one bit unless it was to barbarically swindle him, human dignity was so trampled. Today those circumstances vary little. Nowadays we allow peasants to buy and sell their products, to marry women without first night rights. They can come and go, buy and sell, even meet in assemblies. Yes, everything. Ah! But their slavery is more difficult, it is covered with the subtle veil of hypocrisy.

Workers!

In observing such acclaimed freedom, you can palpably sense your misery, from family to family, generation to generation, that you do not have a place to lay down your tired bodies, and with what you earn you can't even feed yourselves. The bountiful riches produced by coffee, sugar, tobacco, where are they? Isn't your work productive? And the exploiters, from whom do they extract so many thousands of dollars? They are so cynical that they will say Nature is productive, but your work is worthless, that it does need human intervention, right? They are capable of saying this.

Workers, you are in a state of slavery worse than ancient slavery, aren't you in a hurry to be released from it? Don't forget that you hold your own redemption in your hands.

Yes, you do not yield, as in the past most of what you produce to your master, nor do you relinquish the wedding night of your daughters. But in exchange, you die of hunger and degenerate visibly, without the right to enjoy the inventions and fruits of modern scientific progress.

Peasants! From generation to generation you have seen things pass by without greater abundance in your homes. Your slavery has not disappeared; before your master maintained you, depriving you of your will. Now he has left your will free, but he deprives you of the means of using that will. It is the same type of slavery with different methods. They oppress you, they humiliate you, tie you down to the land, to the machine, to the humiliating work that annihilates and brutalizes you, thereby stripping you of your status of free men, putting obstacles in the way of universal redemption. And still, you do not worry about anything except politics, which will offer you nothing, nor defend your rights, they use your ignorance to tie you down and wear you down always against your will.

ɑ൙   ɑ൙   ɑ൙

I left Aguadilla and I arrived in Mayagüez between two and three in the afternoon. I visted the print shop "Unión Obrera" (Worker's Union) and met the distinguished journalist and friend Rafael Martínez Nadal.

I remained in this unique and poetic city for several days. In those days they were celebrating a meeting of the Executive Committee and the Advisory Board of the tobacco union, and I attended. We celebrated a public meeting in honor of July 14th, organized by Julio Aybar, director of "Worker's Union", one of our most enthusiastic comrades.

I enjoyed a delightful stay, dividing my time between pleasant and fun activities, and joining with my comrades in work, struggle, fatigue, and ideals.

In groups we would go for walks, to the table, to the sessions, and like brothers we joyfully passed away hours and had fun.

I remember that right in the middle of the session our comrades

Alejandro Escalet, Alfonso Torres, and Antonio Olavarría had to leave with suitcase in hand to fulfill their sacred duties demanded by the valuable and worthy "Ideals Crusade", whose goal was to disseminate the beautiful ideals of worker redemption in the towns and cities, countryside and villages, planting the radiant and fruitful seed which in the future will reap the most precious fruit, creating the elements for an educated proletariat, and thereby stimulate the appreciation of the precious labor made by our brave comrades, leaders who receive no reward other than the general good of the workers.

On rickety horses and under the rays of a brilliant sun, they went from town to town, taking the good news of our redemptive ideals; and at midnight you could hear the last calls of alert to the workers from the red tribunes.

Lucky are the peoples who listen to the propagation of truth not driven by profit. Happy are the men who understand, and have such courage and gather in the brilliant insignias of their intelligence the suggestive phrases of harmony pouring forth like pearls from the lips of redeemers.

Ah! You honorable propagandists, that, without having studied in the most renowned schools, without having been driven by academic prestige or power, know how to tell the truth with more faithfulness than those who have had lucrative careers, and who have the means and personal comfort to educate the people.

You do not receive awards, or diplomas, or honorary mentions, nor are statues erected in your name. Why?

You do not desire this, you go to your daily labor, and your idea of rest is to agitate for the workers from the platform.

Martyrs of truth, heroic defenders of human freedom, why not trail flowers along your path? Let me spread them about, to console your anguish and disillusions… The solemn hour will arrive, where you can enjoy the bountiful gifts of Nature. You have fulfilled your duty, and in your presence humanity will discover itself.

ভ ভ ভ

I left Mayagüez headed to San Germán. In this gorgeous city, with its enchanting hills, I stayed for a day and a night. The night of my arrival I visited the "Love and Charity" center, where a meeting was being held. There I met Celedonio Carbonell, and after making several eulogies to Anarchism because of its egalitarian synthesis, some in the audience said I was a materialist...I, a materialist? Why? I don't know: all I know is that I feel human, profoundly human.

Materialist? And, so, what of it? Am I the only one, or are materialists to be despised? Is it because I am not —like a sophist— speaking of God in a brutalizing way and saying things like "Oh God, you are everywhere, Sublime Creator, your name is written in the heavens with luminous stars; you vibrate in the depths of the ocean and in the mysterious abysses! Oh! You, Celestial Creator that swells in every flower, in the sighing breeze as it kisses the flowers, your very name is being spoken!"

"You are in the microbe that lives in a drop of water, God you are also in the bacillus that destroys thousands of lives! You close in powerfully like the eagle that majestically crosses the skies, you are in the lion's roar that makes the jungles tremble."

"The turtle dove sings to you from its branch, the nightingale from the forest; and you are in the panther and tiger that stalk the useful sheep."

"You are light and shadow. You stir in the heat, and tremble in the cold. You are in everything. You, Oh God! And by being in everything, in the ignorant soul who seeks the opportunity to plunge a knife into the breast of a brother to take his watch and wallet; similarly you are in those intelligent but hypocritical folks who for centuries have deceived their brothers in your Name. The atoms and molecules pronounce you Powerful Lord of their dominions, and the sunrise sweetly speaks your Name!"

"And the birds flying gleefully intone hymns to you, Powerful Creator, who is uncreated".

Well, tell me now that I have praised, exalted, and adored God. Have I done something sublime?

Oh fools! And you call yourself rationalists? The poor soul who lacks all that is necessary, what do they obtain by praising God? The exploited washerwoman who is deprived of food so that she can pay the landlord, and because of her poorly fed organism her nerves are shot, and any small thing makes her desperate. What good are praises to God for her? And my praises, what good are they to God? One would think that God is nourished only by praise and prayer.

I cannot accept this type of ignorance. I am a rationalist and reason is severe, it does not need praise.

Truth does not need such practices. These customs are the remnants of past errors established in order to subject the masses under the noose of tyranny and despotism.

We rationalists are set upon demolishing all the pernicious customs that do not allow peoples to think with complete freedom, without fear of supposed reprisals in exploring the unknown regions that scientific investigation has not been able to find.

All human beings are free to live according to natural laws, not the ones imposed by human error. I know that those who want to travel in a balloon or on a steamship, do not have to entrust themselves to anybody —human or divine—because all their petitions will be futile.

There are human beings who feel that nothing will happen to them even when they undergo the utmost danger. There is no human power that can destroy them, being immune from any attempt at destruction. How many occupy themselves in addressing prayers to harm others, how many pray with self-interest, and if those prayers were heard what would happen to the life and liberty of each one of us? We would be at the whim of any furious and bad intentioned individual, badly influenced by his ignorance. I do not deny or doubt that in many cases spirits have intervened to protect or save a persecuted friend since there are endless cases of this type, but they have not needed prayers far removed from human intervention.

I remember having read in the "Buen Sentido" (Good Sense) about the fortunate case of a priest who was riding in a train and wanted to arrive at his destination as quickly as possible to attend a party, except the train didn't stop at that location. Shortly before arriving at the desired stop the alarm bell went off, because there was an obstacle on the tracks. All of the passengers were scared, and when it arrived at the designated spot, the train stopped and let the young minister get off. The passengers were informed of the reason for the alarm and the locomotive engineer said there were two persons on the track wearing nuns' habits. People looked, but no one was there. Only the engineer had seen them. I don't doubt this. I've never doubted these stories since I find them quite natural. But this will not make me believe in the efficacy of prayer. If they told me that this was due to a highly developed willpower, I would accept it, or about the perseverance in wanting something, in the power of determination, well, yes, because mental strength is extremely powerful.

But to say, as I've heard on many occasions, that it was the Heavenly Father that sent good spirits, is simplistic and naïve. It implies directing thought in an uncertain fashion. The best way to obtain positive from good influences is to place oneself in the conditions to obtain them. But if you are choleric, lazy, vice-ridden, or a bad human being, if you pray all your life to the Heavenly Father you will not get what you want. Place yourself in the way of useful practices that benefit you and others, and the rest will come on its own. It is logical that if you drink too much you will get drunk, if you say bad things about another, the same will happen to you. Don't believe in superstitions, everything flows from within ourselves. We are so free that even justice lies within us.

There is an adage or maxim that says: "Your own conscience should be the judge, do not suffer later for what you do now."

But you can do many things ignorantly, and in this case you can later reform yourself.

How true and how often repeated that ignorance is the mother of all crime.

Let us enlighten ourselves well, then later step back to reflect and put into practice what we have thought, which has to be a better course than doing something before reflecting upon it.

Humanity has always precipitated itself along erroneous paths, fell sway to excessive self-love without prior analysis.

The excess of self-love is egotistical, and the person blinded by it will make errors.

Excessive self-love leads to crime, by mistaking what is true dignity and honor, and wanting to make it superior to natural laws.

The jealous lover, who cannot admit that his lover can leave him: this leads to a crime of vengeance fed by this self-love, which is egoism.

One can tolerate egoisms that do not harm another individual or bother another's will. The contrary is perverse and leads to harsh or bitter pain.

Through excess of idolatrous love, a mother who wants to benefit her children can harm another mother's children; this should not be accepted or practiced: "what you do not want done to you, you should not do unto others". Everyone guided by such a sublime maxim has the true notion of freedom, equality, and fraternity.

I have tried to control in myself anything that harms, even indirectly, another person.

Indifference is criminal: someone who is indifferent is not human.

It is necessary that the true concept of natural law be understood, for the benefit of all. The person who fails to obey natural law harms humanity.

What is understood by honor and honesty, according to social formulas, are aberrations, mistakes of an ignorant humanity.

There is nothing in natural laws that is dishonest or disgraceful.

Everything against natural law is the invention of human egoism, the errors of self-interest.

But all these blunders will disappear: all of the social system of the family as it is now constituted, the entire commercial system, will disappear and give way to a free family and a free commerce within natural law, in other words, exercising free will for the benefit of all.

Established customs against the spontaneity of nature will disappear.

The education system will be substituted for another more in agreement with the common good.

Education will be adapted without distinction of nationality; the absurd and idolatrous respect shown to governments will be abolished in a future system geared to learning.

The religious ideal to be established in the schools will be brotherhood as supreme law, regardless of national boundaries, or divisions of race, color, or language.

Society's emblem will be the common good, and its slogan will be truth above all things.

The only religious ideal: "Love one another", which will be engraved in the hearts of all.

CR   CR   CR

From San Germán I went to Yauco. In this town I met the renowned writer and poet Doña Fidela M. de Rodríguez; I had the distinct honor of greeting her. She was very correct as always, a genuine expression of distinction that is characteristic of poets.

My affectionate greeting goes to such a distinguished friend and comrade.

From Yauco I went to Arecibo, my home town, where I write down some pages[1] that I read to my children with the idea of interesting them in human suffering. And in August I set out to San Juan, at an unfortunate moment, to see my dear friend J. Barreiro, then the director of "El Carnaval" (The Carnival), who was in prison or about to be jailed because I went to his office several times but did not find him. Luckily I found and met the esteemed and cultured novelist and friend José E. Levis, who accompanied me to various printing presses, among them the one run by the gallant and genteel gentleman J. Pérez Lozada and the no less distinguished and learned Mr. S. Dalmau Canet, and the most attentive Mrs. Timothée. And I almost forgot the virile poet and the eminent comrade Luis Muñoz Rivera, whom I did not meet because he was in New York. But I did have the great satisfaction to meet and greet the prolific writer Mariano Abril, who I had wanted to meet for a long time, and I don't remember who else. Oh! at the gathering at "La Correspondencia," I greeted Blandino and that timely chronicler Joaquín Pujals (Semper). And who else? Nobody. Later I went to see my comrades and friends E. Sánchez López, Rafael Alonso, and Santiago Iglesias, propagandists and tireless strugglers on behalf of the proletariat, those who uphold the most advanced ideas within the current regime, those who run the only institution that energetically and doggedly defends the working class.

Upon arriving to San Juan I was planning to stay somewhere, well placed or not; I also needed to run another printing of my first pamphlet and be able to take it to the factory. Then go to Caguas where the "Ideal Crusade" led by J.B. Delgado and J. Ferrer y Ferrer was being waged, initiated by the Free Federation, and there I

---

[1]"Truth and Justice," which will go into a second edition.

had the opportunity to attend and contribute with my modest help to the workers' talks in Caguas, Juncos, Gurabo, and then go to back to San Juan, then to Arecibo to help with the literature for the tobacco union in Utuado, where we remained for a few days and held several meetings. David Storer also took part in the meetings, with his caustic oratory, speaking his fiery truths. Nicolás María de Jesús and I also took part. I attacked Catholic fanaticism energetically and because of this some rather insolent and impolite broadsheets were published, according to what I was told. I can't pass judgment, I don't censure it, I think it's appropriate they defend themselves, but within the bounds of reason and science. For example, they replied if it is just —being the belief of many— to not baptize someone because they do not contribute to the church, even if they don't have enough to eat, then what is the USEFULNESS of baptism? Or the usefulness and illustrative nature that so many youths that are heads of family, have formed a congregation called San Luis, wearing green bands; and that instead of dealing with the situation of workers and their misery, they waste their time in kneeling and praying in places that priests claim are the house of God.

I have not been able to go back to that group of people. I will go on to energetically defend what I previously stated; that is, to expose the synthesis of the only and true religion: "Love one another", bless your enemies, pray for those who slander and persecute you.

Do not exploit or usurp from your brother the fruits of his labor; don't deceive, don't adulterate the goods of prime necessity for a healthy life.

Don't cheat on nor feign love for any woman if you don't truly feel it. Don't make the sexual act of human procreation, the most sacred and beautiful, the object of impure and vice-ridden pleasures that will harm future generations.

Don't take women as mere objects of pleasure, respect her as the representation of motherhood in the human species.

Be useful and just and you will be happy. Don't lie.

At last, I finished my trip. I stopped in Arecibo and returned to the San Juan of my joys.

I became an Agent for "Unión Obrera" (Worker's Union), and later founded the magazine "La Mujer" (Women).

Naturally, since I had been saturated by the ills that beset society, I found it convenient to rawly present the crimes and vices that are produced by this bundle of stupid preoccupations for the ill development of women.

I started to deal with the issue of sexuality from the point of view of "Free Love", as explained by Magdalena Vernet, and there is no woman, no matter how mystical or modest she might pretend to be, who, after reading this explanation will not find her words reasonable and prudent, but the obstacles placed by social formulas make women be silent.

I know of a man who thinks he is the perfect gentleman, who has no companion, and, according to him, does not use women, who dared to criticize a young lady who had subscribed to the paper. The young lady stopped receiving the paper, because she was called immoral. And I didn't take it to her, nor touch upon the reasons for doing so, since I wanted to avoid an unpleasant situation. This man who thinks he is a perfect gentleman is mistaken if he does not form a union with a woman. Just like you heard it, dear sir.

The article was not inducing women to go off with their lovers or boy friends; the only thing I explained were the mistakes and slavery of women.

And a young lady, who graduated as a Doctor, rejected the paper indirectly, but I don't accept these types of palliatives. And I ask myself, to what degree of fanaticism does the comedy of honesty lead us that even with scientific books in hand that advance the cause of women, women deny this, thereby becoming accomplices of endless errors that are produced by these misjudgments with regard to the sexes?

If the act of procreation were not confused with pleasure instead of being acknowledged as a necessity regulated by science, by study and by self-control, surely there would not be so many lunatics, idiots, deformities, criminals, and lascivious people. But most people have children by chance, because of bestial passions, or in a state of inebriation, and in these kinds of conditions, what kind of generation will be procreated, since the generative act becomes a cesspool of vice, abuse, and contamination? Can a generation be educated if it does not understand what duties it must exercise nor the purpose for which it was created?

An endless number of youth think they have been born to only and exclusively satisfy their carnal instincts, without caring in which way they achieve it.

And from an early age they want to enjoy the rights given to their corresponding age, which hurts their health and is a detriment to the generation that they will procreate.

Tell me, if those who are supposed to bring light into the world do not do so because it is dishonest or "immoral", then who will take charge of telling the truth without dallying?

What can be expected of a youth that at the age of twelve or fourteen knows the minute details of the sexual act?

The lack of centers or societies that deal with sports and gymnastics only contributes to these customs.

It is necessary to increase social hygiene, and persons in the study of the humanities and sciences need to uproot this evil for the benefit of future generations. We need to establish research centers, sports complexes, and gymnasiums in order to prevent the wasting away and degeneration of the race.

Doctors, professors, and parents are the ones needed to deal with this matter of extreme importance for our future.

Thinking of You
For M.L., Arecibo

Oh the moon, how beautiful it is! How many times did I contemplate the moon in my youth, almost entire evenings, in mute contemplation, in front of a tiny orchard with some plants and flowers that I was growing.

Sitting there for endless hours of eternal waiting, seeing small clouds drift by that could not cover the beauty of its splendor, nor the limpidity of the sky, those white clouds adorned the horizon as they went by. There I had the great pleasure to wait for my beloved.

Ay!!! That moon, the way I contemplated it, I have never contemplated it this way ever again.

And as I remember that amorous in-tranquility, which rested on my being unaware of life's struggles, its lies and betrayals, painful tears pour out of me, . . . remembering who I waited for all those endless nights in an incredible solitude, draping myself in that memory so that I could be comfortable in thinking about and waiting for the bronze knob to sound so that my yearning would stop, a yearning that destroyed my illusions and cruelly mortified me, beset by the desire to have next to me the lord of my thoughts and feelings, the one who made life bloom in me, sprouting into two souls, product of my spontaneous love without fetters, evasions, hypocrisies, and self-interest . . . a love spoiled, perverted by only one obstacle: a woman-mother that for me symbolized social formulas.

But it was not important that she was opposed, and always opposed to our being together. My great satisfaction is that I have nothing material of his, I keep only the inperishable memory of the freedom with which I loved him (without wanting pearls or jewelry, cars or palaces): my two children.

Behold the only inheritance of my love. It has been a while since

I live from my own work; he perhaps thought he had the obligation to maintain me, and truly he does. That doesn't bother me, but I have wanted to demonstrate that I could maintain myself and be productive, without being ridiculous or making an exaggerated fuss of it.

So here I am with the eternal pain of wanting companionship. I write this, but no one admires it and he who reads this forgets it when they see me, because I do not show my sadness.

And yet, when I am alone, without knowing why, I feel sad, and needing to dissipate this sadness, I start reading and studying, and reading some paragraphs from Castelar, on the one hand, remembering that moon I contemplated so many times waiting for him and the tears moistened my face, and so I got up to write these hastily scribbled lines of unerasable memories, the eternal companions of my anguished soul, a "wounded turtle dove" . . . and, well, it's that I still love you . . . and "despite time and distance, I will keep your memory in my heart like a uniquely fragrant flower."

I have wanted to become deeply moved again, I have wanted to love . . . but it is not possible . . . I cannot love the way I loved him.

That beautiful illusion that made me delirious, where has it gone? What happened to that treasured illusion that nurtured my soul, that forged my entire life, that I struggled to hold on to, that unraveled like foam on the crest of a wave that is undone on the sand?

And I tried to nurture new dreams for my soul, new fires for my mind, and I tried to dream and seek experiences to alleviate my sad solitude, and . . . they were erased . . . I could not fool myself.

I imbided new nectars of love in order to quench my thirst, and to forget my pain, but the nectar would run out, and the thirst went unabated, nor did the pain diminish . . . And with a smile on my lips, entrenched in a supreme struggle and with supreme calm, I said to myself, I will wait for my next life.

As I reread, will I say what Pierrot said? "Oh, moon! White and pallid moon, when will I return to the ecstasy of contemplating and waiting for my beloved?" Or will I say like Castelar: "What silvery shimmers your rays give to the meandering brook! How your gloomy radiance filters among the branches of the elm!" Even Byron was inspired by the moon's rays, and Byron the skeptic said: "The Moon bathed him with her very soft rays!"

Luisa Capetillo.

MI OPINION.

SOBRE LAS LIBERTADES, DERECHOS Y DEBERES

DE LA MUJER.

COMO COMPAÑERA, MADRE Y SER INDEPENDIENTE.

La mujer en el hogar, en la familia, en el gobierno.

AÑO. 1911.

THE TIMES PUB CO.

PRIMICIAS

DEDICO

ESTE LIBRO A TODOS MIS PAISANOS.

A los trabajadores en general del universo.

A mis hijos.

RECUERDO.

A TI, por quién he suspirado y suspiro....

------

*A tí madre mía que jamás me impusistes,
ni obligastes á pensar de acuerdo con la tradición. Y me dejastes indagar libremente, repro-
chando solamente, lo que tu suponías exageraciones, sin violentarme.*

LA AUTORA.

San Juan, Octubre 1910.

PREFACIO

Al publicar estas opiniones, lo hago sin pretender, recójer elogios, ni glorias, ni aplausos. Sin preocuparme de la crítica de los escritores de experiencia.

El único móvil que me impulsa á dar á la publicidad este tomo, es decir la verdad; la cual, aún aquellos que están en mejores condiciones y con mas talento para decirlo no lo hacen. ¿Porqué? por suceptibilidades de opinión, por no apoyar conceptos de una idea, cuya doctrina, la consideran utópica. Ese modo de juzgar no es suficiente para no publicar las verdades que encierra.

Todo lo que no puede realizarse inmediatamente es utópico. El éxito en un negocio es utópico, pues lo mismo hay probabilidades de ganancia, que de pérdida.

Todo lo que se asegura para época futura, de cualquier índole que sea es utópico. Pues no hay la completa seguridad de que resulte como pensamos.

Diréis que esto es equivocación de conceptos, que no es utopía. Es cuestion; de opinión.... Mas yo entiendo que lo que otros consideran utópico, és en mi concepto realizable.

La idea de "La Fraternidad Social y Benéfica" era utópica para muchos.

¿Y queréis una idea más fácil de practicar? No era Anarquía; no se llamó Socialismo. Sinembargo, muchos que vieron el fondo de igualdad, temieron, y se opusieron, diciendo que era utópico, que era un medio de explotación. Era Comunismo. Era todo amor. Los que acusaron á los iniciadores, de encubridores de una nueva forma política: de explotadores, ¿quienes eran?

Los que vivían y viven de la ignorancia del pueblo trabajador. ¿Dijeron verdad? No, falsearon los hechos, calumniaron á sus apóstoles! ¿Qué conceptos tenemos de los que se oponen á todas las ideas de igualdad, y libertad humana? La de traidores y judas del Maestro. Todos los que juzgan una idea llevada á la práctica, utópica, son obstáculos, y los obstáculos deben empujarse á un lado. Son los que entorpecen las grandes iniciativas, las obras de bien.

Y aun así, se llaman patriotas y padres de la patria.

¿Qué concepto de la patria tendrán? Un concepto egoista, que empieza en ellos y termina en ellos. Ellos lo son todo.

*
* *

No hay nada más perjudicial al éxito de una empresa, que la timidez, el apocamiento, la duda. Una especie de cobardía, que creo que

solamente la pоséen los vagos. No creo nada
imposible; ni me asombro de ningún invento ni
descubrimiento, por eso no encuentro utópica
ninguna idea. Lo esencial es llevarla á la práctica. Empezar! Lo demás, es debilidad, y un
concepto errado del poder humano.
¡Querer es poder!

* *
*

Hace tiempo que deseaba exponer mi opinión
sobre la vida de la mujer en sus diversas manifestaciones. Después de ligeros estudios, heme
aquí en mi tarea árdua y difícil; para un sistema social tan contrario á mis ideales. Estudios
ligeros, he dicho. Sí: debido á que el mayor
estudio lo he tenido en mí misma. Es recojido
de sucesos, acontecimientos y equivocaciones
que durante algunos años he observado en mi
existencia. Relativamente corta, para detallar-
lo completo: Pero más tarde, podré ofrecer
otro estudio
Por lo pronto, necesito reconozcan estos conceptos, que formado tengo en el transcurso de
algunos años de la libertad exigua de la mujer.
Consecuencia del análisis, y el estudio á que me
he dedicado.
La mujer como factor importante en la civilización humana es digna de obtener toda libertad.
Si fuéramos á detallar el influjo poderoso de
la mujer desde las antiguas épocas de los tiem-

pos primitivos, sería interminable, y no es mi
propósito. Esos detalles importantes los ha
publicado en su libro «Mujeres Célebres» Emilio Castelar, en el cual expone con minuciosos
detalles la historia general de la esclavitud, so-
beranía, intelectualidad, sentimientos de la
mujer, desde los tiempos primitivos á la fecha.
¿Necesitamos repetirlo ó plagiarlo? Nó, léa-
se su obra.

Unicamenté deseamos exponer que la mujer
debe adquirir más libertades y derechos.

El actual sistema social, con todos sus errores, se sostiene, por la ignorancia y la esclavitud de la mujer.

Vamos á empezar narrando la esclavitud de
la mujer en el matrimonio. Los inconvenientes
que proporciona el no instruirse. La consecuencia de su desdicha reflejadas en sus hijos.

Como debe entender la educación para que
pueda explicarla á sus hijos. Porque debe ilustrarse, para libertarse de una esclavitud que la
inutiliza como mujer y como madre. Cual mé-
todo debe adoptar para educar sus hijos y su
marido.

Luego de terminada la parte dedicada á la
mujer y sus libertades y derechos.

Continuará, con algunas dedicatorias y explicaciones sobre asuntos importantes que intere-
san á todos.

Esperando que perdonaréis estimados lectores,
los defectos en que haya podido incurrir.

Encontraréis contradiciones debido á la lucha
de mis ideas con el medio ambiente en que me
agito; que trata de ahogar mis ideales.

No importa. Analizad el fin que persigo, y
me basta.

Octubre 1,910, San Juan, P. R.

LA AUTORA.

La mujer en el hogar, en la familia, en el gobierno.

La verdadera madre de familia debe saber hacerlo todo, tanto en la parte intelectual como manual.

Es de imprescindible necesidad que sepa no solamente confeccionar un traje, y disponer la combinación de colores y de encajes si es necesario. Sí, también debe tener talento y gusto para preparar un plato desde el más modesto, al más exquisito trufado. Debe conocer el modo de preparar platos de postres, desde los más sencillos, á los más delicados: sin ensuciarse, sin revolver la cocina y con todo el aseo posible. ¿Que se «curten» ó se afean las manos? Si podéis, recurrid á unos guantes viejos, ó que no necesitéis. Pues unas manos útiles son preferibles á unas simplemente bellas.

Si acertais en uniros á un buen y leal marido, unas manos útiles os ayudarán, á cimentar vuestra felicidad doméstica. Pues si no tenéis alguna práctica para desenvolver vuestra habilidad con facilidad, bambolea la paz del hogar, una mujer limpia, exacta, cariñosa, indulgente y persuasiva, hará las delicias del marido. Si él es bueno, atento y cariñoso, haréis una pareja ideal. Si por el contrario es áspero es incomplaciente y egoista, tratad de educarlo, procurad persuadirlo y tened suma paciencia para conservar la paz; no os pongais á contestarle con asperezas, al igual que él. Todo lo más suave y armoniosa que podais No le demostréis que tenéis más razón que él, esperad que él os la dé, de acuerdo con el sistema actual, que no reconoce que la mujer pueda tener razón.

Procurad haceros lo más agradable posible. Se puede hacer estos sacrificios cuando el marido es casero, cuando no se pueda sufrir: el divorcio.

Igualmente dígole á los maridos: sed pacientes, dulces, amorosos y estad en el hogar, ó salid pero con élla. De lo contrario es inútil el matrimonio. (1)

De modo que siendo un cariñoso compañero, no son inútiles todos los esfuerzos que por complacerlo se hagan; sacrificios, como el moderarse, ser pacientes.

_____

(1) Tal como yo lo entiendo dos simplemente unidos. Sin fórmulas.

No otros, que estén en contra de la naturaleza. Cuando corresponde de un modo leal á todas las atenciones por amor, no por fórmulas.

Compromisos de amor, no de etiqueta ó por costumbres adquiridas por las tradiciones de familia, ó de sociedad.

No se concibe una mujer que no sepa arreglar la casa, la ropa, que no sepa administrar el orden de una casa. Pues las hay sí señor que no saben, ni fregar un plato, ni hacer desaparecer una mancha del piso, ni surcir, ni cocinar.

Qué les espera, en un cambio de estado, ? malos ratos, sinsabores y desencantos.

La mujer actual por regla general, su afán, toda su atención, la dedica al figurín, no se preocupa, de otra cosa que de vestir á la última moda, toda su intelegencia la malgasta en procurar ser más bonita, y si fuera de un modo prático, provechoso é higiénico, como haciendo gimnasia, ejercicio al aire libre, bañándose todas las mañanas.

Pero no, ha de ser, con muchas cintas y encajes, falta de respiración con el uso excesivo del corset, muy ajustado. Y esto significa pérdida de tiempo, de salud y de dinero. (1)

La mujer debe procurar por todos los medios naturales, ser más bella pero de una belleza efectiva, real y duradera, por medio de una sana alimentación, sin comer carne, ni tomar

---

(1) NOTA: Me expreso de acuerdo con el sistema social actual.

licores alcohólicos, gimnasia y paseos al aire libre. No una belleza ficticia como lo es solamente el adorno, desprendida de sus adornos no es la misma.

La mujer debe ser naturalmente bella, sin ridículos adornos, por su constitución fuerte, no excesivamente gruesa, ni muy delgada; por su dulzura de carácter, su paciencia, su sencillez su honestidad (1) todo aunado forma un precioso ramillete, que toda mujer debe conservar, sin dejar marchitar algunas de sus flores.

En tiempo de mis abuelos, se opinaba que los adornos más excelentes y apreciables de la mujer, eran.

‹El silencio, la modestia, el retiro, su continua laboriosidad, su habilidad para las costuras y demás labores propios del sexo, su constante aplicación, para el gobierno de la casa, su desprecio á los atavíos y galanuras. El olvido y aún la ignorancia misma que debe demostrar de su belleza, y habilidades, que la admiren, y que parezca que ella sola lo ignora. Debe ser dulce, sencilla, amable y cuerda. Sus manos no despreciar ni huir el trabajo, debe preveer las cosas y hacerlas á su tiempo: su mayor orgullo, el buen orden de la casa. Su espíritu y cuerpo no deben pagarse de vanos adornos.›

Todo esto, es magnífico para la mujer-madre,

---

(1) No la confundo con la supuesta honestidad que impone la sociedad, esta es hipocresía. La verdadera honestidad de acuerdo con las leyes naturales. Todo lo que esta en contra, es deshonesto, y perjudicial al organismo.

(pues no resulta, que su marido ó hijos la esperen, y ella esté revisando adornos en las tiendas).
Con todo estoy de acuerdo; ahora falta que el marido secunde á la mujer y contribuya á que cumpla élla.
Pero si él dá lugar ú ocasión para que élla no sea buena, entonces no hay que acusar á la mujer sola.
El debe estar en casa con élla, y compartir la difícil tarea de educar los hijos.

¿Podrá existir verdadera felicidad en el matrimonio (1) siendo el hombre el único que puede resolver, y disponer de su albedrío, y satisfacer sus deseos, sin observar si le gusta ó no á su mujer? Acostumbrado á la obediencia pasiva de la mujer, no se preocupa de indagar si está ó no satisfecha de su conducta.   Y si no lo está, no procura complacerla ni adaptarse á una nueva vida.
¿Cómo podra la sacerdotiza del hogar conservar el fuego sagrado del amor en el hogar si oficia sola?   ¿Donde está el objetivo principal de su sacerdocio? Buscadlo fuera del hogar en las horas que debe estar al lado de su compañera.
¿Se cimentará de un modo sólido la felicidad do-

(1) No quiero decir que esté sancionado por el juez ó el cura. Para formar matrimonio no se necesita sanción de las leyes ni seguir costumbre alguna establecida. La voluntad de dos seres humanos de ambos sexos es suficiente para formarlo y constituir un hogar.

méstica con este proceder? Nó. El hombre
tiene derecho para hacer y deshacer, sin su
compañera. Va al baile de disfraz ó nó, al
casino, al juego, á todas....y entre tanto pobre
mujer! ¡pobre felicidad doméstica! expuesta á
la triste soledad, de días y noches sucesivas,
huérfana de amor de atenciones delicadas, de
alegrías, mientras el compañero expresado jue-
ga, baila....ó se enamora.

¡Cuán tristes y amargas son las decepciones
amorosas, y cuán largas las horas que se espe-
ran, en noches interminables esperando, siempre esperando....

¡Oh! que desagradable es, esperar...horas...
y más horas....Días y más días....Las que
habeis pasado por esas amarguras, que trae tan
fatales consecuencias, si no se tiene experiencia,
si no se sabe luchar, sola sin amigos....sin diversiones....

¡Pobre mujer! Pobre felicidad!

De esa soledad surge el engaño, la perfidia,
la hipocresía....ó se rompe esa mal enlazada
unión.

¿Porqué el hombre puede estar al lado de la
mujer, en el baile, en el teatro, antes de contraer matrimonio, y luego que la tiene por compañera la deja sola en hogar y el vá con otras.
¿Por la novedad?, por la variedad de mujeres?
No lo sé.

El verdadero amor no procede así; si no siente el hombre verdadero amor por una mujer,

no debe sacrificarla en holocausto, á sus deseos, como mero instrumento de placer, es injusto. Un hogar solitario, del cual, han huído las delicadas atenciones, las caricias, ¿qué atractivo puede tener?

Y así en esas condiciones puede la mujer conservar su fidelidad amorosa? Aparentemente puede conservarla por formulismos, pero su corazón como está, sus ilusiones do se fueron? Pobre corazón y pobres ilusiones.

Si esa mujer siente simpatías por otro, que durante su soledad, le dedica su simpatía, y llega á olvidar su marido y sus hijos. ¿Quién es culpable?

¿Acaso es justo que ese hombre pueda serle infiel, sin que nadie le crea culpable, y aún así crée tener derecho para exigir fidelidad?

Entiendo que si un hombre tiene una mujer y por satisfar vicios recurre á otras y deja la que lo ama y le es fiel, que no pertenece á otros como las que él visita. Y dá lugar á que ésta esclava rompa las cadenas de su esclavitud. Si ésta mujer no se siente dispuesta por su temperamento, por su educación á envejecer prematuramente, aceptando una moral que no comprende, porque está en contra de las leyes naturales, y una virtud de nombre, no tiene derecho para acusarla.

¿Esto es moralidad? ¡Y se atreven á exigirla á las mujeres!

Si ésta mujer no entiende porque su amante
ó marido, la deja sola siempre, porque la sociedad se lo ordena, ó su orgullo se lo impide ó la
opinión de su madre se lo impone, ni comprende, como este hombre que desea fidelidad en
su mujer, vá donde mujeres que pertenecen á
muchos, faltando él á la fidelidad que debe
practicar para poder exigirla á élla.

Y si esta mujer en esas condiciones y halaga-
da por la simpatía de otro que en su soledad le
agrada y la conquista por su asiduidad, encontrando en él más cariño, y siguiendo los impul-
sos naturales accede á la simpatía y se abraza
á su asíduo adorador, faltando á la fidelidad,
que una moral impuesta y una virtud violenta y
criminal establecida por tiranos de la mujer que
desde antiguas edades la oprimen. ¿Tiene derecho el amante, que no pierde ocasión en serle
infiel y de un modo estúpido, en castigarla?
No, únicamente, en separarse; (¿he dicho en
separarse? Si nunca vivieron juntos) en no volver más donde ella. Pero tampoco, es razonable, ¿por qué si no le agrada que su amante sea
de otro, él prefiere ir donde otras que son de
individuos enfermos y de todas clases? ¡Es in-
comprensible esta moral! El le repugna que su
amante le pertenezca á una persona distinguida,
culta é higiénica, y no tiene reparos en ir donde mujeres que la brutalidad de los tiranos han
empujado, á pertenecer á muchos, y que reco-
jen enfermedades y aún enfermándose desaira

á la que contínuamente le espera, y vuelve á verle infiel.

¿En qué consiste esto? Cual es la moralidad que exije esta sociedad?

¿Qué derecho tiene el hombre en esas condiciones para exigir fidelidad? ¿Acaso á comprado á su mujer como á una esclava, y en forma que ella no puede disponer de sí misma? ¿Si ese hombre no sabe ó no puede cumplir con los deberes de marido, por qué exije á su mujer que los cumpla?

¿Qué moral es ésta?

No tiene derecho para acusarla. El no se ha separado de ella para serle infiel, y ella teme dejarlo ó separarse. En conclusión el hombre que le es infiel á su mujer no la quiere, y si ella termina por no quererlo, y no se atreve á separarse de su lado es una estúpida.

La mujer tiene derecho á separarse del marido infiel, y para esto debe saber trabajar, si es que desea conservar su libertad. Pero si antes de separarse, ha usado de su libertad para aceptar otro hombre. El será el que podrá jactarse de que le ha sido infiel y querrá presentarla como una mujer viciosa. Si tienen hijos entonces el padre de los niños, tiene la obligación de sostenerlos y atenderlos hasta que ellos sean mayores. La mujer en este caso, debe alegar sus derechos y no admitir que tomen pretextos para quitarles sus hijos.

El padre tiene la obligación de sostener á sus

hijos, hasta un nuevo régimen. Pero por ahora, no hay otro.

Todos debemos contribuir, con nuestras energías, y voluntad á sustituir las caducas costumbres tradicionales que son obstáculos en la vía
del progreso Todos debemos de un modo
tenaz y perseverante, intruirnos convenientemente. La mujer madre es la primera que
educa, dirige, al futuro monarca, como al ministro y presidente; al útil bracero y el inteligente educador. Ella forma, modela cuidado-
samente, pero de un modo á veces equivocado,
por falta de educación, casi siempre los futuros
lejisladores y revolucionarios.

Si la mujer estuviera convenientemente ilustrada, educada y emancipada de formulismos
rutinarios, la política de los pueblos sería distinta.

Pero élla enervada por el fanatismo de las religiones, fabrica las cadenas que han de aprisio-
nar á sus hijos y nietos. Sin medir su extensión
ni su fortaleza. Observad que la madre desde los
primeros años, va infiltrando creyéndolo .bueno
y conveniente, las ideas que sustenta sin haberlas analizado y seleccionado, unicamente por
haberlas recibido de sus padres como legado
espiritual. Y continúa aturdiendo el cerebro
de sus hijos en creencias políticas y religiosas
que le atrofían el cerebro, y lo imposibilitan
para analizar la verdad de las leyes naturales.
Esta influencia maternal, es poderosa cuando

pueden los hijos estar contínuamente á su lado, hasta que formen ó nó nueva familia. Si antes ha podido emanciparse de la tutela doméstica seguramente cambiará, si desde pequeño pierde la madre ó está por circunstancias distintas obligado á separarse, ya no hay que pensar en que pueda conservar las ideas como en la infancia le inculcaron. Han sucedido casos excepcionales, pero las circunstancias que le rodearon influyó en tal ó cual idea.

No hay duda que la primera y mejor escuela es el hogar. La mejor y superior maestra para el niño, és, la madre instruída. La madre, tiene el alto deber de inculcar á sus hijos sentimientos de bondad, de ilustrarlos en los rudimentos de la instrucción primaria. Siempre que se le proporcionen medios, que no se vea precisado á salir fuera á buscar trabajo, en este caso pierde el niño su mejor y más superior directora La mujer educada é ilustrada, es buena madre y buena esposa. Claro está que debe encont.ar en su marido, el complemento, que se amolde perfectamente á su carácter y naturaleza y los dos dirijir la prole.

La armonía en el matrimonio influye grandemente en la educación de los niños, futuros ciudadanos. ¡Cuantas veces, las lágrimas vertidas en horas de dolor y contradicciones por la madre, ha influído poderosamente en los hijos!

Recuerdo un caso que refiere Guy de Maupasant, de un niño que jugaba en el jardín de su

casa, y corriendo por sus callecitas, oyó ruido,
se puso á observar, y por entre el ramaje vió á
su padre que oprimía por un brazo á su madre
y violentamente quería obligarla á que firmara
un documento. Ella se resistió, y no lo hizo,
y él en un acceso de cólera, la sujeta ambos
brazos, y le abofeteó al rostro, de un modo
cruel y villano. Fué tal la impresión que produjo en el niño aquella escena, que dió un grito
y huyó pero lejos, muy lejos......

Era de noche y el niño no aparecía, por fin lo
encontraron al día siguiente en el bosque, y al
llegar y ver á su madre cayó de rodillas lloran-
do. Este niño fué hombre, y siempre tenía
presente esa escena, fué como su eterna sombra, pues para alejarla de su mente se pasaba en
el café pidiendo "Mozo un bur" Mozo otro bur.
Y cuando veía algún antiguo conocido refería
aquella escena que lo había hecho vivir retirado
del mundo y solo, sin más compañía ni recuerdo
que el de aquella escena.

El documento que no quiso firmar la madre,
era la dote destinada á su hijo que el padre quería utilizarla.

¡Cuantas escenas domésticas han influído é
influyen poderosamente en los niños y los hacen
buenos ó malos.

Cuantos padres por su proceder incorrecto
ocasionan disturbios y proporcionan medios
para separarlos de la madre. La madre que se
ha sacrificado, que les ha dado su salud y be-

lleza, vé con dolor que tiene que separarse de
sus hijos, y confiar su educación á gentes de
opiniones y conceptos erróneos, por terquedad
de un padre que quiere imponer su voluntad,
por sobre las conveniencias de sus hijos, que
debe dejar al lado de su madre, hasta los 12 ó
14 años. Y no buscar pretextos para privarlos
de influencia tan benéfica.

¿Debe este padre privar á esta madre, de educar á sus hijos? Nó. Debe proporcionarle medios, y no obligarla por la miseria á que los
deje. Su obligación. era proporcionarles medios para que ella los atendiera, y no tuviera
que separarse de ellos para que otros traten de
dirijir lo que á la madre pertenece, formar y
educar el alma, el corazón de sus hijos de acuerdo con las prédicas de Jesús, y de libertad humana, entonces pueden estos educarse sin temores.

Por eso la mujer debe ilustrarse y educarse,
hay que distinguir, pues ilustración abarca
todos los ramos de la ciencia humana, Fisiología, Fisonomía, Geología, Geografía, Química,
Física, Astronomía, Ingeniería, Agricultura,
Geometría, Historia, Música y Pintura. Pero
la Educación es distinta, pues se puede ser
instruído y no educado. La educación es muy
bella y necesaria. En ella está basada la armonía de la familia y los pueblos. La educación
es importante y muy útil en la mujer madre.
Vamos á dar algunas explicaciones de cultura.

Un niño en la mesa, comete una torpeza, derrama un poco de agua ó rompe un objeto del servicio, una madre educada, que ha cultivado la paciencia, lo tranquiliza por el susto que ha pasado y lo dirije dulcemente y recoje los pedazos rotos ó seca el agua y hace que el niño la ayude. Una madre no educada, de un "tirón" baja al niño de la silla, le pega, lo empuja, y lo maltrata y lo pone de rodillas y sigue hablando de economía y de gastos y de miles historias hasta que el marido se incomoda y se marcha sin almorzar. Y esa mujer que alborota tanto y maltrata á su hijo, por un vaso, copa ó plato, que dió un meeting de economía, malgasta el dinero en objetos fútiles, y tiene pulseras y está repleta de encajes que parece un bazar   Educación es, cultivar la paciencia, la tolerancia, la dulzura, la concordia, la abnegación, la templanza. Todo el que cultiva estas virtudes es educado.

¿Si no se instruye, y educa la mujer, podrá educar, aconsejar y dirigir convenientemente á sus hijos? Nó. Y es un asunto importante que debe interesar á la mujer. Siendo el hogar la primera y más necesaria escuela, lo que vé hacer y decir á la madre, eso observa y aprende el niño.

Si la madre es violenta y colérica en sus modales, el niño la imita. Le decimos, "los niños no mienten", y en el mismo momento llaman á la puerta, y dice la madre, "dí que no estoy" y

se aleja, abre el niño, y dice: "mamá no está"
O de otro modo, ofrecerle cualquier objeto,
después que lo ha contrariado sin motivo, por
capricho, por ejercer imperio, sobre el niño y
luego no le cumple lo ofrecido; "te voy á
llevar á paseo", y se esconde y se vá sola. ¿Por
qué hace eso una madre cariñosa? Creo que
es ignorancia de su cargo.

Hay muchas mujeres que créen que el ser
madres es contradecir al niño, y pegarle luego
y ordenarle tonterías por el solo hecho de man-
darle, para verse obedecida ordenar al niño que
no corra, que no salte, que no grite, en fin un
sin número de ignorancias, pues prohibirle todo
eso es prohibirle que sea saludable. A las
niñas porque son niñas, como si el organismo
de las niñas no tiene que desarrollarse, para
que crezca hermosa y fuerte: y no raquítica y
pálida, que llegan á ser madres, para estar continuamente llenas de enfermedados y dolores.

Créen que.ser madres autoriza para maltratar
y ordenar al niño caprichos, y obligarlo á hacer
cosas contra su voluntad, es un error.

Muchas dicen yo soy pobre y mi hijo tiene
que ayudarme, y por eso crée que el niño debe
abstenerse de jugar, pues cada vez que lo necesita dice, "mira, tú no piensas nada más que en
el juego". ¿En que ha de pensar? ¿en que su
madre es pobre?; el niño no comprende eso, si
es niña, la obliga muy pequeña, sin haber
disfrutado de los juegos infantiles, con toda

comodidad; á lavar, á tostar café, á fregar el
piso, y élla, se vá á casa del vecino á conversar,
ó no vá, de todos modos es grave que si se le
quema el café, expuesta lo niña á quemarse, un
puntapié, ó un golpe con el palo de la escoba,
ó un empujón que la hace caer. Esa niña ultrajada así, después de estar haciendo un trabajo superior á su edad, siente la necesidad de
huir, al verse mal tratada. Cuantas pagan las
rabietas ó celos y contrariedades de sus madres,
sin motivo que lo justifiquen solamente por
desbordarse y no poder hacerlo con el marido.

De ningún modo, esto debe hacerlo una
madre, es una herejía, una-crueldad, que no
resuelve nada ni aminora sus contrariedades.

Pues si el niño ó la niña rompe algo, eso la
demuestra que es élla la que debe hacerlo. Y
si el marido se está fuera de casa más de lo
necesario ó se enamora, es culpa de élla y no de
la niña. En este caso debe de procurar hacer
el hogar y su persona más agradable y risueña,
y no ser majadera ni gastadora y ser educada y
tolerante con los defectos del marido, (pues élla
también los tiene) ó si es que le molesta su
marido ó está cansada de él, debe separarse, y
no estar con pretextos. Si la mujer fuera ins-
truida y conociera sus derechos, no pasara
esto. El hombre no se atrevería á engañarla.

Por ejemplo, ninguna mujer debe aceptar un
hombre que esté comprometido, sin exijirle que
deje su mujer ó amante si no lo quiere ya. Y si

ésta amante ó esposa no quiere dejarlo, tendrá
que admitir que su marido tenga otra mujer,
pues no puede obligarlo á que la quiera á ella
si no ha tenido en sí gracia ó influencia para
retenerlo para sí, ó no ha sabido procurar
aguardarle. Este hombre debe tener la libertad, de escojer otra y vivir con ella. Y esta
mujer debe buscar otro para marido. Y si es la
mujer la que está aburrida y cansada de su
esposo, y este apesar de conocer ó comprender
que molesta, que fastidia; persiste en la idea de
retenerla por que la quiere, pero no ha sabido ó
no ha querido c ptarse sus simpatías ó su cariño, ó no ha querido, ó le ha sido indiferente,
creyendo que por que ella está casada con el
tiene la obligación de aceptarlo sin haberla con-
quistado, es un..... grosero, y ésta mujer está
en su derecho y deber natural de repararse por
todos los medios y no engañarse á sí misma, ni
engañar á los demás. El hombre que toma una
mujer y que cree que ella está en el deber de
esperarlo todos los días hasta las 12 ó la una, es
un egoista. Si ella por complacencia lo espera
muy bien, no tiene derecho á quejarse. Pero
la que llora y desea libertarse de aquella
desigualdad hágalo en buena hora y demuestre el valor de sus sentimientos, sin temor
alguno. La mujer que acepta una esclavitud
por no saber trabajar, es una idiota. La mujer
debe penetrar en todas las galerías del saber
humano, y presentarse dueña de su libertad y

de sus derechos. La mujer que para que la
sostengan muellemente descansada ó lujosa-
mente ataviada, consiente ó tolera y admite casarse con un viejo y engañarlo, es una estúpida
y el viejo un ridículo. O que sufre y se calla
y envejece porque no se atreve quejarse, ó
reclamar su derecho, por temor de cambiar de
posición ó por la opinión, es una esclava.

La mujer que se siente herida en sus derechos, libertades y en su naturaleza de mujer,
debe reponerse y reclamar, y cambiar de situación, cueste lo que cueste. La moral establecida, ó lo que se llama moral, no lo es, no se
puede aceptar una moral que está en contra de
la libertad y de los derechos de cada uno de los
humanos. No hay que temer á una moralidad
que solo existe de nombre. Vamos á establecer la verdadera moralidad la que no obliga ni
contraría los derechos establecidos por la naturaleza. Lo demás es ficticio, es engañador
y falso, y no debemos continuar admitiéndolo.
Cada cual tiene el derecho de ser feliz, y no se
puede ser feliz si la persona que ha de formar
ó completar nuestro yo, no lo es. Y si no se
busca el modo de agradar y de hacer sentir
bienestar, á la persona amada, no debe obligar-
se á ella ó á el, á vivir de un modo contrario
á sus aspiraciones ó deseos. Dejar que libremente elija su gusto.

Otro pretexto el de los hijos, que por los hijos
no pueden separarse dos que están disgustados

y no pueden tolerarse sin grandes violencias.
Sí señor; pueden separarse, y tiene el deber el
padre que puede colocarse ó tiene un empleo de
sostener en debida forma, á los hijos y la
madre; pues esta no puede trabajar fuera; y
cuando sean mayores, ya ellos se proporciona-
rán lo que necesitan. De todos modos es pre-
ferible á que vivan riñendo siempre.

*
* *

Hoy no es aceptable eso del "silencio y el
retiro, en la mujer", pues hoy la mujer en
Europa aspira á compartir los puestos públicos
y á gobernar, administrar pueblos, sin perder
su personalidad femenina, ni sus deberes de
madre y esposa.

Opina la autora de (1) "La Mujer Moderna
en la familia", "que es bueno que la mujer moderna justifique que sabe estudiar tanto como el
hombre para obtener un título académico, que
sabe manejar hábilmente el bisturí del cirujano,
el microscopio del naturalista, y el buril del
grabador, lo cual demuestra lo erróneo de la
teoría de la inferioridad del cerebro femenino.
Bueno es que la mujer demuestre que sabe
desempeñar un cargo público con tanto acierto
como el hombre; que la capacidad, la conciencia, la fidelidad, en las obligaciones no son pri-

(1) No conocemos el nombre: en ese libro su autora se
esconde tras una A...... así.

vilegios del sexo fuerte que sabe mantenerse á
sí mismo y mantener tambien á su marido."
Se ha dicho infinidad de veces, que la mujer
en ese terreno perdería, perjudicando el hogar,
la familia y los hijos!
Pero los que opinan de ese modo olvidan que
la dama, de alta y cómoda posición, vá á las
tiendas, visitas, museos y teatros, y modistas, y
el hogar solo, sus hijos con las sirvientas, ó
nodrizas únicamente, los ven un momento, los
besan y vuelven á salir, y esto es diariamente.
No les alcanza el tiempo para su tocador y
atender á las visitas de cortesía, á la modista y
al paseo; en el Pardo ó Prado, el "Boix de
Boulogue", ó los Campos Eliseos. Todos estos
paseos se hacen á determinada hora para encon-
trarse allí y satifacer la vanidad y seguir la
moda. ¿Como los maridos de esas elegantes
damas no se ocupan de observar si se perjudica
ó nó el hogar y los hijos en esa soledad continua? Los niños, no ven á la madre un momento. Pues en estos casos es más útil que se
dedicara á estudiar ó escoger cualquier empleo
que le proporcionara medios de ser útil. La
mujer posee en alto grado, penetración sagaci-
dad, prontitud, buen sentido administrativo.
¿Porqué no desempeña cualquier puesto administrativo?
Porque se ha de pensar en que se perjudica-
ría el hogar para esto.
Y no se perjudica cuando la mujer no quiere

lactar á su hijo y no quiere acompañar á su
marido al teatro, por ir á la iglesia á confesarse?
Y no se perjudica la familia, cuando se la pasa
todo el día entre la iglesia y las visitas y los
paseos. Pues no puede perjudicarse, porque
contribuya con su talento y actividad al desarrollo de los pueblos.

Y la mujer obrera que deja sus hijos, por
cuidar los de las ricas y concurrir á las fabricas
y talleres, ¿no perjudica su hogar?

El hogar obrero, el campesino y su mujer que
abandona su hogar y no tiene á quien dejar para
que lo cuide y al volver encuentra á su hijo
carbonizado, ¿no se perjudica?

De modo que perjudica el hogar! se perjudica
la familia! se confunde la dama en macho!
Pero es el hogar del rico! es la familia aristó-
crata!, es la dama linajuda!

Pero el hogar pobre, la familia obrera, ¿no
se perjudica?, la infeliz sirvienta ó campesina
que se alquila á lactar el hijo del acomodado y
abandona los suyos ¿no sufre?, ¿ni tiene sentimientos naturales? La pobre mujer que tiene
que ir á empujar la carretilla en las minas,
confundida con el hombre, que va y vuelve
sola, no se convierte en macho. La que marcha
á labrar la tierra, tampoco. ¡Qué vá! ¡Si esas
gentes son de bronce, no sienten!....La infeliz
esposa de un trabajador de ingenio ó carretera
que solamente gana 60 á 50 centavos por día,
que no le alcanza para atender á 4 ó 6 hijos que

tiene que vestirlos y calzarlos y no puede hacerlo, y para ayudarse, se alquila á lavar ú á
otros oficios y deja sin atender á sus hijos, ¿nó
se perjudica?

Porque el hogar protejido por las leyes, y las
riquezas, se beneficia y se proteje más y se olvida
el hogar pobre. Se olvida que la familia pobre,
en vez de enviar á sus hijos á la escuela los
utiliza vendiendo frutas ó los tiene que alquilar,
ó hacer trabajos superiores á su edad. ¿No los
perjudica? ¿Por qué? No se procura atender á
esos niños que no pueden ir á la escuela por
falta de ropa y calzado y que los padres no
pueden alimentar y para eso tienen que enviar-
los á vender dulces ó frutas. Deben de proporcionarles alimentación é instrucción, las familias ricas, en combinación con el Estado.

Mis ideales me están recordando que no se
debe pedir, que se debe instruir al pueblo para
que se tome lo que necesite sin recurrir á medios artificiosos á incompletos. Porque pedir
que las familias ricas y el Estado contribuyan con
una limosna para atender á los hijos de los que
han proporcionado á esos ricos su capital, y
sostienen el Estado. ¡Es ridículo! Pues hay
quien, á pesar de razonar y comprender que sin
el pueblo trabajador no habría riquezas, ni mu-
nicipios, ni empleados, encuentra muy justo el
que se vaya á mendigar á los mismos que viven
usurpando el sudor, el trabajo de la clase trabajadora.

No debemos continuar con nuestra indiferencia, continuar remachando las cadenas de la esclavitud del salario mezquino y degradante que recibe el obrero en general. El trabajo de cada ciudadano, debe de cubrir todas sus necesidades, gustos y diversiones de acuerdo con la higiene y el progreso actual. No se debe continuar diciendo: "que el campesino y su estado, debe permanecer sin educación, por ser innecesario á su trabajo", pero no hay que olvidar, que los que así se expresan son los amantes del progreso de su patria! ¿Sabéis quienes son? Los patriotas políticos!

¡Bien por los patriotas de cartulina!.....

**

La mujer que teniendo su marido dueño de ingenio ó hacienda y conozca, ó se llame espiritista ó cristiana debe procurar no ataviarse con lujo, ni usar prendas, ni hacer gastos inútiles. Debe visitar las familias de sus peones, que le producen la riqueza que poseen y continuan aumentándola y observar en que forma viven, si carecen de lo útil y necesario, como lo son las camas, sillas y demás utensilios; si la casa en que viven no se moja, y si se puede habitar en ellas de acuerdo con la higiene. Si ella viviría con gusto en ella.

Luego de visitar sus peones, expondrá á su marido en que estado y condiciones se encuentran los infelices que le producen su capital y conseguir el aumento del salario, y ella con dis-

creta economía en vez de llevar prendas, y adornar con objetos inútiles, su cuerpo y su hogar;
ir á llevar consuelos y salud, á los tristes hogares de las víctimas de la explotación. Llevarles
ropa, calzado, libros, y procurar instruirlos
leyéndoles, é influir que haya escuelas en el
barrio para que se ilustren los hijos de ellos.

¡Cuán hermosa y bella sería una mujer sembrando el bien, cumpliendo con un deber
humano!

Con qué luminosos destellos alumbraría su
alma!

Cuán dulce y exenta de disgustos pasaría la
existencia!

La mujer que empieze á practicar estas accio-
nes y estableciera la fraternidad ú igualdad
social, se elevaría á un nivel tan alto sobre las
mezquindades y egoismos humanos, que graba-
ría su nombre en todas las conciencias y tendría
un lugar sagrado en cada corazón que le rin-
diera culto. Y en la futura existencia ¿qué le
esperaba? cuando sus mismos hechos, de amor
y justicia, trazarán el luminoso sendero que
hubiese de conducirla á disfrutar las consecuencias del bien que sombró.

¡Oh tú, mujer! que pudiendo sembrar justicia
estás dispuesta á hacerlo; no te turbes, ni te
inquietes, ni huyas, adelante! y en provecho de
las futuras gereraciones coloca la primera piedra para el edificio de la igualdad social de un
modo firme y sereno, con todo el derecho que

te pertenece, sin bajar la frente, que ya no eres
la antigua material é intelectual esclava. Tu
iniciativa será coronada por el éxito, haciéndose
por tu propio esfuerzo tu alma, luminosa y
bella como un sol de verdad y justicia.

¡Mujer rica! tu puedes redimir á tus hermanos explotados! redímelos que tuya será la
gloria!

Y si encuentras oposición en tu marido, si es
cruel y egoista que se opone como obstáculo á
tus grandes y justas aspiraciones! no le culpes y
no le temas; que en él, veras representado el
símbolo de la ignorancia, tratando de conservar
sus dominios.

No le temas y continúa tu marcha que como
á Isabel de Hungría, se convertirán tus dona-
tivos en hermosas y perfumadas rosas que ali-
gerará tus pasos, y te evitarán. el disgusto de
contradecir á tu tirano.

Grande y digno ejemplo darías tú, oh mujer!
rompiendo las tradicionales costumbres, injustas
y tiranas, símbolos de la ignorancia para establecer el reinado de la Libertad, Igualdad y
Fraternidad, símbolos de la verdad y la justicia!

No temas la crítica, ni la burla ni el escarnio,
son los aullidos de la impotencia, asciende, asciende, más alto, más alto! cual otro Jesús al
Calvario, y establece la redención del proletariado puertorriqueño, que será el prefacio de la
redención universal!

*
* *

¡Cómo podrá la mujer ilustrarse de un modo
verdad, si no vé ni observa las cosas tal como
son?

Para élla todo está oculto tras un velo miste-
rioso, que no la deja ver de un modo real; si
está en un baíle, si en el teatro, en el hogar todo y todos la engañan, sin ella darse cuenta.

Ella es la eterna ciega á quien conduce por
regla general un libertino; que continuamente
le dice: "Haz lo que te digo y no lo que hago",
y la mujer sigue creyendo á este pérfido sin
darse cuenta que es engañada. Y engañada
vive, y así con engaños la educan y la pervierten, sin notarlo élla. Cuando niña le dicen:
"las niñas no deben hacer esto, ni aquello, por
que las niñas deben creer, en lo de aquí, y en
lo de más allá" y empieza por ser víctima del
rutinarismo de los padres, y luego de los caprichos sociales, y más tarde ó al mismo tiempo, de las extravagancias del novio, y luego
de la tiranía del marido, y así de este modo la
mujer tiene que ser pura y no mentir.

¡Cuán engañados están!

Y cuando la mujer se da exacta cuenta
de la vil é infame comedia que para engañarla
sin élla saberlo, se ha utilizado; y se han pervertido utilizándola. Y cuando toma libertades
por su cuenta entonces no hay pretextos ni
frases, ni razonamientos, ni modo alguno que
la detengan. Y en este caso, ¿para que se ha

querido engañarla? Para esclavizarla por
egoismos carnales y estúpidos.

Y después de tanta precaución de los padres
para que ignore lo que realmente debe conocer;
(que es, el procedimiento de los hombres con la
mujer, desde tiempos muy remotos, la forma
en que la han considerado y como la han utilizado, y los vicios que le han enseñado) pase al
nuevo hogar á ser víctima de su ignorancia.
Una mujer instruída en lo que concierne á su
sexo, antes y después de unida á su marido
natural ó nó, tiene que saber defenderse. Y si
no lo hace porque esté ciega, sabiéndolo ya de
todos modos es beneficioso, pues aunque se
hiciera cómplice del marido, siempre tendría
oportunidad de pensar en lo inconveniente de
sus actos y terminará por execrarlos. Es conveniente que la mujer se ilustre de un modo
científico. "La higiene del matrimonio", debe
ser leída por solteras y casadas. No puede
aconsejar esto sin pensar en los enemigos ó
contrarios á que las mujeres se enteren de que
existen ó aprenden sin saberlo, prácticas obscenas, enseñados por los que siempre y en todas
ocasiones critican á la mujer, siendo sus dis-
cípulas. Pero creo que de igual modo que se
atreve el hombre á presenciar y á facilitar un
parto difícil con su título de doctor: opino
también que la mujer debe estudiar los vicios
y enfermedades de los hombres para preservar
de adquirir costumbres impuras y obscenas ó

indecentes. Y los que se atrevan á creerlo inmoral, es porque realmente son culpables y temen ser descubiertos por su mujer. Y á estos hay que darles un fuerte correctivo sin temor. ¡Mujeres de todas las posiciones defendeos, que el enemigo es formidable, pero no le temáis, que según es el tamaño es su cobardía!

Los que crean que la libertad de la mujer, tiene límites especiales se equivocan. Los padres que contribuyen á que sus hijas no se casen á su debido tiempo son causantes de lo que le suceda luego. Por cualquier tontería ridícula se oponen á que se verifique su enlace, sin fijarse en el daño que ocasiona.

Y los que no las ilustran en las prácticas de la vida marital cometen un error que lamentarán y no podrán evitarlo.

El procedimiento que se emplea actualmente es contra la moral. Yo opino que el hombre no debe pertenecer á ninguna mujer antes de su completo desarrollo y llegado este debe escojer la que realmente ame con toda su alma y hacerla su mujer, y crear una familia. Si no congenian y se ven obligados á separarse puede cada uno elegir de nuevo.

Esto es lo correcto y lo natural. Para mi el matrimonio es un error, tal como está establecido. En la actual sociedad la mujer se casa por seguir la costumbre.

Y el hombre á veces para tener una ayuda ó esclava. Y de este modo se atreven á hablar

de moralidad, una sociedad que encuentra
inmoral que la novia huya con su amante y
viva con él y crean una familia, y no se espanta
de que ambos sexos cometan actos contra lo
natural atrofiando el cerebro y la belleza y pervirtiendo el acto de más importancia para los
humanos; la procreación. Demostrando que
tales desvaríos criminales se cometen por ignorancia de ellos, é imprudencia de los padres.
Y los jóvenes no protestan que en vez de ir á
sus brazos como ordena la ley natural; se entre-
guen á la masturbación ó al delito contra natura del mismo sexo. Y las damas ó señoras que
lo saben, tampoco protestan cuando se verifica
en el sexo contrario.

Pero como van á protestar? si eso es moralidad!.... moralidad!.... lo esencial es la apariencia de "*virtud*" de "*honestidad*" como si
la virtud y la honestidad estuvieran fuera
de las leyes de la naturaleza.

No puede haber virtud ni moralidad, ni honestidad, que no esté comprendida en las leyes
naturales. Estos son el compendio de todas las
virtudes.

La naturaleza nos indica el verdadero camino
del bien, pero queremos ser más sabios que ella,
y he ahí el origen de todos nuestros errores,
en querer modificar las leyes naturales, que es
donde está la belleza, la salud, la armonía, la
verdad.

¿Y á donde iremos por caminos errados? Al

crimen, á la prostitución, al adulterio, á la
muerte de nuestro espíritu.

Una cuestión importante para las madres

Es costumbre generalizada, el quejarse las
madres de tener hijas y alegrarse de tener hijos.
¿Por qué esta lamentación? "Yo desearía que
todos nuestros hijos fueran varones y no tener
hembras". ¿Por qué? Porque los varones no
dan tanto *que hacer* y las mujeres hay que
vigilarlas y ser responsables de lo que hacen.
—No hay tal—aquí la generalidad de las madres se equivocan, pues á quién hay que educar
es á los varones, pues estos como no reciben
aviso alguno á ellas solas las culpan. Los que pudiendo educarlos, no lo hicieron.—Los que le
han dicho una y mil veces,—el hombre siempre
sale bien,—y han consentido que burlen,(al menos así lo creen) y se les importe poco el sufri-
miento. de las mujeres, esos son los culpables.
Lo mejor es destruir fórmulas vacías y crear
costumbres sanas y naturales. No indispongáis
á la mujer contra el hombre, dejadlos libres y
naturalmente se amarán ó repelerán Sin temores ridículos. Es de suponer que con las actuales costumbres haya mujeres despreciadas y
perjudicadas, estas infelices no tienen la culpa.
Ese es el resultado del sistema egoista de educación masculina; el joven tiene una hermana y teme la enamoren, pero al mismo tiempo enamora á

una joven que tiene hermanos, y no desearía que ese otro joven enamorase la suya.

Así somos, pero realmente estoy colocada fuera de esas costumbres y de esas fórmulas estúpidas. La ley que en E. U. prohibe, hayan casas de prostitución es magnífica. ¿Por qué ha de haber un cierto número de mujeres dedicadas á eso? Eso es cruel é injusto, todas deben estar consideradas y estimadas. De igual modo que no hay hombres con esa ocupación, no debe haber mujeres, todos con los mismos derechos y libertades y haríamos un mundo mejor. Pero como no se educa á la joven rica para el trabajo, si, se la instruye para que procure contraer matrimonio con un hombre rico. He ahí el mal; he ahí la turbación de la mujer cuando su amante ó marido la abandona. No siente su separación tanto, lo que la perturba es el sustento, el pago de casa; las necesidades sin cubrir que eran sufragadas por el marido ó amante y he aquí, que como no sabe lo que cuesta el proporcionárselo, sea gastadora y superflua en sus gastos. ¿Y continuaremos educando á la mujer así, no la prepararemos, para que pueda desenvolverse libremente y con comodidad en las luchas por la existencia, para que no sea víctima de una burla y de una deshonra, ilusoria y mentira.?

Pues no hay tal burla ni deshonra. Lo que hay son leyes naturales que cumplir y que es un crimen el violar esas leyes, ó imponerlas inventadas por los hombres egoistas. Egoistas y crueles, pues el solo acto de gustarle una mujer es bastante para que quieran, sin saber si á esa mujer le gusta; poseerla y luego, si les agrada, entonces querer imponerse por temor de que se enamore de otro. Es decir que no trata de gustarle á ella; de ser bueno y complaciente para que ella se conmueva y lo quiera, nó, eso nó; basta su deseo y voluntad para querer ser complacidos, sin tratar de agradarla y hacerse necesario á esa mujer que sería lo más correcto y natural.

Primero ver si á ella le gusta, para luego ir tratando de intesarle y hacerse necesario. Ahora yo comprendo que todas y todos tienen el derecho de dirigirse y aceptarse mútuamente sin rodeos, ni privilegios de alguna clase, pero estas libertades hay que conseguirlas, no están establecidas; vamos á luchar por ellas que es luchar por la verdad y la justicia. Para disfrutar de ellas, tenéis que trabajar por conseguirlo. Emancipemos á la mujer del rutinarismo enervante llamado religioso, que las hace ver en una ley natural, un acto deshonesto y bochornoso. Si es agradable pasear, oir una deliciosa música, comer un manjar exquisito, ¿por qué negarlo, y avergonzarse en demostrarlo? Siendo cosas necesarias establecidas por leyes naturales.

El Hombre y la Mujer.

No me esplico por qué el hombre crée tener siempre derechos sobre la mujer. Por ejemplo un joven, no importa la edad, aspira siempre á unirse á una. joven virgen sin conocimientos de la vida. Aunque el haya probado y haya disfrutado de todos los placeres, y conozca todos los vicios, crée que es muy natural aspirar unirse á una joven moderada y honesta.

Esto lo han permitido las fórmulas sociales. Mejor dicho lo hemos tolerado nosotras, por la supuesta debilidad de que siempre nos han acusado.

Cuando tengo ocasión de contemplar á un joven enamorando á una joven y me fijo en ambas fisonomías, me asombro y protesto de que este hombre se atreva no estando en iguales condiciones de moralidad á pretenderla. Él ajado y hasta gastado, ella bella sugestiva y casta y aún así, encuentra que es un gran favor que le hace á la mujer con casarse.

Nosotras tenemos que hacer variar este sistema, tenemos que transformar estas costumbres. Ninguna mujer debe aceptar á un hombre que no esté en sus condiciones; si ellos no quieren dejar estas costumbres, tendrán que convenir en concedernoslas á nosotras.

Porque es ridículo, estúpido que dos enamo-

rados no puedan pertenecerse, porque es inmoral, por formulismos caducos y que al separarse
vayan á saciar su pasión contenida donde otra
mujer, y ella ó se masturba ó tiene "relaciones"
sexuales con otra mujer, atrofiando de este
modo su cerebro y perjudicando su belleza. Esto es criminal, odioso y bochornoso, antinatu-
ral, y son culpables los padres. Lo natural es
que este hombre y esta mujer se completen haciendo uso de los derechos que les ha concedido
la naturaleza, sin temores estúpidos.

Lo natural sería que cuando llegue el hombre
a su completo desarrollo y sienta necesidad de
buscar compañera, escoja la de su agrado y si
ello lo acepta, los dos formen un nido y crean
una familia, sin más preámbulos, ni ridiculeces.
Eso sería lo ideal, lo sublime lo correcto, lo que
la naturaleza ordena. Hombre y mujer se pertenecen vírgenes, y así no hay temores de prostitución ni adulterios.

El hombre no debe hacer uso de sus necesidades sexuales hasta que esté en su completo
desarrollo y entonces, busca la mujer amada y
la lleva al hogar y forman la familia.

Con esta práctica tendríamos una generación
sana, fuerte, robusta y felíz.

Ningún hombre debe pertenecer á otra mujer
que á la que ha de escojer para crear familia.
Entonces podríamos hablar de buenas costumbres, de moralidad, pero en la forma en que

estamos, todos prostituídos, hablar de moralidad es irónico, estúpido é inútil.

Vamos á llevar á la práctica este sistema, y entonces llevaremos el amor á su verdadero estado. Este es el amor libre, que nos critican y tratan de profanar y difamar, diciendo que es inmoral, cuando la inmoralidad y los desórdenes y vicios están establecidos actualmente. El hombre actual crée muy correcto, decente, ir á realizar actos sexuales, con una mujer que no le pertenece á el solo y tener derecho de ir á enamorar luego á una joven casta ó que lo parece, al menos así lo crée. En lo que me fijo es en que no busca una mujer en condiciones iguales á la de él. Nó, ha de buscar la virgen; y así en esta desigualdad, se atreve á hablar del bien. Y la mujer actual que tiene iguales derechos, ha de privarse por una supuesta honestidad, de pertenecerle á su novio para luego martirizarse y enfermarse aniquilando su organismo, atrofiando su cerebro, envejeciéndose prematuramente, sufriendo miles achaques, vahídos, se pone histérica, ríe y llora sin saber por qué, todo esto por no conocer sus derechos ni lo que realmente la haría felíz, que es pertenecerle al hombre que ama (1) sin temores, quitándole de este modo el derecho á su amante que es el que debe disfrutar de las primicias de su amor. Y el hombre á veces numerosos casos por no contagiarse, por no entregarse en brazos de una mujer que no ama comete actos contra la naturaleza. ¿Quienes son los culpables de tales aberraciones?

¡Los moralistas tienen la palabra!.....

Quién ha contribuído á que el acto mas hermoso, más sublime realizado por dos que se amen, haya sido convertido en mero pasatiempo de placer, sin reproducir la especie humana.

Los "religiosos" célibes y demás partidarios tienen la palabra.......

¿Quienes son los culpables de que un hombre y una mujer, por su estado de miseria, no quieran tener hijos porque no tienen con qué sostenerlos y recurran al fraude conyugal?

Habiendo en la naturaleza lo suficiente para alimentarse humanidades como la actual, sin explotaciones, ni fraudes, ni miseria?

Tienen la palabra los egoistas y explotadores.......

Contestad hipócritas, quién ha deformado la humanidad así? y la ha llenado de vicios y miserias siendo tan pródiga la naturaleza. Decid, á que no os atrevéis á contestar "hermanos"..

(1) Nota! al final.

Entendiendo desde luego que este hombre realmente la ame y constituya un hogar, y crea una familia, sin permiso del Juez ni del cura.

Este hombre debe ser un hombre sano, que no tenga malas costumbres y que no haya pertenecido á otra mujer.

Para establecer estas costumbres puras, necesítanse individuos puros.

Todos los que apoyan, y continúan explotando, son los que sostienen el estado de miseria del pueblo y por tanto son los sostenedores de las cárceles, presidios ó mejor dicho los creadores de ladrones, de asesinos, de locos y fanáticos religiosos y políticos. Porque si no fuera por temor á la miseria, no habría fanáticos, políticos y religiosos.

El temor á la miseria ó la miseria misma hace cometer torpezas, que degeneran en crímenes, injusticias y locuras, por los cuales tenemos cárceles y manicomios desigualdades é injusticias.

La Revolución Social, será la que hará desaparecer tantas iniquidades.

Y la revolución surgirá por la propaganda y el estudio ó investigación científica. Y la propaganda la hacemos los libertarios y el estudio está al alcance de todos.

Estudiemos y preparemos nuestra generación para las luchas futuras, que se avecinan.

———

EL AMOR LIBRE

POR
MAGDALENA VERNET

Traducido y editado
Por la agrupación "Nueva Vida"
DE BARCELONA.

I

Sería necesario buscar y probar que el amor para ser justo y sano no puede ser de otra manera que libre, puesto que los pintores nos lo presentan en los lienzos como un bello niño alado, y los poetas, en sus cantos alegres, fantásticos ó tristes, nos lo muestran caprichoso, volátil, cambiador, siempre en busca de horizontes nuevos y de nuevas sensaciones.

¡L'amour est enfant de Bohéme!...

Y esto es verdad; ninguno de nosotros puede responder de la estabilidad del amor. Mucho

más que todos los otros sentimientos del ser
humano, él es el más variador y fugaz, porque
no representa solamente un afecto del corazón,
sino un deseo de sentido y una necesidad física

Que no se confunda el amor con el matrimonio. El matrimonio es una conveniencia social;
el amor es una ley natural. El matrimonio es
un contrato; el amor es un besar. El matrimonio es una cárcel; el amor es un apasionamiento.
El matrimonio es la prostitución del amor.

Para el que conserva su pureza y dignidad el
amor lo ha de practicar libremente; y no puede
hacerlo de otra manera que libre si se rige por
su única ley. No puede haber sobre este capricho de consideraciones de orden material y
moral que dos seres se aman, se desean, se lo
dicen; ellos han de tener el derecho de entregarse el uno hacia el otro sin que ningún extraño intervenga en sus deseos; como deben tener
el derecho absoluto de separarse el día que uno
de ellos no se desee más.

Y yo no digo: «el día que no se amen más»;
más bien el día que ellos hayan cesado de de-
searse. Pues eso son dos cosas distintas. Uno
puede acabar de desear á una mujer y amarla
todavía; una no puede querer más al amante y
continuar siendo fiel al amigo.

Esto es un caso psicológico muy bien conocido, porque los hay; pero el lado sobre el cual
yo pretendo insistir es el que concierne á la
mujer.

Para la mujer es generalmente admitido que
la vida sexual es nula ó está subordinada á la
del compañero—legal ó no—que ella ha escogido. Ella debe vivir y sentir por él; ser apasio-
nada si él lo es, y sostenerse en un estado
neutral si él es frío   Hasta hoy el hombre ha
considerado el deseo sensual como debe regirse
esencialmente, no queriendo reconocer en la
mujer un ser moral y físicamente organizado
como él mismo.

Es en esta cuestión que yo me sxtenderé hasta donde me sea pssible, dentro de este estudio
del amor libre.

***

He dicho precedentemente que para estudiar
las grandes leyes naturales ha sido necesario re-
montarnos á las eras primitivas, estudiar la
Naturaleza dentro de la vida animal.

Pues bien; en los animales la hembra lleva
una vida sexual que es curiosa; ella tiene necesidades sexuales, deseos que satisface con la
misma libertad, la misma regularidad que el
macho.

Nadie contestará que las leyes fisiológicas que
rigen al animal no sean las mismas por el hombre. ¿Por qué, pues, en este caso, no querer
admitir para la mujer la misma similitud fisio-
lógica entre ella y el animal, lo cual uno admite
muy bien que existe entre el animal y el hombre? ¿Por qué reprochar en la mujer una vida

natural? ¿Por qué hacer del amor una necesidad exclusiva del hombre?

Hasta hoy, rigiéndose como maestro sobre esta cuestión como sobre las demás, el hombre ha respondido: «porque la mujer no tiene necesidades; porque ella no desea nada; porque ella no sufre nunca la privación de satisfacciones carnales.»

Pero ¿qué es lo que sabe el hombre, si la mujer tiene ó no necesidades? ¿quién mejor que la mujer, que ella misma, para juzgarse y decidirse?

Todavía tengo presente esta afirmación de un médico: «El celibato de la mujer es más monstruoso que el celibato del cura. Condenar á las mujeres á la abstinencia es una iniquidad, pues esto es privar el desarrollo integral del ser femenino.»

De lo dicho por este médico, la virginidad demasiado prolongada de la mujer provoca una tiranía para su evolución intelectual y física.

Si existen realmente mujeres frías, sin deseos de sentir, ¿qué es lo que prueba ésto? También hay hombres refractarios á la sensualidad. Pero nunca es la mayoría la que se encuentra en este caso; y séame permitido decirlo: jamás la mayoría de las mujeres son refractarias al amor.

Actualmente, con la educación defectuosa que recibe la mujer, es mala, juzgada bajo el punto de vista de las sensaciones y los deseos.

Ella no analiza nunca su vida interior, y á menudo sufre sin saber por qué.

La virgen exhuberante de salud, donde la sangre ardiente le quema las sienes y le enrojece los labios, quizá no sabrá que la virginidad es la que la pone nerviosa, inquieta. Ella no sabe que es la necesidad del amor la que la hace llorar ó reir sin motivo; no obstante, porque ella no lo sabe definir, no deja de ser una gran verdad que es la ley natural de amor quien la conmueve.

Eso que la mujer ignora, el matrimonio le hará comprender; el matrimonio, al cual será llevada ciegamente, porque habrá evocado dos brazos vencedores donde poder encontrar un refugio; entonces, cuando ella «estará» iniciada á la vida sexual, su carne se pondrá vibrante y se dará cuenta exacta de que está ligada á un hombre que quizá no puede amar. Y según sea su temperamento irá hacia el amante ó se resignará al deber conyugal.

Y, si ella se resigna, si acepta el deber sin amor, entonces verá muy bien lo mismo en las otras que en sí misma que no tiene deseos; si no aprueba ninguna necesidad carnal, equivocará simplemente á las demás y á ella misma. No obstante, la necesidad carnal habrá existido en ella, pero no habiendo encontrado el ambiente necesario á su apasionamiento, será atrofiada ó adormecida. Si esta misma mujer hubiese seguido la vida libre; si dejando el compañero

que no respondía á sus deseos se hubiese dirigido hacia el hombre que la hubièra hecho vibrar
completamente su vida amorosa, es muy probable que no habría llegado á ser una mujer fría.

Dentro nuestros amores actuales, le es mucho
más fácil á un hombre juzgar si él «es frío» ó
si no lo es. Libre como es de dar curso á sus
deseos, sencillamente podrá—después de haber
pasado en los brazos de varias mujeres—decla-
rarse en pró ó en contra de la sensualidad.
Pero la mujer—condenada á no conocer más
que un sólo hombre—no puede saber en realidad si eso que no ha hallado dentro los brazos
de este hombre, lo hubiese encontrado en los
brazos de otro.

Por consiguiente, es imposible poder decir
exactamente lo que son las mujeres bajo el punto de vista de la sensualidad No obstante, si
uno quiere observar bien la vida animal, contestará que la anomalía de la no sensualidad
raramente se presenta en la hembra. Ella no
se presenta nunca dentro de las especies salvajes; y si se presenta algunas veces en las especies domésticas, es porque la domesticación les
ha deformado. Entonces nosotros podemos
contestar que la hembra camina privada de la
satisfacción sexual, se estropea y se quita una
cuarta parte de su existencia.

No hay ninguna duda que si la mujer viviese
normalmente, que si no hubiese sido también
deformada por la contrata física y moral, el

número de mujeres «frías» sería muy reducido.
Pero yo supongo que hubiera un cincuenta por
ciento verdaderamente sensuales, estas cincuenta tienen derecho á una vida integral, y sería
inícuo condenar á la mutilación de una partida
de ellas mismas, por la' sencilla razón de que
existen cincuenta perfectamente satisfechas de
su suerte.

La libertad en amor así para la mujer como
para el hombre, no es más que una gran justi-
cia· Eso no forzará nunca á las «frías» á ser
apasionadas, pero permitirá á las apasionadas
no sufrir más la cautividad de leyes convencionales y sociales.

***

He dicho al principio que no debe confundirse el amor con el matrimonio. Pues bien; antes
de salir del terreno fisiológico iré más lejos, y
diré que no debe confundirse el' amor con
el deseo.

El amor es la comunión completa de dos ce-
rebros, de dos corazones, de dos sensualidades.
El deseo no es más que el capricho de dos seres
que una misma voluptuosidad reune. Nada es
tan pasajero ó poco estable como el deseo; no
obstante, ninguno de nosotros se escapa de él.
Si todas las mujeres quisieran ser bien francas
con ellas mismas, verían que algunas veces se
han entregado virtualmente á un hombre que lo
habrán visto algunas horas—ó un corto instan-

te,—del cual ignoran sus sentimientos y su mismo nombre. Pero le habrá bastado una presión de mano, el cambio de una mirada ó la emisión de la voz, para que nazca el deseo; y, que ella lo haya querido ó no, la mujer que ha sentido este deseo habrá pertenecido á este hombre desconocido, que no la poseerá nunca, porque quizá ella le olvidará mañana.

Nosotros no podemos ser dueños del deseo carnal, como tampoco lo podemos ser de la tirania de nuestro estómago. Los dos son inherentes á nuestro ser físico; ellos son el resultado de dos necesidades naturales y también legítimas así la una como la otra. Si el hambre no se satisface, viene el decaimiento y después la muerte.

Yo insisto todavía sobre la diferencia que hay entre el amor y el deseo, porque siempre se es llevado á confundirlos el uno con el otro, y esta confusión lleva á menudo disgustos que dan tristes resultados.

—«¡El espíritu es rápido; la carne es débil!»—nos dice la Escritura. Sí, es verdad; la carne es débil. ¿En qué consiste que hay tiempo en que el deseo nos hace realizar un acto? Y este acto ¿es siempre cumplido, voluntario y conscientemente? Hay horas en que la noción de cosas reales desaparece, y nada nos domina tanto á nosotros como la sensación del momento.

Una de las cosas mejores que hemos visto en la Naturaleza es la siguiente:

Cuando en la primavera los árboles florecen, cubriendo las hojas todas las ramas; cuando la florescencia de vida nace de todas partes—de la Tierra, del Sol, del bosque y de todas las plantas,—el deseo nacido también debajo del pecho conmueve los corazones, haciéndoles volver frenéticos. Y por las noches de estío, noches calurosas y perfumadas, ¿quién negará que la necesidad de la voluptuosidad no sea más intensa? Preguntadlo á los apasionados, quienes en algunas noches se han encontrado solos; ellos saben algo de esto; ellos os dirán todo lo que han sufrido en la soledad de aquellas noches.

Pues si existen días y horas en que la sensualidad exaspera al individuo, no tiene nada de extraño que «la carne sea débil». Basta para esto que el azar ponga frente por frente á dos individuos de sexo diferente.

Realmente esto no es el amor; esto no es más que el deseo, deseo que algunas veces recibe todas las apariencias del amor; pero que satisfecho, deja á los dos amantes perfectamente extraños el uno del otro, lo mismo que el hambriento, que cuando ha saciado su hambre se marcha de la mesa sin dolerle.

Que no se haga una conclusión de esta última frase en que yo condeno un deseo. ¿Por qué lo condenaría yo, si vengo á demostrar que está naturalmente ligado á nuestra vida sexual? Es-

to que yo quiero decir es solamente dejar bien
sentado la diferencia que hay entre el deseo y
el amor.

II

El matrimonio, el amor y el deseo son tres
cosas distintas.
El matrimonio es la cadena que tiene al hombre y á la mujer prisioneros el uno del otro.
El amor es la unión integral de los dos.
El deseo es el capricho de dos sensualidades.
Yo dejo el matrimonio, del cual soy adversa-
ria, para venir á la cuestión del amor libre.
Yo digo que el amor debe ser absolutamente
libre, tanto para la mujer como para el hombre;
y todavía añado: el amor no puede verdaderamente existir más que con la condición de ser
libre   Sin la libertad absoluta, el amor es pros-
tituído.
El hecho de vender el cuerpo á un precio más
ó menos elevado á una numerosa clientela no
constituye solamente la prostitución. La prostitución no sólo es herencia de la mujer; el
hombre también se prostituye cuando por un
interés cualquiera da caricias sin sentirlas.
No solamente el matrimonio legal es una
prostitución, sino que generalmente es una es-
peculación de uno de los dos esposos sobre el
otro, y siempre es una prostitución, toda vez
que la virgen ignora lo que hace contrayendo
matrimonio,

En cuanto al deber conyugal, eso no es más
ni menos que la prostitución.

Prostitución la sumisión al marido; prostitución la resignación y la pasividad.

Prostitución todavía cuando la unión libre
pasa del amor á la costumbre.

Prostitución, en fin; todo eso que reprochan
los sexos fuera del deseo y del amor.

***

Una de las razones de que el amor debe ser
absolutamente libre, es precisamente la similitud del amor y del deseo de que yo he hablado
á la vez, pidiendo que no se haga confusión entre los dos términos.

Racionalmente, dos seres pueden concertar
un lazo, pero, ¿les es posible saber si lo podrán
continuar? ¿Tiene uno el derecho de ligar dos
elementos cuando ignora la afinidad que existe
entre ellos? Dentro del matrimonio legal siempre hay una duda: la mujer alguna vez es engañada; el marido no ha encontrado en su esposa
lo que creía adivinar. Por lo tanto, hételes ahí
atacándose el uno al otro.

El matrimonio suele tener por base el amor
recíproco, y al poco tiempo puede haber un
obstáculo que impida la armonía de los dos cón-
yuges. Esto sucede porque dicho amor no era
más que un deseo nacido de la pasión; y si los
dos esposos se hubiesen entregado libremente
ante la legislación, la experiencia les hubiera
hecho ver que ellos no eran nacidos para llevar

vida común ; y con todo esto, se ve claramente
que la legislación para la unión de los individuos siempre ha sido innecesaria; al propio
tiempo es una prueba en favor de la necesidad
del amor libre.

El amor puede nacer de un deseo, pero nunca
es posible poderlo afirmar. Cuando el amor ha
llegado sin antes haber pasado por el corazón y
el cerebro, su duración es muy aventurada ;
pero cuando sólo tiene por base el deseo sexual,
es muy probable que se extinga si durante su
existencia no ha podido ganar el cerebro y el
corazón.

En fin—puesto que yo hago un análisis detenido de este estud o, debo ir hasta el fondo de
la verdad—yo diré que el deseo sexual, puede
unir á dos seres por un período de tiempo más
ó menos largo sin hacer nacer el amor completo.

Un hombre y una mujer pueden tener relaciones íntimas sin jamás ser atraídos por otra
cosa que por el deseo sexual. Sus sentimientos
y sus pensamientos pueden estar en perfecto
desacuerdo en el momento de satisfacer su necesidad carnal.

Esto—yo tengo que hacerlo observar bien—
de ninguna manera puede ser comparado á la
prostitución, puesto que el sentimiento que atrae
á estos dos indivuos—sin que sea exclusivamente sensual—es sincero de una parte y de otra.
No puede haber prostitución más que allí donde

hay venta, contrata, ignorancia ó pasividad.
Esto no es el caso, puesto que los dos amantes
son atraídos el uno hacia el otro por una misma
sensación dentro del lazo pactado libremente
por los dos.

La verdad de todo lo expuesto lleva la conde-
nación de la monogamia:

En efecto, de la diversidad de sentimientos
nace la diversidad de deseos, y si se admite
como ley esencialmente natural, de ninguna manera se puede sostener la ley monogámica. La
monogamia todavía es una prostitución : prostitución del hombre á la mujer y de la mujer al
hombre.

Sobre la cuestión de la vida sexual de los individuos no puede existir más que una sola ley
y una sola moral para los dos sexoe : la libertad
absoluta del amor.

La unión de la carne no puede ser regida por
una regla única, idéntica para todos los individuos : no puede estar sometida á ninguna ley
determinada, inmutable ; por consiguiente, no
se han de crear deberes ni constituir derechos,
si se quiere conservar la libertad completa del
amor.

¿No es un ilogismo que la palabra deber vaya
ligada con la palabra amor? Fácilmente se ve la
ironía que hay en el fondo de estas palabras
inscritas en los libros de moral infantil : «El

primer deber de un niño es amar á sus pa-
rientes.»

Dentro de la moral corriente también se dice:
«La madre tiene que amar á sus hijos ; la mujer
tiene que amar á su esposo.»

Esas palabras son irrisorias. El amor, á cualquier orden que pertenezca, ¿puede ser nunca
un deber? Pues ¿no es muy natural que el niño
ame á su madre por agradecimiento de haberle
cuidado durante su vida infantil; que la madre
ame al niño que le cuesta muchos pesares, el
cual es un recuerdo de dulces caricias recibidas?
¿No es muy natural también que la mujer ame
al compañero que ha escogido, al amigo que le
ha ayudado á desarrollar su vida de mujer? Si
un niño no ama á su madre; si una mujer no
ama á sus hijos; si una mujer no ama á su compañero, ¿qué es lo que se puede hacer con esto?
Nada. Todas las sentencias de los Códigos, todas
las declamaciones morales y religiosas no harán
nacer nunca el amor si él no ha nacido naturalmente.

De la misma manera que el amor no puede
crear deberes, no puede hacer nacer derechos.
El derecho del hombre sobre la mujer y el de
la mujer sobre el marido, es la opresión, y la
opresión mata el amor. El esclavo nunca puede amar á su tirano.

El hecho de que una mujer ame á un hombre
y se entregue á él no debe alegarse como privi-
legio de este hombre sobre dicha mujer. Por

el sólo hecho de haberse entregado esa mujer,
tampoco ha de tener ninguna autoridad sobre su
compañero. Libres antes de vivir juntos, se
amaron libremente; unidos libremente, el hombre y la mujer también han de ser autónomos
en todas sus manifestaciones después de su
unión.

Resumiendo, pues, este estudio, concluyo diciendo:

El amor ha de ser integralmente libre; ninguna ley, ninguna moral puede regirlo ni sujetarlo en ningún sentido.

Ninguna diferencia ha de haber entre los dos
sexos en lo que concierne al amor.

En una palabra: los rendimientos sexuales no
deben crear entre los individuos obligaciones,
ni deberes, ni derechos.

III

Yo no ignoro que á primera lectura, mi teoría sobre el amor parecerá á muchas personas
un hecho inmoral. Algunas de entre ellas ve-
rán ó querrán ver una consagración al libertinaje.

Si se quiere razonar ó profundizar un poco
la cuestión, se estará de acuerdo conmigo para
declarar que el amor libre, lejos de ser una
charca de inmoralidad, será el regulador natural de felicidad y de perfecta moralidad.

¿Y qué es la inmoralidad? Para definirla es
preciso sustraerse del atavismo, que nos hace

considerar como ley natural todo lo que no es
más que convencionalismo social.

Para mi la inmoralidad es todo lo que es contrario á la Naturaleza; todo eso que contrata el
individuo haciéndole salir de las reglas naturales de la vida para sujetarlo á las reglas pura-
mente convencionales; todo lo que traba el apasionamiento del ser humano en nombre de consideraciones sin ningún valor para el que quiere
profundizar bien.

La inmoralidad es la prostitución—legal ó nó;
—es el celibato forzado de la mujer; es la venta
del cuerpo femenino; es la sumisión de la esposa; es la mentira del marido hacia la que ha cesado de amar.   Pero el amor libre no puede ser
fuente de inmoralidad, puesto que es una ley
natural: el deseo sexual tampoco puede ser inmoral toda vez que es un deseo natural de nuestra vida física.

Si la necesidad sexual fuera inmoral, en este
caso no hay más que anatematizar de inmoral el
hambre, el sueño y todos los fenómenos fisioló-
gicos que rigen el cuerpo humano.

Si observáramos bien nuestros amores actuales, ¡qué charca de inmoralidad encontraríamos
en ellos! Matrimonios sin ninguna afectuosidad,
en los cuales el compra una dote y la mujer una
situación; adulterios de la esposa y del marido;
violencias de todas clases, ventas carnales; mentiras de sentimiento, contratos diversos llevando
al ignorante al libertinaje y la pobreza al explo-

tador, quien especula siempre sobre su hambre.
Aunque el amor libre no estuviese en regla,
no habría en él más inmoralidad de la que existe
hoy Admitiendo que la situación no cambiase
en su fondo, al menos tendría el mérito de la
franqueza en cuanto á su forma.

Estoy completamente convencida de que el
amor libre será la liberación moral de los individuos, puesto que libertará á los sexos de las
contratas y servidumbres físicas.

¿Por qué creer que el individuo libre será
inmoral? En los animales libres no hay inmoralidad. Estos no conocen ninguno de los desórdenes físicos que son la herencia del hombre,
y esto es porque ellos no se rigen por ninguna
otra ley que la natural. Lo que crea la inmoralidad es la mentira forzada del hombre hacia los
otros y hacia á sí mismo; y el amor libre, liber-
tando al hombre de la mentira, pondrá fin á los
desórdenes y al libertinaje.

Cuando el hombre sea completamente libre;
cuando esté regenerado por una educación mejor,
encontrará en sí mismo el equilibrio natural de
sus facultades físicas y morales, y al mismo
tiempo se convertirá en un ser normal y sano.

Nosotros tenemos un sentimiento de instinto
que vela sobre nuestro ser: el sentimiento de
conservación. Cuando no tenemos más hambre
no comemos más porque sabemos los perjuicios
que nos podría acarrear; cuando la marcha nos
ha fatigado, tenemos el buen cuidado de reposar;

cuando la fatiga cierra nuestros párpados sabemos que hemos de dormir. De la misma manera encontraremos el regulador natural á nuestra vida sexual en el curso sexual de la misma.

El animal obedece á este sentimiento de conservación. ¿Por qué el hombre libre ha de ser inferior? No quisiera injuriar á la especie humana para atacar esta última hipótesis.

—No: el desenvolvimiento integral de los individuos libres no será inmoral. Lo que verdaderamente es inmoral es el falsear las conciencias falseando las verdades de la Naturaleza; es el de quitar á los individuos de vivir sanos y fuertes en nombre de dogmas, de leyes, de convencionalismos contrarios á la harmonía y á la pureza de la vida.

VARIEDADES

FEMENISMO

(De *L'Avenir Médical* de París.)

Las elecciones legislativas, que acaban de verificarse, no han sido favorables al femenismo. Apenas si se ha presentado alguna que otra candidata; pero ninguna ha podido sostener hasta el fin una lucha verdadera. Mas no por eso van á desalentarse los apóstoles de las faldas. Todos los países continuarán oyendo sus aspiraciones, ya bajo la apariencia tímida, como en Francia, ó ya con profusión y algazara, como en Inglaterra ó en ciertas regiones americanas.

De hecho, la causa del femenismo ha tenido entre el sexo fuerte muy eminentes partidarios. En 1877, Victor Hugo la defendía en calorosos términos en una carta á Leon Richer: «La mujer, escribía el poeta, es menor civilmente, y moralmente es esclava. Su educación adolece de ese doble carácter de inferioridad; y de ahí tantas penas de que participa el hombre, lo cual es injusto. El hombre ha cargado desigualmente la balanza del Código, en cuyo equilibrio se halla interesada la conciencia humana, poniendo en su platillo todos los derechos y en el platillo de la mujer todos los deberes. De ahí, el profundo trastorno; de ahí, la esclavitud de la mujer. Hacese necesaria una reforma, y ésta se realizará en beneficio de la civilización, de la sociedad, de la luz.»

Por su parte, el célebre filósofo STUART MILL, ha escrito: «Todas las inclinaciones egoistas, el culto de sí mismo, la injusta preferencia de sí mismo, que dominan la humanidad, tienen su origen y raiz en la actual manera de ser de las relaciones entre el hombre y la mujer, y de ellas dimana su fuerza principal. Pensad en lo que puede engreirse un joven que pasa á su edad viril convencido de que, sin mérito alguno, sin haber hecho por su parte cosa alguna, y aún siendo el más frívolo y más incapáz de los hombres, solo por haber nacido perteneciendo al sexo masculino es de derecho superior á toda una mitad del género humano sin excepción ninguna, siendo así que en dicha mitad pueden hallarse personas cuya superioridad es capaz de pesar sobre él cada día y á cada momento. Al dar á las mujeres la libertad de usar de sus facultades, dejándolas escoger libremente la manera de emplearlas, abriendolas el mismo campo de ocupaciones y proponiéndoles los mismos estímulos que á los hombres, uno de los principales beneficios que de todo ello se podría obtener sería el poder dupliear la suma de facultades intelectuales que la humanidad tendría á su servicio.»

Pero, sin seguir, tal vez, tan lejos en esta vía á dichos autores, y en lo que á nuestra profesión concierne, podemos convenir en que varias mujeres la han acometido con buen éxito. Ya en las más distanciadas épocas se las ve tomarse interés por nuestro arte. En Francia, Diana de Poitiers y Margarita de Valois son conocidas por haber practicado las obras de medicina de los antiguos.

Madame Necker, esposa del ilustre ministro de Luis XVI. es á quien se debe la reorganización de los hospitales franceses.

En Alemania, las mujeres médicos fueron numerosas en la edad media, y más aún en los siglos XIV y XV.

Por fin, en nuestra época son muchas las mujeres que se han dedicado á la medicina. Miss Elisabeth Blackwell, que había sido profesora de primera enseñanza, es la primera que en América obtiene el título de Doctor en la Universidad de Boston. en 1847, habiendo seguido, además, cursos complementarios en Ginebra y en París. Después de Boston, no se transcurrieron ocho años sin que la Universidad de Filadelfia admitiese á las mujeres á los estudios medicales, y este ejemplo fué imitado rápidamente por otras universidades. En 1874, por vez prim ra, Madame PUTMAN–JACOBI llega á desempeñar el cargo de profesor en el hospital del Mont-Sinai. Luego, ha habido mujeres que han sido empleadas en calidad de médicos al servicio del ejército, y cítase como ejemplo el caso de Madame Mac-Gée, nombrada cirujano militar en Puerto-Rico, con el grado de Teniente. La señorita María Walcher desempeñó las mismas funciones en el ejército federal, durante la guerra Separatista.

Sin dar á este estudio mayor alcance y aún sin reconocer en las mujeres una aptitud igual á la del hombre para estudios tan árduos como los estudios medicales, sea permitido concluir, de los ejemplos que acabamos de citar que la mujer, á fuerza de voluntad y energía, es efectivamente capaz de participar en ciertos trabajos de que ha sido excluída hasta hoy. Contra esta teoría se oye invocar de contínuo la inferioridad atribbuída á la diferencia de sexo y que se dice parece ser una regla inmutable de la naturaleza. Pero, nada más falso que pretender sostener así la permanente superioridad del sexo masculino. Numerosos son los animales entre los que esta regla se ve quebrantada. Los elefantes, por ejemplo, cuando en ocasión de sus transmigraciones cruzan una región accidentada, no dejan de enviar por delante del rebaño sus hembras, pues que estas son tenidas como más aptas para encontrar el mejor camino.

Entre los pájaros, es á menudo la hembra el personaje preponderante de la pareja. La

hembra del gorrión no se priva de suministrar
al macho ásperas correcciones; la hembra lo
echa fuera del nido cuando no hay de comer
para dos. La hembra del palomo lo asienta
sobre los huevos y le obliga á covar todos los
días de diez á cuatro horas, mientras ella va á
tomar el aire.

Entre las aves de presa, la hembra es más
feroz que el macho; bien lo saben los halcone-
ros, y aquella les es preferida; tan poca ternura
tiene, que, prisionera, le ocurre matar á su
compañero.

Hasta entre los insectos la suerte del marido
es de la más humillantes muy frecuentemente.
La reina de las abejas tiene muchos pretendien-
tes. Oblígalos á seguirla á la carrera; el más
ágil la alcanza y es aceptado; pero es bien efí-
mera la dicha de este esposo porque muere desde luego. Mejor parece el destino de los riva-
les á quienes aquél sobrepujó. Bien nutridos
estos, y sin trabajar, toman los andares de bellos señores; pero llega una buena mañana en
que las obreras se aperciben de que alimentan
seres holgazanes é inútiles, y de ellos hacen una
matanza general.

Pero el triunfo del sexo femenino en la escala
animal es la araña quien lo alcanza. En esta
especie, la hembra es mucho más gruesa y más
fuerte que el macho; por esto queda éste reducido á la esclavitud inmediatamente y hasta el
momento de la fecundación. Pasada esta época,

y pues que ya no hay necesidad de sus servicios, es devorado.

Elegante solución de los problemas conyugales! Pero confiamos en que no tienden aún á ella las amables personas del sexo femenino, á pesar de abrumarnos por doquier con sus revindicaciones y de saludar ya en la Eva liberta, según la frase de Mlle. Odette Laguerre, la generadora de una humanidad mejor.

Doctor PAUL VIGNE.

1910.   París.

IMPORTANTE !

No es posible que no reproduzca algunos párrafos de «La Comedia Humana,» conferencia del Doctor Luis Gámbara.

Dice:

«La comedia humana es la comedia de la honestidad, dividida en tres males : la hipocresía de la educación, la hipocresía en la mujer y la hipocresía social. Haré algunas observaciones, y tales que sean suficientes para poner en evidencia la hipocresía de la educación actual, que parece no tuviera otro programa sino el de despertar en los hijos sentimientos de bondad y de egoísmo.

Porque está basada sobre la mentira y se nutre de las apariencias ; tenemos loros bien instruidos, que recitan admirablemente su lección, pero el corazón está desprovisto de sentimiento, la mente vacía, la espiga corrompida.

¿ Los sistemas que imponen en la instrucción secundaria, no son acaso el triunfo cotidiano de

195

la apariencia que se apoya sobre los programas enciclopédicos ?

Libros, libros y libros; programas voluminosos y todo por la pasada del examen. ¿Pero después? Un gran vacío, una muchedumbre de laureados en la ciencia de los topos, fatalmente condenados á quemar incienso á la exterioridad.»

Otro :

«Siempre y en cualquier parte superficialidad. En las familias pudientes con la ayuda de jóvenes institutrices, inexpertas, se preparan señoritas, que saben un poco de todo y nada de bueno, sin ideas propias, sin convicciones propias, que piensan como piensan los otros, á los cuales se enseña no la virtud, si bien el pudor convencional.

La alta misión maternal, hablo en general, es un peso. De ella no se siente ni la importancia ni el deber, y se confía á las institutrices que la comprenden menos todavía.

La rica burguesía imita, copia, por aquella ciega ciega idolatría que ella siente por todo lo que le parece distinguida.

La burguesía semiacomodada imita como y cuanto puede, pero imita siempre : fabrica jóvenes que en el paseo, en el teatro pueden ser confundidas con los otros. En las clases sociales pobres, falta tiempo y medios para educar, y se duermen tranquilos pensando que la escuela lo remedia todo. ¡Buen Dios! es

ya un sacrificio enviar á la escuela estos
hijos !

¡ Señores !

¿ Cómo son estos hijos?

¿ Cuáles tendencias tienen ?

¿ Cuál organismo fisiopsíquico?

¿ Quién se cura de ellos?

Con amor de sociólogo escribía el gran Spencer y ¡ ojalá ! muchos se ocuparan de las futuras generaciones como se ocupó él. «Sabéis producir el buey para el trabajo y para tablado las ovejas de lana, el caballo para carreras, los gallos para riñas, los toros para corridas. Sabéis producir animales de cualquier calidad, pero mirad el extraño caso, vosotros aceptáis vuestros hijos como vienen, no os preocupa saber de antemano si serán sanos ó enfermizos, débiles ó fuertes, avaros ó pródigos, resueltos y enérgicos ó pusilánimes y flojos.»

Así escribía Spencer :

Dice Gámbara :

«Rasguemos los velos ; por ejemplo aquellos que esconden los pudores artificiales, y hé aquí una moral con doble fondo, como los baú es de los contrabandistas, especialmente usada por las señoritas, las futuras madres.

¡ Pobres señoritas condenadas á ruborizarse según la ocasión !

Estudien los padres á sus hijos en el período en que la niña se vuelve mujer y el

niño idóneo es apto para la procreación. Este
período es el más crítico para la niña que de
repente entra en la vía que llega á la mater-
nidad.

«No hipocresías, no mentiras pueriles, no ilusiones dañosas ; sepa la niña por el casto labio
de la madre,—antes que lo aprenda por los
otros—que ella se vuelve mujer, que una vida
nueva se le abre delante, y los sagrados mis-
terios de la naturaleza no sean contaminadas
con cuentos vulgares, que tarde ó temprano,
de otro modo comprendidos, crearan malicias,
pervertimientos, vicios, que no nacerían si la
verdad hubiese sido manifestada para dirigir
la nueva mujer en el camino de la virtud,
desde que la madre es guía, consuelo, consejo. ¡No reneguéis de la naturaleza que habla
su lenguaje sincero ; no encubráis con cortinas
en nombre de una moral falsa, que de inmoralidad es madre ; sed, madres, las amigas, las
confidentes de vuestras hijas! ¡Que aprendan
de vuestra boca qué es la vida, y así ellas
no lo preguntarán á la criada, á la institutriz.
al primer enamorado, que serán más mentí-
rosos que vos—si vos habéis mentido—ó maes-
tros de vicios que no habrían nunca ni leja-
namente dejado entrever á la fantasía de vuestras hijas! Así hablo, señores y tengo la conciencia de hablar la verdad. Convengo en que
es el hombre el que contribuye en la mayor
parte, con su despotismo oriental, á formarla

como la vemos hoy, en general, falsa.»
En fin, no debo continuar copiando párrafos,
sintetizaré brevemente.

Entiende Gámbara y explica que la vanidad
de la mujer, debido á la educación falsa, es
en extremo fenomenal y frenética. Y yo entiendo con él, que es debido á que el hombre
por regla general, toma á la mujer como instrumento de placer y no como futura madre;
y, claro, si procrea es por casualidad, no por
que se quiere realmente reproducirse; y repito con él: «Es la corrupción la que mina la
familia, porque se quiere amar sin procrear,
pervirtiendo la mujer y aumentando el número
de las cortesanas y de los crímenes».

«Es la fiebre de la perversión que consume
el organismo del hombre en este pobre siglo.»

Si examinamos la moda, vemos que ella crea
muchas víctimas. El deseo de ser ó de pa-
recer lindas hace vestir á la moda, generadora
de hipocresías sociales, porque todos aquellos
que no tienen los medios para seguirla en sus
contínuas evoluciones caprichosas, sacrifican á
la apariencia y afirman con la exterioridad lo
que en substancia no son. ¿Cuántas jóvenes
no venden su honor por un vestido elegante
que sea de moda? ¿Cuántos hacen faltar pan
al estómago para tener guantes? ¿Cuántas dicen: cada úno tiene su amor propio?

Hay necesidad de tutelar el decoro.

No se puede ser menos que otros.

No quiero figurar mal ; no quiero ,pasar por un andrajoso.

Todo esto constituye la apología de la hipocresía, cantada en homenaje á la «moda,» que crea amarguras, desengaños, rivalidades, inmoralidades, deli os; y precisamente de aquella moda fascinadora, conquistadora, porque en la vida elegante tiene un culto profundo, que por vanidad, servilismo é irritación, recluta sacerdotes en todas las clases sociales. La moda crea el lujo, así lo que es fuente de placer y de gusto, también para aquellos que tienen lo superfluo, para hacer daño cien veces más á aquellos que posean sólamente lo necesario. De aquí un número mayor de abandonados, de infelices ; y un desarrollo más vigoroso de la hipocresía social. Decidme, señores, ¿no es la escuela de la hipocresía ésta de cantar la civilización actual, el progreso, el adelanto, y dejar sin previsión todas las miserias que á cada paso se nos paran adelante? ¡ Oh, ustedes todos, los que con la sonrisa en los labios, con la alegría en el corazón os sentáis al alegre banquete de la vida, y gustáis sus goces! ¿Habéis nunca pensado en la tristísima condición del niño abandonado?

¿No habéis nunca oído sus lamentos, no los habéis nunca hecho narrar su historia, no habéis nunca visto sus lágrimas, no habéis nunca entrado en las profundidades de su co-

razón, para indagar sus dolores, sus torturas
y sus lágrimas?

¿No lo habéis hecho nunca?»....

¡Leed por humanidad el libro de Gámbara
«Sociología Criminal» y «La Comedia Humana:»

Estos libros no deben faltar en ninguna biblioteca. Llevan la expresión del dolor humano, en caracteres de imprenta, para arrancar la máscara de hipocresía de una sociedad
que se llama cristiana y que permite, tolera
y aprueba las injusticias, crímenes y desórdenes bestiales.

Cuando el cristianismo en su esencia, es el
comunismo anárquico: que no tolera privilegios, ni tiranías, ni imposiciones, ni amos ni
criados, ni distinciones de clase alguna. Que
practica y ordena la fraternidad. que no admite acumulación de bienes, ni acaparamien-
tos de riquezas. ¿Dónde está ei cristianismo
primitivo, el verdadero amor al prójimo? Está
escondido por el Vaticano, oculto por la sotana
que antepone sus dogmas embrutecedoras á
las máximas del hombre abnegado y justo que
predicó la verdad. ¿Debemos hecernos cómplices de los crímenes que actualmente se
cometen, en vez de protestar y procurar obtener un modo de vivir de acuerdo con lo justo
y lo natural?

SOBRE LA HONESTIDAD

El falso concepto que se han formado de la honestidad me obliga á escribir sobre este asunto.

Individuos de ambos sexos hemos caído en el error de creer que solamente el hombre tiene derecho á usar su libertad del modo que le plazca.

La mujer tiene el deber de conservar su belleza, ella no puede conservarla, con los prejuicios que lo atan al poste del convencionalismo de la hipocresía social. «La Comedia Humana» como ha dicho Gámbaro es la comedia de la honestidad. Se quiere aparecer «HONESTO» con una honestidad ficticia, criminal, en contra de la salud y la vida, en contra de las leyes naturales.

Oigamos al Dr. Drysdall que escribe en «Salud y Fuerza» de Barcelona.

«Muy corrientemente se engaña uno sobre los deseos sexuales de las mujeres. Experimentar fuertes pasiones sexuales se considera como vergonzoso en una mujer, y esas pasiones son despreciadas como si fueran cosa animal, sensual, grosero y vituperable. Se mira con bue-

nos ojos las emociones morales del amor en la
mujer, pero las emociones físicas son miradas
como degradantes y poco femeninas. Es un
gran error. En la mujer como en el hombre,
el vigor de los apetitos sexuales es una gran
virtud, pues es el signo de una constitución
robusta de órganos sanos y de una disposición
sexual naturalmente desarrollada.

Lo mismo ocurre en el apetito venereo, como
en el apetito ordinario. Si una mujer goza de
perfecta salud y que su cuerpo se halla fortale-
cido por el ejercicio, y por una vida conforme
á la naturaleza humana, comerá con buen apetito y placer: sucede lo propio con los deseos
sexuales. Los dos son los grandes regulariza-
dores de la salud á condición del ejercicio que
no debe ser excesivo ni insuficiente. En vez de
despreciar una joven que posée fuertes pasiones
sexuales, debe considerarse que existe en ella
una de las más bellas virtudes, mientras que los
deseos débiles ó mórbidos son al contrario el
signo de una constitución imperfecta ó enfer-
miza. A menudo he sido consultado en casos
donde, según los informes facilitados por la
familia, esperaba hallar una enfermedad sin
gravedad, y no obstante resultaba ser casi des-
esperada.

Desgraciadamente nada hay mas cierto que
una debilidad delicada, y menstruaciones irre-
gulares son ahora, por lo menos, en las ciuda-

des, mas pronto la regla general que la excepción en nuestras jóvenes mugeres.

El tipo *de la salud* femenina está muy bajo. Si recorremos una ciudad cualquiera, veremos que las jóvenes por lo general son pálidas, flacas y desmedradas. Cuando las facultades vitales se hallan en una tan baja condición, es casi una enfermedad, y en todos los casos eso produce efectos innumerables.

La clorosis y el histerismo de la mujer son análogos á la espermatorrea del hombre. Las dos enfermedades son una debilidad una postración de la constitución y se relacionan á la debilidad genital.

Hemos visto que el único remedio verdadero y natural contra la espermatorrea es el ejercicio saludable y suficiente de los órganos sexuales, un campo de acción para las emociones y las pasiones del amor. Lo mismo ocurre para la mujer. Su naturaleza languidece en la ausencia del estimulante natural que sus órganos solamente pueden dar. Su espíritu y sus sentimientos tórnanse mórbidos por la misma causa y el único remedio verdadero y permanente es el ejercicio sexual. Ese ejercicio estimularía su constitución, satisfacería las pasiones naturales que consumen su fuerza y daría á su espíritu sentimientos naturales y sanos en vez de la vergüenza sexual y de la timidez mórbida que la aplastan. El comercio sexual es necesario sobre todo cuando la clorosis es el resultado

de la masturbación, pues en ese caso no se trata
solamente de establecer una costumbre natural
del ejercicio sexual, si que también de arrancar
una que no es natural: la masturbación, cosa
difícil á veces en los dos sexos. De hecho solo
hay un medio al cual fiarse para combatir la
costumbre de la masturbación en los dos sexos
y es la satisfacción normal del apetito venereo.
Si esa satisfacción llegase á ser posible, rara
vez se recurriría al placer solitario de la masturbación, una de las causas, las más frecuentes
de enfermedades corporales y mentales, resul-
taría extirpada.

Ya se cuantos prejuicios se oponen á reconocer el comercio sexual como el gran remedio
contra la debilidad genital de la mujer, más
hállome íntimamente convencido, que al fin será
reconocido á pesar del empeño en mantener el
asunto en el misterio. Por más que anatemati-
cemos á los poetas, á los filósofos, á los médicos, que buscan un nuevo c mino para salir del
laberinto de las dolencias sexuales, todos quedan sordos á reconocer el libre comercio sexual
normal y suficiente, puesto que se lo veda el
enorme fardo de los prejuicios religiosos. Para
prevenir esa importante enfermedad, requiere
hacer cuanto se pueda á fin de aumentar las
facultades físicas de la mujer desde la tierna
infancia. Es preciso cambiar por completo la
educación de las jóvenes y renunciar á las ideas
enervantes, srbre las conveniencias femeninas.

Hay que fortificar su cuerpo lo mismo que se fortifica el de los muchachos y adultos por medio de los juegos expansivos y la gimnasia. Es menester enseñarlos á enorgullecerse tanto de sus facultades mentales. No es para ellos solos que engrandecerán su potencia corporal, es también para sus hijos que vendrán luego, pues madres pálidas engendran vástagos pálidos y enfermizos. A toda costa hay que comunicarles conocimientos sólidos y reales. Sobre todo hay que enseñarles una cosa esencial en la educación de los hombres y las mujeres la creencia del cuerpo y del espíritu. Sin el estudio de la anatomía y de la fisiología en una palabra; sin el estudio de la naturaleza humana, la educación no merece tal nombre La ignorancia y la falsa delicadeza de la mujer traen los mismos defectos en el hombre, pues no se puede discutir libremente ninguna cuestión sexual mientras la mujer no se halle en condiciones de razonar sobre ese sugeto.

LO QUE HACEN LOS HOMBRES

Tenemos costumbres muy singulares y muy distintas entre los hombres y las mujeres.

Un hombre de cualquier posición, educación y raza puede decir francamente, sin rodeos: "yo me enamoré de la bailarina tal, ó cual, ¡oh!

muy buena muchacha, sobre todo buena hembra!....

Otros en diversas formas y ocasiones dicen también: "Yo enamoré á Lilia, muy bonita joven, algo tonta y presumida, muy coqueta.... y embustera, me cansé pronto de ella y enamoré á Margot preciosa chica, muy lista é instruída, conoce francés y habla el inglés perfectamente, toca piano y baila que es un primor!.... pero chico el padre me habló, (un día que ella estaba en un paseo) con mucho misterio de mis visitas y terminó señalando fecha para nuestro enlace salí de allí y no volví más. Después me volví loco por Carolina una deliciosa chiquilla de 16 á 18 años, pulcra y bella excesivamente sensible y cariñosa, un ángel.... pero no me dejaba tocarle una mano, estuve haciéndole el amor unas cuantas semanas, ella me atendía, y no salía con nadie solo conmigo y una amiga íntima. Me cansé de la monotonía de su carácter placentero, pero esquivo y á los dos meses le dí "calabazas por una morena soberbia de unos ojos negros abrasadores, de mirar atrevido y profundos; gallardo cuerpo y magestuoso andar. Me tenía desquiciado, me concedía entrevistas, de á 5 minutos, y á los tres meses desesperado, le dije no podía seguir viéndola, de ese modo, y me marché para no volver.

De ese modo proceden infinidad de hombres, juegan y se ríen de muchísimas mujeres.

Las mujeres no tienen derecho de hacer lo

mismo en nuestra sociedad actual que es preciso cambiar lo antes posible.

Es indispensable que la "Igualdad" deje de ser una vana frase muy usada, que los derechos de ambos sean iguales. Si alguna mujer se enamora y dice "yo me enamoré del tenor ó artista tal, y lo visité varias veces, pero él estaba muy preocupado y no me atendió.

Y después me enamoré del joven aquel que es agente de negocios, pero era un excéptico y lo dejé.

Pero la mujer no encuentra igual sinceridad en el hombre, que el hombre encuentra en la mujer. La mujer cuando un joven la enamora, si á ella le agrada, es sincera y afectuosa, y atenta y fiel, el hombre cuando esa mujer lo enamora, es pedante, injusto, grosero, importuno, y por fin la desprecia.

Todo esto es debido á las costumbres establecidas, pero después que se acostumbren ambos, á ser libres, ya variarán de procedimiento. Yo no culpo al hombre porque cuando él se dirije á una mujer acostumbrado á tener ese derecho, olvida, que puede interesar á alguno, y herirlo, y la mujer se figura que cuando él se dirije á ella es porque la ama.

Y él, cuando la mujer lo enamora, ó le demuestra que está enamorada, él crée que ella es una ligera, una descarada, cualquier cosa, y empieza á rebajarla en su mente y creerla indigna de prestarle atención.

He aquí el escollo, pero destruyamos ese es-
coyo con nuestra persistencia, y demostremos
que tenemos iguales derechos y realmente el
hombre variará de procedimientos.

El hombre desea cuando enamora á una mujer, poseerla, sin preocuparse de el resultado; si
lo aceptan, juzga á la mujer muy débil, y cree
que ha desmerecido, y no se atreve á continuar
siendo su amante porque desconfía. Entiendo
que este hombre, ó todos en general deben
acostumbrarse á no enamorar, sino á la mujer
que realmente quieran y con la cual estén dispuestos á crear una familia.

Lo fundamental está ahí, en que el hombre
adquiera dominio sobre sí, y no se dirija á ninguna mujer que no quiera, y espere á los 18 ó
20 años para eso.

En un sistema social comunista en que los
individuos tengan derecho sobre todo lo que
produce la naturaleza y el ingenio de todos, podrá haber más libertad, y el hombre podrá crear
una familia sin preocupaciones económicas ni
sociales. Pero aún no hemos llegado á esa
época, no tardará en ser establecido entre los
humanos, ese hermoso procedimiento común.

A pesar de la oposición, de los que creen serán
perjudicados, esas costumbres llegarán y se es-
tablecerán, haciendo la felicidad del género
humano.

Es natural que en el actual sistema la mujer
se perjudique, al tener un hijo, y que el autor,

ó padre no esté con ella. Si los dos, franca y
lealmente se quieren, y preparan hogar y se
marchan á vivir juntos á formar una familia.
Esto no puede perjudicar á ninguno de los dos,
y si la sociedad se cree perjudicada, ya se acos-
tumbrará á no ver delito, donde solamente debe
ver una ley natural.

El hombre acostumbrado á ver en la mujer
un objeto de placer olvida que está destinada á
ser madre y maestra de una nueva generación

La unión de los sexos es para la procreación
únicamente; que la invención del hombre la
haya colocado á bajo nivel, no quiere decir que
se perpetúe ese estado.

Debido á eso es que afirmo que el hombre
debe dirigirse á una mujer cuando realmente la
ame y sienta la necesidad de vivir con ella, y
hacerla madre de sus hijos. La tolerancia y la
indulgencia son virtudes cristianas, son parte
de la verdadera educación, y ellas permiten que
se contagien en este ambiente social, los no partidarios de esas costumbres.

Pero los pensamientos que brotan del espíritu
son parte esencial del mismo, le librarán del
completo contagio.

FUERZAS NATURALES

Las 12 y minutos de la noche. Voy á reco-
jerme. (A esta hora he regresado del teatro en
el cual trabajaron los excelentes actores Paco

Fuentes y Antonia Arevalo, con mucho gusto,
acierto y arte) Frente á mi cama la ventana
abierta deja entrar libremente una brisa fresca
y vivificante. No hace frío, y estamos en la
época de nuestro invierno. Oigo un rumor de
mil voces que penetra por la ventana.... Escu-
cho.... ¡Es el mar! las olas en sus extraños
y eternos coloquios, llenos de ternura unas veces, otras de imprecaciones como si quisieran
desbordar su inmenso recipiente, por ser pequeño aún para extenderse: otras veces, gi-
miendo como si deseara atraer á su seno algo
que las consuele arrullándolos dulcemente, ó
moviendo apaciblemente con los remos en una
barca, sus agitadas aguas para luego enfurecer-
se repentinamente, y devolver en mil pedazos
á sus playas las embarcaciones confiadas á su
regazo, envolviendo en su blanca espuma los
restos que balancean en su irritada superficie,
como para acariciar lo mismo que ha destro-
zado.

Escribiendo estas cuartillas, le oigo aún, y
me parece ver sus ondas chocando unas contra
otras para llegar á la orilla, y besar la arena.
¡Qué bello es! imponente es el mar! sobre sus
embravecidas ó tranquilas aguas, regresa el
valiente marino de su cotidiana pesca; sobre
ellas cuando se muestran en deliciosa calma, se
desliza la poética barquilla conduciendo dos
enamorados, dos que unidos por iguales aspiraciones enlazará el destino.

Sobre ella, descansan los grandes vapores que nos traen noticias y objetos útiles y necesarios para nuestras necesidades.

Por su inmensa superficie se cruzan miles de barcos, buques y pequeñas embarcaciones, que de paso, de tránsito, ó con larga estancia en nuestro puerto, alegra y dispone la ciudad al movimiento comercial.

Que poderosa admiración sentimos por el mar es casi sugestivo el contemplarlo, ejerce una fuerte atracción sobre nuestro ser. Cuando en noches de luna lo contempláis, luciendo sus aguas mil colores bellos en combinación con los fríos rayos de la luna, parece como que se adormece bajo la claridad que le envía la eterna solitaria nocturna. Y otras veces en pleno día, bajo los ardientes rayos del Sol, que doran su blanca espuma, cuando ésta salpica las rocas, muéstrase orgulloso de lucir su poderosa hermosura, bajo la tutela de nuestro padre Sol; como si conociera su gran influencia calorífica, que le da vida á los miles pecesillos que saltan y juguetean en su seno. Encontramos bello el mar, ¡oh! sí, ¿por qué? Sin el Sol nada habría bello, el Sol, es el que hace producir y multiplicar las plantas y los peces, que nos conserva la salud, nos purifica la vida, nos alegra y embellece la existencia. Es el verdadero manantial, de donde surgen nuestras riquezas por el que se multiplican nuestros tesoros convertidos en bellas y sabrosas frutas, y en frondosos y

corpulentos árboles, que constituyen una de
nuestras principales riquezas del globo, la madera, de diferentes clases con lo que edificamos
nuestros muebles é infinidad de utensilios tan
necesarios. Y las múltiples minas que constituyen nuestros más preciados tesoros, con los
cuales edificamos las vías y ferrocarriles, puen-
tes y columnas para edificios, y subterráneos
todos de hierro transformado en acero y otros
metales. El estaño, la plata, el oro, el nikel,
todo es obra de ese calor solar ¿Qué son sino
las inmensas minas hulleras? Todos los demás
inventos de calor reconcentrado, el vapor, la
luz, la electricidad, todo es trabajo de millares
de siglos de nuestro sol, que se enfría cada
siglo una línea, un ápice, enfriándose también
nuestro planeta y reduciendo el sol su diámetro
de un modo visible, afectando de este modo á
nuestra tierra, que finalmente se enfriará. Se
deduce de esto, la ínfima importancia de ambos,
en el inmenso concierto de sistemas y soles que
giran en el espacio. Igual importancia que tiene (en relación al número de ciudadanos cuidando
se mueve ó se enfría (1) un ser humano en una
ciudad. Luego será una cosa tan natural que
no hay que lamentarlo. De modo que todos
nuestros productos y medios de vida, inventos
y descubrimientos podríamos decir que es luz
solar, acumulada, reconcentrada. Nuestros en-
tusiasmos, nuestras alegrías, es luz solar que

---

(1) Se muere ó desencarna.

irradia de nuestro ser. De modo que no hay
nada de extraño en que los antiguos lo adorasen,
aun sin comprender la poderosa influencia que
ejerce en nuestro planeta y en nuestra vida.

A mi hija Manuela Ledesma Capetillo

"De todas las concepciones y reve-
laciones antiguas y modernas: la de
la pluralidad de existencias, es la
única que satisface plenamente la
lógica y la razón."—BOUCHET.

¡Cuántas veces, hija mía, te he repetido, recordando estas frases de Lumen! ¡Vida eterna,
sin fin posible!.....∴...

Si pudieras alcanzar á comprender esas frases
¡oh! hija de mis primeras ilusiones, angelical
reproducción de mi único y triste amor.....

Si comprendieras la grandeza de esas palabras
que al pronunciarlas, cae uno de rodillas, rin-
diendo culto á la gran fuerza desconocida que
se presiente á través de todos los obstáculos y
todas las negaciones.

Nunca te he enseñado á orar, eso hay que sentirlo. No estás bautizada por rito religioso alguno. Te he conseguido la más ámplia libertad
en cuanto tus gustos y deseos. No me agrada
la violencia.

Lo único que deseo y espero de tí, es que seas
una buena humana, no una cristiana de rutina,
nó. Una intérprete de las máximas de Jesús,
sin oir misa, sin confesar ni comulgar, ni acep-

tar ninguna clase de errores, ni mentiras de las absurdas religiones materializadas.

En vez de ir á oir misa, visitas los pobres y socórrelos, que podrás hacerlo: en vez de confesarte y comulgar, visita los presos, y llévales consuelos, algo que los instruya. No olvides que los abundan en cárceles y presidios son los pobres y los ignorantes, las víctimas de siempre de todas las explotaciones.

Cuando se reforme esta sociedad indiferente y egoísta por la futura, fraternal y altruista, entonces, cuando no se cometan injusticias, cuando no se castiguen inocentes, cuando los jueces no exijan "la verdad, toda la verdad, y nada más que la verdad", siendo los primeros embusteros. Cuando no haya quien robe un bollo de pon, porque carezca de él, Cuando no exista la propiedad privada, y todos nos miremos como hermanos, entonces, y sólo entonces, desaparecerán las cárceles, presidios y las inútiles y perniciosas iglesias. No habrá miseria, odio ni prostitución. Existirá el libre cambio, pues estarán abolidas las fronteras y la verdadera libertad reinará en este planeta.

Procura tú ayudar con la práctica á la realización de estas hermosas ideas humanas para que no perezcan de hambre y de frío, los infelices que no tienen hogar, ni riquezas, en los tristes portales de alguna cochera ó pesebre, ó de algún palacio....¡qué irrisión! ¡Qué humanidad! á dos pasos de opípara mesa y de ricos y abun-

dantes abrigos, perecer de hambre y de frío.
Cerca de la prodigalidad y el despilfarro, el
hambre, el dolor... pobres niños víctimas de la
miseria... Parece un sueño, ó cuento y es una
realidad, que asombra... ¡Qué horror! ¡qué
falsos son los cimientos de esta llamado sociedad,
que está basada en el crímen, el error, y la hipocresía. ....
....

Es necesario apartes de tu mente todo pensamiento que pueda empañar tu natural sencillez,
pues quizás nuestra separación pueda contribuir
á dar cabida á sentimientos de filetes aristocrá-
ticos, que puedan hacerte creer en las diferencias de clases. No olvidarás que todos somos
suceptibles al ambiente en que vivimos, que si
hay alguna diferencia, entre los humanos, en su
carácter, modales, y figura, es debido á la forma de vida y educación y costumbres adquiridas, ú obligadas á aceptar, por la misma, ú explotación.

Oye: Severine, en su libro "En Marcha....."
relata infinidad de suicidios verificados en París,
detallados en miles formas, y en diversidad de
ocasiones y circunstancias.

Es dolorosísimo leer esos relatos, conociendo
el lujo que se derrocha en París, los espléndidos
regalos que se hacen á los artistas, (que merecen más) y olvidando la miseria que consume la
vida de miles de personas. Lo que se derrocha
en Champagne, y en miles de fiestas orgiasticas.

Las sedas y brillantes; tu dirás, ¿nada de ésto
puede usarse? Sí, puede usarse todo hasta la
exageración, al disloque, ó llegar á la locura.
Pero dime, necesitase eso para vivir? según la
sana razón y el recto juicio? Nó: me dirás, y
¿el comercio y la industria, como progresarían?
Perfectamente, pues las miles y millones de
familias que en el mundo carecen de ropa, de
calzado, de muebles, de utensilios de cocina, de
vajillas y cubiertos é infinidad de objetos necesarios que deben y pueden estar en abundancia
en los hogares de los que se envejecen en las
fábricas y luego, imposibilitados para el trabajo,
recurren á la mendicidad, y perecen en los hos-
picios ó en las calles.

Dime, ó medita mejor, cuantos miles y miles
de sábanas, manteles, mesas, sillas, roperos,
medias, calzado é infinidad de todas clases de
artículos necesarios que se pudren hoy en los
depósitos y almacenes; si se les proporcionara
todo lo necesario á esas familias, entonces, la
fabricación de dichos artículos, sería más numerosa, y no habría lugar de que se pudriesen
guardados habiendo quien los necesitase.

De qué modo podremos llegar á realizar estas
ideas, si los explotadores, no aceptan tales inno-
vaciones ni se ocupan de remediar estas miserias, como no sea por medios que les asegure su
poder, sus privilegios y distinciones. Dar limosnas y crear hospitales. Eso es lo que hacen.
Las instituciones religiosas, han ayudado á

fomentar esos privilegios y división de clases.
Si los trabajadores en general por medio de la
instrucción no logran destruir los privilegios de
castas, razas, gerarquías, y miles de majaderías,
que nos perjudican como seres humanos. Entonces la revolución lo hará. Muchos le temen
á la revolución. Pero no hay como pertenecer
á ella, para que el miedo se evapore. Las cosas
vistas desde lejos, producen distinto efecto. De
cerca, se llegan á palpar, y desaparece lo que se
llama efectos de distancia y también de apre-
ciación.

Porque hay que suponer que la revolución
social, no será una asonada de tiros, por
sorpresa.

Yo entiendo como Labriola, que "La clase
obrera no puede emanciparse si no determina
apoderarse de la producción y "absorver" el
poder público." No para utilizarse. Para des-
truirlo. ¿De qué modo empezaremos á apode-
rarnos de los medios de producción? Por el sistema cooperativo; y de este modo, cuando haya-
mos acaparado la tierra y los instrumentos de
un modo general; el gobierno queda anulado.

Hoy todo está en poder del capital. Los
capitalistas no ceden sus "derechos" ni privilegios, la miseria es despiadada y ésta no sale del
hogar obrero. Si cuando sale el rey con toda
su comitiva resplandeciente de lujo, á paseo ó
al Congreso, sea en Rusia, Italia ó España, y en
el trayecto lo encuentra el infelíz padre de fa-

milia, que dejó en su hogar llanto y dolor y hambre, y no encuentra trabajo, ese hombre no se explica, por qué ha de sufrir hambre, mientras el otro sin trabajar derrocha el lujo... y si surge un Mateo Morral, ó Caserio, no es de asombrarse, consecuencia natural de las injusticias. Procura leer en "Sensaciones de un Cronista" de M. Abril, que es un libro delicioso, de lectura amena é interesante, unas páginas que sobre anarquismo ha escrito el distinguido literato y amigo. Recuerdo estos párrafos: "Pero surgen en Francia las huelgas de Cremiex y tras las huelgas, los atentados de Ravachol, y la ejecución de éste." Y Carnot al poco tiempo, cae bajo el puñal de Caserio" Y más adelante otro párrafo: "Llénase el castillo de Montjuich de prisioneros.

"Unos son fusilados y otros sometidos á tormentos tan bárbaros que dejaron muy atrás los realizados, por la inquisición."

Estos tormentos eran arrancarles la lengua, castrarlos, y quemarlos y fusilarlos. Pues apesar de haber escrito ésto, el señor Abril opina hija mía, que "El anarquismo es un cáncer terrible que hay que extirpar" porque supone que, "Esa *secta* fanática y criminal parece formada para el ejercicio de la venganza."

Ahora yo desearía saber, por qué fué que encerraron á los trabajadores en Montjuich ¿por darse el gusto de encerrarlos? Entonces el procedimiento anarquista es más justo. No es venganza, es justicia. Pero bien hija mía, ob-

serva: qué derecho tenía Cánovas para encar-
celar, martirizar, triturar y destruir las vidas
de los infelices trabajadores? solamente porque
se declararon en huelga para reclamar aumento
de salario. (Creo que las minas eran del gobierno).

Cuantos infelices inocentes han sido ejecuta-
dos y encarcelados, por épocas interminables, y
por solamente ser pobres gentes, sin representación, sin riquezas, han pasado desapercibidos.
¿Y sus hijos y esposas? En la más cruel situación. En otro párrafo recuerdo que dice: "El
hierro y el fuego no dan resultado?

"Pues apélese á la confraternidad humana."
Con ella logró el cristianismo acabar con el poder de los Césares." Estas frases van dirigidas
á los anarquistas: y á quien deben dirigirse es
á los gobernantes y explotadores. Hija mía, no
soy partidaria de la violencia. Pero nosotros
decimos (1) "¡Que empiecen por dar el ejemplo los de arriba! No hemos de usar del derecho
de lejítima defensa, cuando se nos explota, se
nos oprime, se nos encarcela, cuando se nos fu-
sila, ó se nos agarrota, solamente por reclamar
nuestros derechos y propagar ideales de justicia
y fraternidad! Sensible es la muerte violenta
de un hombre, mendigo ó rey, burgués, ó pro-
letario, pero...... ¿Quién hace el ataque?
¿Quién ejerce primero de victimario, de ver-
dugo, de asesino? Vale más la vida de un po-.

---

1) NOTA.—Fragmento de ¡Tierra! de la Habana.

deroso que la vida de un desarrapado"?... de
¡Tierra!"

Hija mía, si no hubieran atormentado y des-
pedazado y fusilado los pobres trabajadores (que
dejan numerosas familias) en Montjuich, cuando la huelga de mineros en España, Cánovas del
Castillo no hubiera caído bajo el puñal de Angiolillo.

El gobierno emplea sumas fabulosas en mu-
niciones, pólvora, espadas, fusiles, para y por
los trabajadores, para que si el burgués los explota, amenazarlos si se quejan. Y si se decla-
ran en huelga fusilarlos. ¿Con cuales derechos?
Con el de la fuerza y la ignorancia.

También en otro párrafo dice Abril. "Czolgostz asesinó (¿por qué?) fría, serenamente al
hombre que eligió por víctima, sin odio, sin ensa-
ñamiento, guiado por una pasión, por una aluci-
nación malvada creyendo como todo fanático
que realiza una obra redentora." (Los gobiernos realizan alguna obra redentora, con las
guerras, y encarcelando huelguistas y martiri-
zandolos, y dejando de este modo innumerables
familias en la miseria?) "Y á Czolgostz se le
mata poco á poco, se le atormenta, se le des-
garra el alma primero, y se le pulveriza después.
Czolgostz para sus jueces, no simboliza nada,
ni siquiera es un hombre, es una fiera encerrada
en su cúbil, á la que se pincha y atenacea."

*
* *

Bien; ahora surge otra cuestión de ideas, soy
creyente de la diversidad de existencias, y por
tanto, de la inmortalidad del alma. Pero dicen
muchos que los espiritistas y anarquistas son
distintos Y muchos no quieren aceptar que la
anarquía y el espiritismo sean idénticos en el
fin que persiguen. Pues bien, supongamos que
no sean iguales. Los anarquistas dicen que el
haber nacido les dá derecho á disfrutar de todo
lo existente y que no están conformes con carecer de todo lo necesario, y después de una vida
laboriosa, recurrir al hospital ó á pedir limosna.
Los espiritistas opinan que no hay efecto sin
causa y que los que pasan hambre es porque la
han hecho pasar; y los que sufren injusticias es
porque la han hecho sufrir. Muy bien, todo
esto será una verdad; pero los anarquistas no se
conforman con eso y están en la obligación
de llevarles á sus hijos pan, y hay que conseguirlo. Los espiritistas no tienen á menos de
utilizar la explotación para atender á sus necesidades y disfrutar por todos los medios posibles
de las comodidades. Y aunque estos medios no
sean violentos ¿dejarán de ser perversos y artificiosos? Nó. Los anarquistas prefieren recurrir á medios prácticos, justos y valientes,
antes que pedir limosna, ó explotar por medios
fraudulentos y criminales.

Hija mía, escoje, analiza, reflexiona, ¿quienes
son más razonables? Los espiritistas se atreven

á decir al hambriento, al pordiosero: "hay que
tener paciencia, no sabemos que hizo usted en
la otra existencia."

Los anarquistas le dicen, estúpido, Vd. se degra-
da, se siente usted inferior á los demás y después
de una existencia de trabajo, se ve usted obligado
á pedir? pues antes de llegar á ese estado, reclamen sus derechos. Y no siente deseos de dar limosna, no porque sienta menos, si porque se irrita
con las injusticias, y dice que el limosnero es producto del régimen capitalista. Es natural que
un cajón lleno pese más que uno vacío; si se
acumula sin medida, dinero y más dinero, por
una parte, la otra tiene que carecer de él. Si se
pudren los productos de la industria y la agricultura en los depósitos, es natural que hayan
hambrientos y desnudos.

Por tanto, los anarquistas no están dispuestos
á consolar, como hacen los frailes aun, diciendo
"Bienaventurados los pobres porque de ellos
será el reino de los cielos" Ellos dicen que el
reino de los cielos está aquí y que los causantes
de este estado, son los usurpadores del trabajo
ageno.

Ahora, si los espiritistas están dispuestos á decir á los trabajadores que no reclamen sus derechos, que no pidan aumento de salario, que se
conformen con la explotación de que son objeto,
que no se declaren en huelga, que sufran con
paciencia el hambre y la desnudez, porque ellos
en otra existencia hicieron lo mismo.

¡Yo no se lo digo! y en nombre del espiritismo, menos!, ya sin dejar de ser espiritista, les digo, que tan criminal es que ellos se dejen morir de hambre y desnudez, como que por llevarle pan mataran, y que antes de matar que asalten todas las ganaderías y puéstos de pan ó establecimientos de comestibles.

Los espiritistas no se atreven á decirle á los trabajadores, que asalten las tahonas de pan. ¿Por qué? ¿De qué manera adquirió el dueño esa panadería, si sólo tenía $1.00 y ahora tiene miles? ¿Y cómo los que trabajan en la tahona no tienen un centavo? Misterio!....... Ese es, el modo y la forma artificiosa y silenciosa de la explotación: es violenta, pues en contra de la voluntad de los trabajadores sostiene ese sistema. Los espiritistas dicen que se debe respetar la propiedad privada, ¿aunque se muera la gente de hambre? ¿Vale más la propiedad de uno ó dos individuos que la vida y salud de miles de personas? Las bases ó principios de esa propiedad, ¿cuáles son? El fraude y engaño, violento y artificioso.

Los anarquistas dicen, esa propiedad hecha de ese modo (y no hay ninguna hecha de otro) es un crimen; sustraer diaria y cautelosamente á miles de trabajadores una peseta de su jornal, para formar un capital, es un robo; la ley no castiga ese robo hipócrita con antifaz de virtud y honradez y nosotros le quitaremos el antifaz. de un modo persuasivo y le haremos compren-

der que está en un error; si no quiere se lo
arrancaremos. No es posible que éste derroche
sin trabajar, lo que otros han trabajado. Los
anarquistas convencidos del acto de justicia que
realizan, no pueden respetar la propiedad que
es un robo.

Los espiritistas se llaman racionalistas, y los
anarquistas también, y sinembargo los espiritis-
tes no se atreven á atacar la propiedad conociendo su formación, y dejan mejor perecer la gente
de hambre, y eso no es racionalismo.

Porque aunque sea privándose de comer, un
individuo no debe hacer capital habiendo hambrientos y desnudos.

Los anarquistas no pueden respetar la propiedad privada, porque saben que es hecha por
la explotación, y si la respetasen serían tan hipócritas como los que la hicieron, y no sería racionalismo. Lo que está basado en la razón, se
analiza y no se oculta.

Yo acepto todas las misiones habidas y por
haber pero en cuanto hay desnudos y hambrientos protesto. Si alguno ha escogido la misión
de venir á vivir aquí á pasar hambre y desnudez, sabiendo que las leyes lo castigan, lo encarcelan, y allí lo visten y le dan comida! Así
la misión no resulta. Esto de misiones son
difíciles de analizar. Es en lo único que difiere
el Anarquismo y el Espiritismo. En cuanto se
llega al problema de la miseria, todos se equi-

vocan. Los más acertados de acuerdo con la razón, hasta ahora son los Ácratas.

Esto no es una crítica, es una comparación, hija mía, para que observes de cuál está la razón.

Son las ideas más elevadas, más de acuerdo con el progreso del siglo.

En todo lo demás, estamos de acuerdo, pluralidad de existencias, diversos mundos habitables, en fin la paz y concordia que debe haber entre enemigos, por la encarnación entre ellos, es decir la armonía universal, por la diversidad de existencias.

Tú aceptarás lo más razonable sin imposición de ninguna clase.

Necesitamos propagar para destruir el fanatismo que enerva y destruye toda clase de iniciativas. Los ignorantes creen que su salvación está en las oraciones, aunque su vida haya sido y sea un cúmulo de injusticias y egoísmos.

¿Qué clase de oración, y hacia donde van dirigidas, si es creada por un corazón cruel. "Porque de lo que está en el corazón habla la boca."

Entiendo que la oración es innecesaria. Pero acepto que se envíen pensamientos de fuerza mental para contribuir al éxito, ó á la tranquilidad de todos, ó de alguno. Entiendo que nunca se debe pensar en que una acción ó propósito, no se obténga como se desea. Nunca, jamás he pensado, cuando he concebido algún proyecto,

que no podré hacerlo. Esto era y es natural
en mí: yo así lo sentía y ejecutaba, pero no sa-
bía cómo se llamaba. Luegó varias cartas
que recibí del "Club Exito" Segno de Angeles
California, en las que me remitió unas tarjetas,
en una de las cuales dice: "La confianza y la
constancia, son las últimas pruebas de la habilidad."

Es decir que yo practicaba sin saberlo, por
conocimiento innato en mí; la fuerza mental,
misteriosa é invisible, en pró de mis empresas.
Yo deseo una cosa, y sólamente el desearla con
tenacidad me proporciona la satisfacción de
tenerla. Estas fuerzas educadas y robustecidas
con algún procedimiento, supongo que debe ser
el de la práctica: pueden llegar á ser poderosas.

Jamás me he propuesto hacer una cosa, que
no la obtenga. Y cuando pienso que puedo llegar á ser capitalista, me aterrorizo y me impon-
go, y digo: "No quiero" "No quiero" con
toda mi fuerza mental. Y prefiero estar, in-
cierta en cuestión económica, antes que utilizar
los medios de la actual explotación. No quiero
contagiarme. Toda la fuerza mental que utili-
zara, no sería suficiente para destruir la suges-
tión de la riqueza. Es tan perniciosa la riqueza en el actual estado de vida, que destruye
todos los sentimientos humanos. Esto no quiere indicar el desprecio á las comodidades y
abundancia, de una sociedad comunista Pero
actualmente sí, porque para obtener comodida-

des, necesitamos despojar á otros. Siempre he
estado en la duda, si era que yo presentía, ó
que deseaba, pero son las dos, desear y presentir.
Si muchas cosas que he pensado, me hubiera
propuesto obtenerlas, lo hubiera conseguido.
Pero me he detenido á pensar antes, que si hacía bien ó mal, sino era violencia, ó contrario á
la libertad como yo la entiendo.. Y me he abs-
tenido en decidirme, por temor á beneficiar mi
proyecto, de un modo contrario á mis ideales.

Hé aquí porqué cuando se piensa, ó se propo-
ne llevar á cabo un proyecto debe inmediatamente ponerse en práctica, llevarse á ejecutar
sin temores, ni rodeos; porque se pierde la
decisión y no hay igual firmeza. Debido á esa
indecisión es que has estado en el colegio católico. Me hubiera propuesto, y no hay poder
humano que lo hubiera impedido.

¡Ésto hay que sentirlo! sí, sentir el deseo
vehementísimo, de realizar, lo que está en la
mente formado ya, y que nos impulsa á
verificarlo.

De modo que nuestra fuerza mental, desarrollada á determinado grado, nos hace poderosos.
Pero este individuo, para tener poder, necesita
que sea de buenas costumbres, para que el aura
que de él dimane, ó le circunde, posea la fuerza de atracción hacia todo lo bueno, lo grande
y lo justo. Un individuo colérico, impaciente,
jugador, perezoso, el aura que le rodea, sólamente, puede atraer lo que esté en iguales con-

diciones, cuando dispone su voluntad para preparar ó emprender algún negocio, ó desear
algún empleo) esa aura que es como reflectora
de su modo de er, al ser impulsada por la voluntad á establecer la corriente, entre lo que ha
de proporcionar lo que desea. Sólamente puede establecer relación y atraer elementos y corrientes de sus mismas condiciones, de modo
que puede obtener éxito, pero dentro del
radio en que se agita, vive ó se desenvuelve.

Este hombre ó mujer puede adquirir mejores
condiciones.

Hay individuos de todas categorías que fuman y no beben, que beben y no fuman, pero
creo que es difícil encontrar un jugador, que no
haga las tres cosas á la vez; jugar, fumar y beber. Parece que se necesitan las tres para
completarse y formar la trilogía. El que no ha
jugado nunca y adquiere ese «nuevo oficio»
adquirirá también el grado de fumar y beber.
Son costumbres del oficio. Todos perniciosos.
De modo que fumar y beber por vicio y costumbre, sólo debe ser de jugadores y perezosos
de oficio. Hay quien aprende á fumar y á
beber sin jugar y hasta odiando y despreciando
el juego y á los jugadores. Pero me atrevo á
asegurar que no tardará mucho en terminar por
ir á jugar y codearse y amistarse con jugadores.
Por que el ambiente atrae y ya el aura de éste,
casi está en iguales condiciones que los de la
trilogía. Tenemos jóvenes de ambos sexos, que

prefieren, los más, ser jugadores y bebedores, antes que ocuparse en un empleo, que según su opinión le proporciona desdenes, pues hay mucha gente que desdeña al individuo que no viva derrochando en licores y en jolgorios, aunque sea á costa del crimen y claro está, estos individuos no tienen fuerza de voluntad para sobreponerse á tales estupideces y hacerles comprender que nada han perdido con ocupar una posición humilde. Y las otras prefieren ser alcahuetas, lujuriosas, y "cuenta-chismes" de una á otra casa, por no ir á una fábrica ó hacer cualquier clase de trabajo y hacer que le alcance para cubrir sus necesidades.

Para observar esto, no se necesitan anteojos. Pues bien; todos estos defectos y vicios, ¿sabéis quién los proporciona, los sostiene y aumenta? El régimen social de actualidad, la perniciosa costumbre de la explotación del hombre por el hombre.

Los padres no le inculcan á sus hijos amor al oficio, de ninguna clase, porque saben que le pagan poco y saben que el fin de los trabajadores de oficio, termina en un hospital ó á pedir limosna.

Los jóvenes con las prédicas de los padres, de que «debe hacerse una persona decente» que «debe hacer y no hacer,» no sabiendo oficio alguno, sino una carrera que la aprendió obligado, no por gusto, no encontrando empleo adecuado á sus ambiciones, pues no le agrada que lo or-

denen, (es natural en todos los seres humanos,
pero algunos llegan á atrofiarse de tal modo,
que no solo le es indiferente que lo manden,
sino que lo insulten y le peguen: por tal de
tener su empleo para sostener su familia, pierden su libertad, su personalidad y dignidad
convirtiéndose en esclavos del presupuesto) y no
pudiendo hacer otra cosa, se dedica á lo más
bajo é indigno. En vez de tener valor para
protestar y luchar por reformar y sustituir este
sistema tan pernicioso que daña generaciones
tras generaciones, sin esperanza de regenera-
ción, y si la hay muy lejana. Porque le temen
á la revolución como á la peste.

Bien, las jóvenes, en iguales circunstancias,
no van á la fábrica, por no ser explotadas, y
enfermarse en un ambiente contaminado, de
este modo recurren á cualquier deformidad,
con tal de aparentar, prefieren acostumbrarse á
referir los defectos de unos y otros, para almorzar en un sitio y luego en otro y así no
tener que pensar en ello.

Así de este modo se agita esta sociedad, y no
tienen valor para protestar.

Con estas deformes costumbres se pervierte
el alma, los sentimientos más puros, se pierde
hasta la noción del bien, y se pierde cuanto
hermoso y noble hay en la naturaleza humana.
¡Puede progresar el espíritu? Que vá! Adquirir
malas costumbres sí. Y debemos hacernos cómplices de estas calamidades? El único afán que

guía á los humanos es vivir de cualquier modo,
se lucha desesperadamente por adquirir medios
de vivir, aunque haya que recurrir á los vicios
y crímenes más odiosos. No se trata de per-
feccionar y hacer habitable esta morada. No, á
vivir de cualquier modo, aunque sea encenegán-
dose en el lodo. ¿Y á esto se le llama perfec-
cionarse y volver á vivir para purificarse? Nó,
esto es igual que si para bañarse fuera necesario meterse en un charco pestilente. Igual
que si una persona cubierta de purulencias, se
lavara con agua contaminada, en vez de utilizar
algún líquido antiséptico.

En condiciones iguales estamos aquí para
perfeccionarnos y cada vez aprendemos más
perversidades. No puede haber modo de per-
feccionarse, con un sistema de vida, tan contrario á las leyes naturales.

De modo que para entrar en vías de perfección, no puede aceptarse los medios que utiliza
la sociedad actual. Todo aquel que valiéndose
de la explotación procura hacer fortuna, no se
perfecciona. El que realmente desea perfec-
cionarse, no debe acomodarse al medio ambiente sin protestar. Se me dirá, que con protestar
no adelantamos nada, sí! ¿cómo vamos á callar
y á seguir la corriente? Debemos exponer algún nuevo sistema ó doctrina, para salir de este
laberinto, en que se pierden todos los sentimientos nobles y las más altruistas aspiraciones.
Tenemos el deber de formar grupos ó sociedades

con determinados fines emancipadores. Aceptar todo lo existente sin proponer nuevos medios de libertad, es una cobardía. Tenemos amplios caminos de emancipación que nos brinda el Socialismo Radical. ¿Por qué no los utilizamos?

¿A quién tememos? Esto no interesa á unos pocos, nó! á todos en general, todos somos víctimas de una explotación inmensa. ¿Por qué no nos defendemos?

Los capitalistas que creén están exentos de preocupaciones, por tener medios de vida, más fácil. También les interesa. Oíd! tenéis hijos, y estos se contagian con las enfermedades originadas por la miseria. Suponed que vuestros hijos se reunen con otros de muy malas costumbres. Lo sabéis, y procuráis evitar el contagio, no dejando reunir vuestros hijos con aquéllos. Pero se encuentran en las escuelas y allí continúa el contagio. Entonces enviáis al colegio á los vuestros. ¿Pero el contagio queda allí y creéis haber preservado á vuestros hijos del contagio? No! en todos los sitios existe la lepra, está generalizada, sóis culpables vosotros por egoísmo! Bién, aquellos niños que tienen igual derecho para que los envíen al colegio, como los vuestros, se quedan en el arroyo, bien; y otros quedan expuestos al contagio. De modo que á quien debíais haber enviado al colegio no es á vuestros hijos que tienen medio de vivir con alguna comodidad. Es á los que están en la miseria. És á los que tenían malas costumbres. Los vuestros no las tenían, ¿porqué los enviastes al colegio? Por egoismo! Creyendo en que hacíais bien, porque no miráis nada más que por vosotros mismos!

Pasáis por el camino rodeando la piedra, en vez de quitarla, para que al llegar la noche, no tropiece el caminante que no la ha visto. Pero por haberla dejado, sufrís la consecuencia, vuelve á casa vuestro hijo del trabajo y tropieza con la piedra, que el padre vió y no la quitó. Si véis un obstáculo en el camino, quitadlo, porque otro pasa sin verlo y se puede caer. Evitad todo el mal posible. Hay muchas clases de obstáculos en el camino de la vida, las tabernas, son unos, las casas de juego otros, las leyes, otros, los tiranos y las congregaciones religiosas y las monarquías, y las cárceles y presidios y los egoístas y usureros atrae una infinidad de obstáculos que las revoluciones se encargan de quitar del camino. ¿Quiénes componen las revoluciones? Hombres y mujeres que no pueden pasar dejando la piedra en el camino porque saben que sus semejantes pueden caerse. Así, pues, todos los que contribuyen á sostener un régimen tan pernicioso como el presente son los que dejan la piedra en el camino, mirándola al pasar, sin importársele que los otros que vengan después de él, que no tengan tiempo para observar y evitar, se estropéen.

Y al hacerlo así se hacen cómplices de los

males que origine. Humanos! vuestra indiferencia y egoísmo ocasiona muchas desgracias y apesar que podéis vivir felices y hacer dichosos á los demás, no lo hacéis, prefiriendo acumular riquezas á costa del trabajo ajeno, sin ocuparos del dolor y las miserias humanas.

*
* *

Algunas líneas más sobre el poder, ó influencia de las costumbres, en la fuerza fluídica ó invisible que llamamos fuerza mental, pero que irradia de todo nuestro sér. Nuestro yo espiritual puede ver, palpar y hacerse visible, sin el cuerpo material; esto no es religión. Es Ciencia! Descubríos!... Es observación metódica, persistente, analítica, de sabios científicos.

Yo me explico perfectamente, por qué no podéis comprender esto así, á primera lectura.

El comprenderlo, no hace á nadie más perfecto. El caso de llamarse espiritista porque se conozca y se acepte la doctrina, (á veces sin comprender el radio que abarcan sus ideas) no quiere decir que sea el individuo perfecto, ni que pueda serlo más pronto; sí, las ideas pueden ayudarlo, pero como quieren adaptar las ideas al medio en que viven, algunos, hasta los romanizan y las ideas se pervierten para el que no observa, que es el individuo pervertido, que atrofia las ideas ó hace unas á su antojo con idéntico nombre. Observamos infinidad de personas que se llaman espiritistas y se unen á su novia por

ritos absurdos y bautizan á sus hijos, y van á
confesarse, y tras las procesiones, y tienen comercio de licores, y venden carne, y adulteran la
leche, y cobran subidos alquileres, y demandan
al que no le paga. Y calumnian, ó injurian, y con-
testan los insultos, y hacen política burguesa. Y
se llaman espiritistas, racionalistas; pues los anarquistas no hacen nada de eso. De modo que llamarse espiritista, no quiere decir que sean más
perfectos, ni medianamente, y estos espiritistas
fraudulentos que usurpan en las pesas y medidas,
que escatiman el jornal del trabajador, que contribuyen á que la pena de muerte subsista, que
ayudan á destruir leyes favorables á los pobres
y débiles, que mienten descaradamente, que son
cobardes, (Jesús fué valiente) y que cometen
miles injusticias, (con muy raras excepciones) se
reunen en un local, para invocar espíritus...
Decidme: ¿qué espíritus ó influencias espirituales, se pondrán en contacto con la fuerza fluídica, ó irradiación fluídica, ó aura que les rodea?
Los que están en iguales condiciones suyas. Por
ejemplo: todo el que acostumbra tomar alcohol,
su aliento es molesto y repugnante, irresistible.
Igual le pasa al que no se baña á menudo, al
que no se cambia la ropa sudada despide mal
olor, igual efecto hace la persona que es colérica y se expresa en tonos ásperos y en formas
incorrectas, estas personas no pueden tener en
buen estado su influencia magnética y sus fluí-
dos están en malas condiciones para invocar á

espíritus algo elevados, pues estos aunque los
invoquen no vienen; se acercan los que están en
iguales condiciones que ellos.

"No es negar á (Dios) la fuerza creadora del universo, el
no creer en la influencia divina, sobre las miserias humanas."
ANTONIO OTERO.

Y un grupo pobre de personas sobrias y altruistas, se reune y obtiene una comunicación
superior, pero la instrucción de este grupo, no
alcanza á interpretarlo y la deforman con el
lenguaje rústico, y los del otro grupo, al saberlo, se burlan y dudan de que hayan obtenido
una mejor y mas altruista comunicación, porque
ellos no la han recibido.

Otros detalles, de modo, que esos del grupo
primero, oyen las prédicas anarquistas, llenas
de altruismo, de un hermoso desinterés y dicen:
¡ah! nosotros no somos partidarios de tirar
bombas, nosotros vamos por vías pacíficas, somos espiritistas!... y realmente se creen que lo
son. Yo desearía me dijeran que quiere decir
espiritista; (si á mí me lo preguntan yo digo
que no sé, porque lo entiendo de un modo tan
distinto!... que no lo aceptarían....

No entiendo el espiritismo, con resíduos de
misticismos, ni fanatismos de otros ideas llamadas religiosas. No acepto el espiritismo con
acatamiento á leyes criminales, ni á régimen
autoritario alguno. No comprendo espiritismo
que acepta costumbres, dogmas y ritos de caducas instituciones, llamadas religiosas. Tampo-

co lo entiendo amoldándose á las prácticas explotadoras del régimen capitalista.

Ni lo comprendo, aceptando la ley de herencia, establecida por pasadas generaciones que constituye privilegios é injusticias. Ni creo sea continuar con privilegios y distinciones odiosas. Ni puedo comprenderlo con el egoísmo que practican los que lo predican ó se llaman así. Repito que hay excepciones de un valor extraordinario, tenemos á don Francisco Vicenty, padre de numerosa familia, muy modesto, muy sobrio, muy humano, que no se ocupa de acaparar ni de preparar herencias para su familia, muy trabajador, muy inteligente, muy desinteresado, y un sin fin de calificativos de alta graduación. Y otros que valen la pena de exhibirlos cómo modelos, pero es muy largo. Y además no quiero exagerar, ni equivocarme al presentarlos, porque mi empeño es esclarecer el concepto de la idea, y no quiero que se me diga, usted se ha equivocado.

Se me olvidaba mencionar que don Francisco Vicenty es profesor de enseñanza superior. Para que alguien no crea que es algún rentista ó algún parásito social. Es un hombre de valer.

Pues bien hay infinidad de personas de ambos sexos, que se llaman espiritistas, y se reunen para celebrar sesiones de experimentación ó estudios, pero estas personas durante el día son coléricos, mal intencionados, calumniadores, exagerados, muy susceptibles de molestarse, glotones, perezosos. Más detallado, aún; está probado que según las condiciones de los que se reunan á invocar, así son los espíritus que se acercan ó se ponen en contacto con las corrientes fluídicas: y si el que evoca se embriaga, aunque en aquel momento no lo haga. Si es colérico, aunque en el momento de la invocación no lo sea, no importa; ya tiene el aura formada, y si en aquel momento no maldice, ni desea mal á su prójimo, ya lo ha hecho.

Estas personas pueden mejorar sus condiciones, dominando su carácter, porque las leyes naturales son inmutables ó inviolables y aunque rece usted miles de oraciones y aparezca hecho un santo, á la hora de invocar; no le dará resultado ni se perfeccionará usted por ese sistema.

Me atrevo asegurar, que la oración es inútil, la reconcentración de pensamiento es una oración, pero si el individuo no se perfecciona esta oración es inútil.

Y además, ¿con qué fin es la oración? para pedir algo? entonces todos tienen derecho á pedir y á que se les conceda. Y he observado que aquellos que siempre están esperando milagros, ó intervención ultraterrena, no logran nada digno de aprecio. Y los estudiosos y observadores científicos, como Edison, no es á la oración que deben sus inventos y descubrimientos. Newton, Fulton, Galvani é infinidad de investigadores, no fué rezando como obtuvieron sus descubrimientos. ¿Estos hombres tenían vicios, costumbres feas, ó perniciosas? unicamente amor al estudio, y á las leyes naturales.

Además, si algún guía, ó espíritu se ocupa de recompensar á los que se dedican á rezar, ¿cuántos hay que contínuamente están rezando? ¡La mayor parte de la humanidad, invocando y ofreciendo ayunos y sacrificios de miles causas! Hasta dejan de comer por comprar reliquias, grabados, lámparas y una infinidad de objetos inútiles para el fin perseguido.

¿Y ésta potencia espiritual necesita tales absurdos, para conceder algo? Para realizar un trabajo ó proyecto beneficioso á la humanidad, no hay que pedir intervención espiritual, porque entiendo que estando en la materia necesitamos ayuda de iguales condiciones, Una intervención de algún prójimo que realmente desea ayudarnos de corazón, con toda su fuerza mental, nos sería más beneficioso.

Del grupo que no rezan ni invocan, han salido los adelantos y descubrimientos mas hermosos y necesarios á la humanidad

Esos humanos que rinden culto á las imágenes y las adornan con seda y oro y miran con indiferencia, infinidad de hombres, mujeres, ó infelices niños, en la más degradante miseria. Cuál santo podrá ver bien y con agrado, que se olviden los dolores y necesidades humanas, que están á nuestro lado, para ir á buscar lo que no está á nuestro alcance y ellos no necesitan. ¿En

qué criterio cabe que un pedazo de madera ó de
yeso mejor ó peor modelado, pueda necesitar lo
adoren y lo cubran de oro, piedras preciosas y
sederías? Se necesita tener el cerebro atrofiado
y haber llegado á un grado de indiferencia muy
grande para cuidar una estatua y dejar hambrientos y desnudos á nuestro alrededor. Aceptando que ιales idiotas creyeran que determinados santos pudieran acercarse á la imagen de su
nombre aunque no se parezca á ella. Pero eso
sería secundar la idolatría y no cabe en lo razonable; porque todas esas apariciones y movimiento de imágenes son cosas de los curas, que
los han colocado en determinado sitio y luego
dijeron que habían aparecido, y por medio de
resortes hacen que llore y se muevan.

Vamos á suponer que puedan recibir los santos los mensajes y oraciones. Entonces, ¿por
qué no atienden á las peticiones que le hacen? y
que vienen haciendo de tiempo inmemorial, por
los que van á la guerra, que se mueren y vuelven sin piernas y sin brazos por miles y miles
de negocios y proyectos que fracasan sin intervención de los santos. Es tiempo perdido mi-
serablemente el de vestir imágenes; y estas mismas personas miran una niña pidiendo un centavo á algún caballero, y dice :—«Mira esa perdida, que su madre no recoje.» Pero no la envía
á llamar y en vez de adornar los ídolos, ador-
narla á ella y enviarla á la escuela.

¡Qué hermoso acto, cuántos beneficios no
proporcionarían á miles de infelices!

Si las mujeres en vez de ir á las iglesias á ex-
hibir sus lujosos trajes, fueran á las pobres viviendas á llevar consuelo. En vez de enviar
aceites y velas á las imágenes, llevadlos á los
pobres que lo necesitan y no lo tienen! los ídolos no lo necesitan. En vez de enviar dinero
para misas ú oraciones novenas y cortinajes y
adornos de la iglesia corruptora y materializada.
Llevadlo á los pobres que no tienen que comer
y ayunan. Si queréis que el cura ó fraile viva
sin trabajar y queréis sostenerlo por decir algunas frases en latin delante de unr imágen. ¿Por
qué cuando una infelíz va á pediros una limosna, ó un pobre campesino le decía "usted está
gordo y colorado, váyase á trabajar," y es el
sol que lo ha coloreado durante el camino. Y á
la infeliz mujer le decis que es una perdida. Y
al reverendo que está tan cuidado y feliz no le
decis que se vaya á trabajar.

!Que de contradicciones, y como salis de un
error para meteros en otro!

¡Cuán equivocadas estais, mujeres al creer
que las novenas, misas y oraciones os van á pu-
rificar. Si no tratais de correjir vuestros defectos, si os creeis superiores é vuestros servi-
dores y los tratais como no quisieran os trataran
á vosotras. Sois gastadoras supérfluas, y sois
engañadas cuando os hacen creer que sereis
perdonadas con los rezos y letanías de los curas.
¡Despertad! y no os asusteis con lo que vais á
seguir leyendo.

No hay quien premie ni castigue   Es una blasfemia.

Nuestra conciencia será nuestro juez, nuestros defectos se quedarán adheridos á nuestro espíritu si no tratamos de corrrejirlos.   Ni el tiempo ni las oraciones podrán borrarlo, si no procurais perfeccionarlos.   Por tanto, mujer ilustrada, madre de familia, obrera infeliz. podeis hacer mucho en beneficio de vuestros hijos.   ¡Despertad! Sacudid la inercia, el fanatismo que os subyugan; y ayudadnos á destruir estos errores sociales.

Observad la miseria de la mayor parte de nuestros hermanos y venid á ayudarnos á conquistar el triunfo de la humanidad sufrida.

De los que siempre trabajan y no tienen jamás razón en sus declaraciones, pués nunca son atendidos.

Este planeta portenece á todos, y no es prvilegio de unos pocos.   ¿Porqué ha de haber tantas injusticias?

Debemos contribuir á nivelar tantas desigualdades.

***

Marchamos hacia una época de bien y paz entre todos los humanos.

Existen infinidad de sociedades con el fin de iniciar á los humanos en ideas de bien general, de interés universal.

Tenemos en Sao Pablo, Brazil, el "Círculo de Comisión del Pensamiento," y tiene por objeto:

1º Promover el estudio de las fuerzas ocultas de la naturaleza y del hombre.

2º Promover el despertar de las energías creativas latentes en el pensamiento de cada asociado de acuerdo con las leyes de las vibraciones invisibles.

3º Hacer que esas energías converjan en el sentido de asegurar el bienestar físico y moral y social de sus miembros, manteniéndoles la salud del cuerpo y del espíritu.

4º Concurrir en la medida de sus fuerzas para que la armonía, el amor, la verdad y la justicia se efectúen entre los hombres.

La sociedad constará de un número indeterminado de socios, de ambos sexos sin distinción de color, nacionalidad y creencia.

Para informes dirijirse al Delegado General, el cual enviará á vuelta de correos Estatutos y demás informaciones en español, italiano y alemán. Dirección: Redacción de la revista "O'peisamento" Rua Senador Feijó, 19 San Pablo, Brasil.

Esto no es como noticia, es un comentario favorable á todas las instituciones ó sociedades

que con este fin se establezcan. Tenemos el
Club Segno que se interesa por el progreso de
los humanos que dirije el Dr. Victor Segno.
El Institute of Sciencies de New York que
dirijen el Dr. La Mote Sage y Ch. Clark.
Tenemos sociedades vegetarianas é infinidad
de libros y revistas que tratan de encaminar
hacia la felicidad humana, terrenal y espiritual.
"Nuestras fuerzas mentales por Prentice Mulford; "La Verdadera Vida" por Tolstoy. "Natura" revista científica. "El arte de ser felíz"
por J. W. Colville. "Las Sentencias del Juez
Magnaud". "La Conquista del Pan" é infinidad que van haciendo comprender á los humanos los errores en que han estado, llamándose
cristianos. Siendo todos intolerantes, vengati-
vos y explotadores. Ya estamos en una época
que las protestas de los explotados se atienden,
y sus reclamos. Ya observamos que todos estos
libros, revistas é instituciones y clubs no aceptan la diferencia de color, ni de raza.

Pues se puede dar el caso de que un hombre
de color escriba á un club de estos y demuestre
aptitudes magníficas para el estudio y su práctica, y el que envía las explicaciones no sabe que
es de color oscuro, amarillo ó rojo ó aceitunado
y atiende y responde su inteligencia á los méto-
dos establecidos para el estudio. Y que después
de instruído y apto ya para el desempeño de su
carrera, le pidieran su retrato. Y que al en-
viarlo, á vuelta de correo, fuera rechazado por

su color. ¿No sería una injusticia? Pues debemos abogar porque las diferencias entre una y otra raza desaparezca y seamos hermanos de un confín á otro del mundo. Propaguemos la abolición de la explotación del hombre por el hombre. Verdad es que en esos Club ó sociedades no pueden todos iniciarse por carecer de medios, pero de todos modos es un gran progreso que proporcionará magníficos resultados. Entiendo que las fuerzas de la naturaleza no están ocultas, si que nosotros no la comprendemos y por eso no las vemos

REFLEXIONES

Si hoy en cualquier parte subiera un hombre ilustrado á una tribuna á exponer los defectos y á proferir insultos contra un hermano de padre y madre, y lo acusara y lo insultara del modo más infamante. Todos los oyentes diríamos ese hombre no es hermano del otro, es una fiera, y sería conceptuado como un ser sin sentimiento, sin delicadeza. Si un hombre hablara mal en contra de su madre, que tratara de infamarla, profiriendo insultos, sería conceptuado como un mal hijo, como un ser que olvida los trabajos que pasó aquella mujer para enseñarlo á ensayar los primeros pasos y las primeras sílabas y le paga con insultos......
Pues bien, los que predicamos y deseamos

que llegue la fraternidad no debemos proferir
insultos, ni tratar de deshonrar á nuestros pró-
jimos, si somos hermanos.   Pues de lo contrario no llegaremos nunca á poder practicar la
fraternidad.   Esto no quiere decir que oculte-
mos la verdad, nó; los atropellos, las hipocresías, las ruindades, las farsas de todas clases,
deben ser expuestas, pues por lo mismo que
somos hermanos, debemos hacerlo comprender
que conocemos nuestros derechos y que si ellos
los atropellan, tenemos el derecho de recordar-
les que nos molestan las injusticias.   Por ejemplo, si por un descuido ó por ligereza nos pisan
un pié, y el que pisa no se da cuenta de que
atropella carne humana, el primer impulso del
adolorido, es empujar seguida al que lo pisa:
porque el dolor no reflexiona, no puede ser cortés, puesto que es antiestético.   Y la cortesía
es una forma de la belleza, y ésta "es la forma
de la verdad" como bien dijo Camile Flammarion.   Bien, al empujar mira mal al objeto que
le ha producido dolor y dice "torpe" ó "usted
no tiene ojos" si es una persona sin cultura. Si
es una persona culta y cortés, procura disimu-
lar su dolor, y el "perdone" ó al "dispense"
del autor; dice "no hay de qué", "eso no es
nada" y otras análogas.   Pero esto lo dice después que no lo pisa, en el acto de pisarlo, todo
su afán es quitarse aquello de encima.   Y luego
pronuncia las frases corteses.

Así como no maltratamos ni volvemos á pisar

al que nos pisó, sino que .ínicamente le recor-
damos que ha molestado nuestra propiedad humana, así debemos portarnos en los demás ata-
ques, hechos á nuestros derechos y libertades,
hacer valer nuestras necesidades y que estas
sean inviolables; ¿ó es que no habrá quien lo
practique en cuanto se trate de intereses y
todos se volverán coléricos, graves, y no harán
caso de tales reclamos?

Pero para eso predicaremos, para persuadir,
convencer y así llegar á la práctica de la fraternidad. No es que seamos tontos ni ridículos al
predicar formas para fraternizar, es que pasan
siglos y no llega y eso demuestra la apatía con
que se ha observado las máximas de Jesús,
aquel valiente y sincero hermano, que nos trazó
luminosa senda para que la humanidad no en-
contrara escollos en su ascención á la cúspide
del progreso. Pero indolentemente hemos leído y vuelto á leer y siempre de generación en
generación, hemos interpretado de un modo
erróneo y abusivo las parábolas y sentencias
por él dictadas. ¿Continuaremos interpretando
mal y sin procurar correjirnos, ni practicar las
sublimes máximas humanas de aquel valeroso
Jesús? Nó, ya los tiempos se acercan, es necesario que desaparezcan de una vez los errores
que han tenido sumida en la más adyecta ignorancia á los humanos. Propaguemos las máximas cristianas, que son las máximas de libertad
humana, propaguemos y prediquemos que los

humanos deben instruirse, para no tener necesidad de gobierno, ni códigos ridículos y anti-humanos, no olvidemos que él dijo "el que se encuentra sin pecado que arroje la primera piedra" y todavía nadie puede arrojarla, por tanto unos pocos no pueden gobernar, ni condenar á los otros. Los menos sin trabajar, no pueden disfrutar de todo mientras los más que siempre trabajan carecen de lo más necesario.

No olvidemos que Jesús díjole al jóven que le preguntó como conseguiría la eternidad. Y Jesús le dijo: "No adulteres" (y "No mates". "No digas falsos testimonios." "No defraudes." "Honra á tu padre y á tu madre." Y el joven dijo: "todo eso lo he guardado." Entonces Jesús mirándolo y éste "mirándolo" quiere decir escudriñando su interior, leyendo en su conciencia y le dijo: Una cosa te falta; vé y todo lo que tienes vende y da á los pobres y tendrás tesoro en el cielo. Ahora vamos á explicar como se entiende esto por medio de la razón, desde el principio que dice Jesús. "No adulteres", yo creo opino, que se adultera cuando se hace lo que no se siente; por ejemplo, aparentar querer al marido, al esposo, cuando en realidad quiere á otro; y tener relaciones ó contacto carnal con el otro y tener hijos y continuar viviendo con el marido haciendo pasar por hijos de el los que son del otro. Y cuando se unen dos que no se aman, es adulterar los sentimientos y hacer del vínculo, la prostitución legalizada.

Esto es adulterio; la que rompe con esas fórmulas y vive con el que realmente quiere no adultera. Pero en esta sociedad estúpida, la mujer que se une á un hombre, por las leyes de las instituciones actuales, está obligada á vivir, á gustarle, y á querer á su marido. Dirán ¿y para qué se casó? ¿Pero no es suceptible el corazón humano de equivocarse? Si se casó cuando le gustaba, pero luego no le gustó por muchas cosas que no son para decir en este libro, y que lo tildarían de escándalo é inmoral. Pero ahí está la "Enciclopedia de la Vida Privada," como un código con letras de fuego, acusando severamente á los que sin temor á las lágrimas, ni á las resistencias de la mujer quieren convertirla en un asqueroso recipiente de vicios, y abusan de su aparente debilidad, mejor dicho, de su falta de instrucción.

Bién, la mujer se abstiene de su libertad por tal de que no se ocupen de ella, y se resigna á vivir en contra de su voluntad de sus deseos, con su marido y este es el adulterio. Y la sociedad actual está basada en eso; y por tanto estamos en el deber de mejorarnos.

"La castidad y la libertad estan inseparablemente unidas, no hay esclavitud tan grosera, no hay cadena más fuerte que aquella del apetito sensual desenfrenado."

"No mates." En los códigos vigentes de nuestra decadente sociedad está escrita la pena de muerte como medio de correción, oh! jueces acusadores! "oh! soldados violentos é im-

pacientes policías."! "Cualquiera que odia á
su hermano es un asesino, y vosotros sabéis que
ningún asesino tiene en sí vida eterna." ¿Por
qué entonces está vigente la pena de muerte?
Es un resto de bestialidad, que aún hay que
destruirla. ¿Podremos con la pena de muerte
regenerar á los humanos errados por ignorancia? No, ése no es el modo, no es el sistema,
la forma, de poder corregir á un pobre hermano descarriado, debemos instruirlo y hacerle
comprender que el crimen no conduce á nada
práctico, pero como la ley le da el mal ejemplo,
no tiene derecho esta misma ley á juzgarlo, ni á
correjirlo, pues como hombres tanto derecho á
matar tiene uno como otro. Lo práctico es que
la ley no autorice el crimen cometiéndolo ella;
al menos que alguien crea, que no sea asesinato
el de la ley al enviar á la horca un hombre, y el
representante de esta ley es un hombre, y este
hombre ordena matar á otro hombre. De este
modo caminamos hácia las épocas salvajes de
bestialidad humana. Lo justo sería que este
representante de la justicia hiciera reflexionar,
meditar y regenerar á este hombre por medios
generosos é instructivos. Esto sería hermoso,
humanamente sublime, un hombre elevando á
otro hombre, que es su hermano. El cristianismo en acción. Oh! jueces, si esto practicá-
rais, veríais que bellos resultados produci-
ríais.

El asesinato cometido por la llamada justicia
humana es una irrisión monstruosa: pues si en-

contramos horrible que un pobre ignorante ce-
gado por la ira, mate á su semejante, tenemos
que encontrar más horroroso que hombres ilus-
tados sin motivo alguno personal. con la calma
necesaria, dicten sentencia ordenando á otro infeliz la ejecute! ¿Con qué derecho castiga el
juez? Y al juez por ordenar tal muerte, ¿quién
lo castiga? En vez de haber un solo criminal
hay varios luego, pues todos los que no han pro-
testado son cómplices de la nueva muerte. Y
ésto agrava más la situación. Si había una familia huérfana, hay dos y esta última en peores
condiciones, por la degradante infamación que
pesa sobre la familia, creada por la misma sociedad. Y esta sociedad después que la coloca en
esa situación la abandona al desprecio. ¿No
hay doble crimen en todo esto? ¿Hay justicia
en este procedimiento bárbaro? ¿Se aminora
el instinto criminal así? Nó; al contrario, aumenta, tenemos los hijos y familiares del ajus-
ticiado que sentirán odio y desprecio por la sociedad, y pasan años y ya nadie se acuerda del
crímen realizado por el hombre, ni el que come-
tió el tribunal. Pero hay quien vela en la sombra; y cuando más tranquilos estamos, surge
otro crimen, mataron al juez, al secretario, ú
á otro que contribuyó con sus acusaciones; ¿y
quién fué el criminal?; el hijo de aquel que
«degolló» la justicia en combinación con otros.
Ah! olvidamos que el espíritu no muere, que al
partir para allá en forma tan violenta, va per-
turbado, y desde luego utiliza su influencia para

que el hijo que estaba exitado con la acción del tribunal vengue la muerte del padre.

Y á estos errores se llama justicia, la verdadera justicia no se equivoca: y ésta justicia, está siempre equivocada, la Pena de Muerte es una equivocación, una de tantas que diariamente cometen estos hombres que créen poseer un alto don de justicia, y son otros tantos ciegos de la humanidad. Ciegos con derecho á ver más, pues á veces llevan la antorcha luminosa de la ciencia en la mano. Pero creo que esto mismo los ha dejado ciegos, su vista es muy imperfecta para ver las cosas con toda claridad.

Oh! jueces si en vez de creeros infalibles, en vuestras sentencias, pensárais que dirigiendo á este hombre que se equivocó al matar á su hermano, hariais un bien, no contagiandoos cometiendo otro error como el asesino. Y pudiérais dirigir por un sentimiento de misericordia á este descarriado, con vuestro esclarecido talento, y ayudárais á levantarlo, y á procurar que se convirtiera en protector de la familia á quien le quitó el padre, el esposo ó el hermano. Y allí ¡cuántas veces no se acordaría de su víctima!, y ese mismo hombre lloraría arrepentido de su acción. Y en vez de otro crímen, realizaría un acto de amor, de fraternidad. Me direis que es un castigo muy suave y que eso no devolvería la vida al interfecto. Esto es muy hermoso realizado de este modo, pues tampoco ejecutándolo devolveis la vida á su víctima. Con la Pena de Muerte, agravais las consecuencias, dejais

otra familia huerfana, de la cual no os ocupareis
ni un segundo, ni le proporcionareis medios de
vida. Haciendo que el autor de la muerte, vaya
á consolar la familia y á ayudarla; el espíritu de
la víctima, tendrá que sentir la necesidad del
perdón, y envolverá en fluidos benéficos á todos.
De este modo hay más justicia, pues no tenemos
la seguridad de saber si en otra existencia fué
víctima éste de aquel. Y con esta duda deben
abstenerse los tribunales de imponer castigos
superiores á sus conocimientos y penetración.
Diréis que de este modo todo el que comete un
crímen, dirá ó se disculpará con la anterior existencia. Muy léjos de eso, pues el que comete
un crimen, está ciego por la ira y no es responsable de ese acto, sea porque lo haya el otro
provocado ó irritado. Esto no es un motivo
desde luego, para matar á un semejante, pero
cuando sucede, están en el deber los inteligentes, los legisladores, los que se atreven á dictar
ó escribir leyes para el pueblo de aminorar y
suavizar educando, y castigando, no se educa.
La Pena de Muerte es un procedimiento muy
bárbaro para que sea utilizado por los llamados
á dirigir á un pueblo, á educar generaciones.
Los que llevan la alta misión de representar la
Justicia deben ser hombres dueños de sí mismo,
impasibles, serenos, que no se asombren ni al-
boroten, ni formen corrillos como los que no
tienen nociones algunas de lo que es la ignorancia. Jueces y Tribunales que se colocan al nivel de
los asesinos, no deben ser llevados á puestos ele-

vados como es el de representar y practicar la Justicia. Ya se ha dicho que "La misericordia es la más alta expresión de la justicia." Y el deber de ésta es aminorar los actos violentos y sanguinarios, no aumentarlos produciendo otros nuevos. Si un hombre mata á su hermano, debemos hacer que este hombre se arrepienta, y procure aminorar las penas de la familia de su víctima y que si él tiene familia se una á la otra. Este es el modo más en armonía con el sentimiento humano, la razón y la lógica. El sentimiento y la razón no se unen? muy bien, pero ni es verdadera razón, ni es buen y puro sentimiento. Porque yo sienta intensamente hayan asesinado á mi hermano ó marido, no es razonable que yo desee la muerte del asesino. Porque él haya sido criminal, yo no debo serlo; lo razonable, lo justo, es que yo acepte tranquila el suceso, sin deseos de venganza, ¿que llore? sí; ¿que me lamente de lo ocurrido? también. Pero esto no me autoriza á vengarme. Pues si yo no siento el deseo de vengarme, ¿por qué los que representan la justicia se han de tomar ese derecho, que sólo pertenece á los familiares de la víctima? Diréis, que toda la sociedad está amenazada con esta muerte, y que esta sociedad en nombre de la víctima necesita lavar el ultraje. Razones que no merecen ser atendidas. ¿Por qué esta sociedad ciega no vé otros ultrajes que perjudican más y solo percibe éste? ¿Por qué esta sociedad, cuando se muere algún hombre en la calle, no busca el culpable? ¿Por qué esta sociedad no se siente herida cuando se realiza un acto deshonesto cometido por altos funcionarios realizado en casas de venta de carne humana? ¿Por qué cuando llevan allí una niña, una infeliz campesina, ó modesta hija de padres pobres y la prostituyen, no sienten el ultraje? ¿Por qué cuando un infeliz trabajador cae de un andamio y se inutiliza y luego se ve obligado á pedir limosnas, esta sociedad no se siente ultrajada? ¿Y este infeliz no encuentra ni abogado que lo defienda, y la sociedad no se ofende ni se ocupa? Porque esta sociedad es hipócrita y cobarde En cambio se han visto juicios de crímenes realizados por personas acomodadas, hijos de ricos, y la sociedad ha transigido en no exigirle su vida igual que á otro cualquiera. ¿Por qué estas desigualdades?; si un rico comete un crimen debe ser castigado en igual forma. Si no se decapita al rico, ¿por qué se ejecuta ó agarrota al que no lo és?

Esto la sociedad no lo vé, y entonces ¿por qué habla de justicia, si no la conoce? Si hay peligro para la sociedad en dejar que permanezca libre el asesino, ¿por qué á los ricos se dejan en completa libertad, y al que no lo es, se encarcela ó encadena perpétuamente sin dejarle ni brindarle medios de corregirse humanamente, y no, como á una fiera encerrarlo. Y el rico puede continuar sin peligros para esa sociedad, frecuentando casinos, paseos públicos, teatros y cafés donde puede embriagarse con Champagne y brindarlo á las jóvenes en los bailes, etc., etc.

¿Y no hay peligro en dejar á este libre? bién, muy bién, pues que no lo haya para el pobre ó el de mediana posición. Si á uno se deja en libertad al otro también. Esto es lo justo lo humano. Y debe siempre de procederse de acuerdo con el sentimiento humano.

El asesinato es terrible, (pero los periódicos le dedican planas describiéndolos), pero, ¿puede lavarse, ó corregirse con otro? No. ¿No sería más humano que reformasemos ó regenerasen al homicida? No debemos olvidar á Caín, de quien Abel no se vengó. ¿Y Caín ahora, donde está? ¿No estará ahora muy alto, muy alto? ¿No guiará hoy á otras regiones más perfectas? ¿No será guía y tierno consejero de los errados y crueles? Seguramente que sin necesidad de haber matado á Caín, ascendió libremente por la escala del progreso y del amor á su prójimo. Y esta es la única liberación que hay que buscar y aceptar. Lo demás es contrario á la justicia, ¿quién puede juzgar á su hermano? ¿y cómo se atreve tomarse el derecho de castigarlo?

Errores que cuestan muy caros á la humana especie. Y que estamos en el deber de corregirlos, para que no se repitan. Los castigos son erróneos, debe educarse humanamente y no violentamente.

"No robes " En verdad, en verdad os digo que el verdadero ladrón es el que posee más de lo que necesita. Esos son los verdaderos ladrones que cada día sienten más deseos de acaparar

y de llenar más y más sus arcas de oro y plata.
Esos son los causantes de todas las deformida-
des, y enfermedades engendradas por la miseria
que ellos originan con su explotación. El que
no tiene trabajo ni dinero, y carece de un pedazo de pan y lo toma para satisfacer una necesidad como la de nutrir el organismo, no es
ladrón.

¡Cuántos se han atrevido á llevar á los tribunales, á infelices, porque le han llevado una in-
significancia que no les hacía falta. Una vez á
un hombre acomodado, le robó un infeliz una
salea vieja y una gorupa, averigua quien fué y
busca testigos y lo llevan al juzgado y oí que lo
condenaban por morirse de hambre, á 6 meses
de cárcel Sres!... Claro está, que salió de allí el
Sr. muy satisfecho de haber castigado al atrevido que se apropió de una porquería, que le per-
tenecía. Hay muchos casos de esos; otra vez
yo observé un muchacho que bostezaba muchas
veces y paseaba frente de un puesto de pan, y
en un descuido cogió un bollo y en dos brincos
desapareció, los que le vieron, dijeron eh! el
pillo! el dueño ó encargado del puesto no podía
abandonarlo. No se veía por allí un policía y
no hubo tiempo. Si lo cojen, á la cárcel con el
hambriento! tenía que ir á degradarse pidiendo
un centavo, que se lo negarían; y además no se
debe pedir. Si la ley prohibe pedir limosna. ¡Por
qué ir á indisponerse con la ley! !A tomar lo
que se necesite allí donde hay mucho en abundancia!. Es más hermoso que pedir. El que

no encuentra trabajo, y vé que los gobiernos,
ni los partidos políticos, ni las religiones, se lo
proporcionan, no debe pedir. Las autoridades
están en el deber de enterarse de los que carecen de trabajo y debe haber un letrero eterno
en los ayuntamientos en esta forma: "El que
no encuentre trabajo, aquí lo encontrará" y de
este modo se le proporciona medios de llevar
diario á su familia.

De lo contrario, ninguno debe pedir es afren-
toso pedir. No pidan, pobres trabajadores,
víctimas de la usura y la explotación; explotados por los partidos políticos, por las religiones,
por el comercio, vosotros sois la eterna mina,
de donde extraen inmensos tesoros la burguesía
y las religiones.

Vosotros sois la inmensa mole donde descansan los gobiernos, sobre vuestras doloridas es-
paldas, ascienden al poder los tiranos. Sois los
eternos peldaños donde confiadamente posan sus
piés reyes y emperadores, ministros y frailes,
repúblicas y monarquías.

Y apesar de ser vosotros las poderosas columnas que los sosteneis con vuestra ignorancia. Aún os encarcelan cuando tomais un pedazo de pan, para alimentaros. Y aún en estas
condiciones, se atreven á imponeros castigos
en carceles y presidios.

Trabajadores! los verdaderos ladrones, son
los que poseen más de lo que necesitan, no lo
olvideis y aunque os encarcelen, no pidais limosnas. Haced que los gobiernos que llevais a

poder con vuestros votos, contraigan el deber
de proporcionaros trabajo cuando no lo haya en
otra parte. Imponed esta petición que es jus-
ta y no es favor, es justicia y no muy explén-
dida.

¡Vosotros, los que adulterais los artículos de
primera necesidad, los que explotais con ellos,
cobrando más de lo que valen.!

¡Vosotros, que cobrais por un miserable cuar-
tucho, precios excesivos y doblais el valor de
vuestra propiedad tres y cuatro veces su valor
y siempre seguís siendo dueño de la casa, apesar de haber cobrado 4 y 5 veces lo que valía.!

¡Vosotros sois los ladrones, yo os señalo al mundo y os acuso de todas las injusticias que se cometen con los pobres!

Vosotros después que cobrais el valor de la
casa, debeis darla á vivir á los que la pagaron
antes. Y hacer otra en las mismas condiciones.

¡Vosotros que comprais harina á muy bajo precio para expender pan en el mercado á precios
que doblen vuestras ganancias.!

Sois unos pícaros y os llamáis caballeros y
despreciais á los que habéis explotado que valen
más que vosotros.

Vosotros todos los que á costa de la explotación vivís y acumulais grandes cantidades de
dinero sois los ladrones, los únicos ladrones que
señala la justicia del análisis y la crítica.

Vosotros que criais hijos en el lujo y el despilfarro para que desprecien á los niños sucios
y rotos que van por las calles de cuya miseria

sois culpables. Vosotros los que despreciais á los que van sucios y descalzos, después de quitarles los medios para hacerlo.

Vosotros los que os atreveis á suponeros de mejor sangre y carne que los que han elaborado vuestro caudal os recuerdo que estais errados, que no sois mejores, sois menos, pues sois inútiles, únicamente servís para acumular el producto del trabajo ajeno. Sois egoistas y soberbios y el reinado de Jesús no pueden sentirlo vuestras conciencias cuando vuestros corazones destilan hiel para vuestros semejantes. La hiel del desprecio y la crueldad; eso dais á vuestros hermanos.

Por eso criticais á los que se burlan de vuestras estupideces y ridículas pretensiones. Más, pronto llegará el día de redención, porque un siglo no es nada, en la e ernidad del tiempo.

"Falso testimonio;" no digas falsos testimonio, no mientas, no engañes, no ca umnies. Todo aquel que se arriesga en afirmar una cosa porque se lo supone, ó porque las apariencias lo engañen, comete un homicidio atroz, pues es proporcionar disgustos, graves, difamar y hacer perder la poca felicidad, que pueden tener uno ó dos indivíduos. ¿Con qué fin se ha de suponer y afirmar una cosa no vista, solamente supuesta? Es cruel y atrevido dejarse llevar

de las apariencias, además de los daños que
proporcionan esas críticas perversas. Además,
¿qué bién se procura el que difama, el que asegura una cosa que no ha visto, pero que se lo
supone. No gana, ni tiempo ni dinero, ¿con
qué fin lo hace? Con el de pasar el tiempo.
En vez de estudiar y hacer algo útil.

La mentira es casi una costumbre, es una
costumbre perniciosa, que debe de apartarse de
nuestra mente. Nos hacemos mucho daño con
mentir, nuestras fuerzas mentales pierden mucho. Una buena opinión que formemos de otra
persona, siempre es muy agradable. No debemos jamás informar mal de otro, aunque hayan
motivos para hacerlo. Es muy poco culto, hablar mal de otra persona, nadie es perfecto, y
jamás debemos decir alguna cosa que pueda
perjudicar á otro. Nos beneficiamos grandemente, encontrando á los demás siempre buenos
y aceptables.

El desprecio y la murmuración hacen muy
mal efecto; es tan agradable hablar, informar
siempre bién de los demás.

Jamás debeis mentir, y por tanto no debeis
hacer uso de lo cual no tengais el valor de sostenerlo. Si comprais barato, decidlo, y si caro
también. No engañeis. El engaño es signo de
atraso y de perversidad.

*_**

«Honra á tu padre y á tu madre.» No se exige más respeto á uno que al otro. Pero cuantas veces el proceder de uno de los dos ha dado ocasión al niño á faltar. Un padre que habla mal de la madre á su hijo, y una madre que habla peor del padre al hijo. Decidme que condiciones de educación proporcionan á los hijos.

Ocurre que los padres, se creen dueños de sus hijos y los obligan á obedecerles en contra de su voluntad. Un niño ó niña, es un futuro ciudadano y debe de ser respetado y atendido. Los padres no tienen derecho á maltratar á sus hijos ni imponerles su voluntad.

Dirán: pero este derecho de "Honra á tu padre y á tu madre," es para reprender á los hijos y no á los padres. Así parece, pero cuan equivocados están los que crean que solamente á los hijos se pedirá cuenta de esto.

¿Hay padres que merecen ser honrados por sus hijos? No; el solo hecho de ser padres no los autoriza para que los respeten, su conducta y austeridad, será el principal concepto. ¿Un padre tiene derecho de llegar á su casa ébrio y fumando y de exigirle a su hijo que no lo haga? ¿Una madre poco cuidadosa y aseada tiene derecho de exigirle á su hija limpieza y orden? No es posible. El dicho de Jesús, es una acusación á los padres, que envían á sus hijos á decir mentiras, que los azotan cruelmente, que los encierran en habitaciones oscuras, para dar satisfacción á sus absurdas iras.

Con el azote ni el castigo se educa, el tono
dulce y persuasivo debe ser el empleado por las
madres y los padres. Pero cuando estos nece-
siten y quieran engañar á sus hijos, entonces el
mandato se vuelve contra ellos. Si teneis que
salir y no quereis llevar á vuestros hijos, en-
viadlos antes á paseo con la sirvienta, aunque
más correcto es que os los lleveis con vosotros y
no los engañeis diciéndoles que los vais á llevar
y no cumplírselo. Habeis faltado á la verdad
y quereis que vuestros hijos os obedezcan y os
estimen. ¿Acaso creeis que como son niños podeis engañarlos?; os equivocais. La ley es una
y para todos igual, no se detiene en edad y tamaño. El niño á pesar de su pequeñez, si sois
buenos y cariñosos, será bueno y cariñoso. Si
sois embusteros y fraudulentos vuestros hijos
os imitarán; no creais que el nombre de padres
os evitará de ser verdaderos y leales con ellos.
Son seres humanos y tienen por su poca edad
más derecho al respeto y la consideración.

El azote es una acusación para vosotros por
vuestra poca paciencia para educarlos. Es una
falta de abnegación maltratarlos. No teneis derecho en azotar sus tiernas carnecitas Debeis
dirigirlos con toda la paciencia posible y necesaria, y responder á todas sus preguntas aunque
os parezcan impertinentes. Pues como es natural, lo que no comprende necesita que se lo
expliquen; y ¿quién puede mejor que los padres
contestarles, dándoles explicaciones? Nadie
todos lo harán, pero ninguno con la buena for-

ma y voluntad de los padres. No debemos engañarlos refiriéndoles mentiras y cosas incomprensibles para su imaginación.

Debemos explicarles las cosas materiales como son, sin añadir ni disminuir.

La verdad debe ser la base fundamental para la educación de la niñez Y los padres tienen la obligación de no engañar á sus hijos, y enseñarlos á no engañar á los demás.

La sentencia dirigida á los niños es una acusación á los padres. El niño nace naturalmente bueno, y según lo dirigen, así será el resultado que dará de acuerdo con las enseñanzas que reciba.

Tiene derecho el padre de castigarlo por un defecto, que él apesar de su edad, su estudio y su experiencia, no ha podido corregir. Los padres deben dirigir y educar al niño, pero no castigarlo. Es un error creer que es una forma de educar el maltratarlos y atormentarlos.

A MARIA LUISA RODRIGUEZ   (1)

TU PAÑUELO NEGRO

Como recuerdo me lo adjudicaste; No lo me-
recía. En este ambiente de hipocresía, las notas del sentimiento desinteresado, del puro
afecto, se ahogan. perecen por asfixia, Tu no lo
comprendes. No sé por qué los sentimientos y
los afectos que anidan las venus mercantiles,
son más puros, más sinceros, más naturales.

Lo guardo junto á mi ropa, pero bien debajo.
para no tenerte presente, porque me hiere el
alma. Yo que padezco de la enfermedad de la
compasión, sin pensar que á mi puedan compa-
decerme. Me es indiferente que me compadez-
can, pero no me agrada la compasión para mí.
¿Los que se equivocan merecen compasión? No

---

(1) Me dirán, estoy seguro, de qué como se me ocurre dedi-
carte esto públicamente. Se ofende la moral pública!... el pudor!... de los que te degradaron (según ellos) los que fueron á
buscar caricias, entre tus brazos. Los que te pidieron más re-
finamientos, más locuras, creyendo te humillaban... esos quieren despreciarte, ríete de ellos! son unos locos!

lo creo. Pues bien aquí tienes una equivocada de la vida. Rindiéndole culto á la sinceridad, donde todo se traiciona A la verdad, donde todo es mentira. A la fraternidad, donde todo es competencia, y egoismo. Al amor, donde todo es interés y odio, envidia y rencores. ¿Qué te parece, flor nacida en el fango de ésta sociedad, que se recrea en el mal de sus hermanos.? Tus perfumes han volado, huyendo de esta atmósfera infectada. ¡Pero no se han perdido! No. Hay un lugar en el espacio para ellos, ya lo recojerás, y perfumarás tu alma. No te aflijas, ni te creas humillada. Alza tu blanca frente, y no temas abrir la vista, que los que deben avergonzarte, se sienten avergonzados y bajan la cabeza. No eres tú. Son ellos los culpables.

Vuelvo á tu pañuelo; no ha muchos días lo tomé, y lo até á mi cuello, me ví en el espejo.... me aflijí pensando en tí, víctima sacrificada á la lujuria bestial de los semi-hombres. Y lo guardé temiendo ajarlo. La primera vez que lo tomé en mis manos, después que lo obsevé en mi casa, me pareció fatídico, sombrío,.... y esquivaba el mirarlo!.... ¡Lo que es la ley de la tradición, y la fuerza de las costumbres! Aquello me pareció un contagio. Perdóname, yo no tengo la culpa: es el ambiente en que vivimos. La fuente en que bebemos, es muy turbia. No hay agua cristalina, y la sed es muy ardiente, y tenemos que beberla. Ya saneará, las reformas se acercan. Pues bien, tu pañuelo negro, para mí es un símbolo. Es la mancha negra, que la sociedad se arroja al rostro, al envilecer y despreciarlas.

No te preocupes, no hay víctima sin verdugos, y en este caso, confórmate; éllos, los verdugos Tú, la víctima. Te desprecian, recibes los desprecios con la sonrisa en los labios, son unos cobardes.

Esos esconden la mano para no levantarte. Niegan la ayuda, para mejor despreciarte. ¡Estúpidos! después que saborearon tus besos y estrecharon tu cuerpo de diosa, te desprecian. Es igual al niño que destrozara el seno que lo formó, y golpeara la nítida paloma de pico rojo que lo alimenta con su blanco líquido. O arrojara al suelo el bellísimo vaso de finísimo cristal en que ha libado sabroso néctar... ¡No lo harán en mi presencia! Los anarquistas no procedemos así, somos los reformadores y practicadores de la verdad.

No temas, te defendemos, eres nuestra; eres de los que sufren, formas parte de nuestro batallón, de los que sufren!....

Hasta luego.

EXTRACTOS ESPECIALES.

He oido decir varias veces, "Se merece un puntapié." Como si esto fuera lo más grosero, el acto más deshonroso. Y los piés son el pedestal del cerebro, sin ellos no se podría ir á ninguna parte. En la base de las estátuas se colocan las coronas dedicadas á honrar y á glorificar á los grandes hombres. No se las colocan en la cabeza. Las dejan colgadas á sus piés, aquí pueden poner muchas. ¡Quién le dijera á la muda piedra que sobre ella descansan los honores de una generación entera!

Por eso, cuando oigo ofrecer puntapiés, dígome: ¿qué le harían al que los recibe? tocarlo ó golpearlo, con la parte más necesaria del cuerpo humano. Es lo mismo que despreciar los retretes, las fregonas y los barrenderos.

Sin los primeros, ¿qué serían los palacios? y los cafés y las cocinas sin las segundas? y las calles sin los terceros?

A veces es más útil á un país un barrendero, que un hombre público, aquél podrá no darle

glorias, pero tampoco le deshonra. A este puede la ambición conducirle al crimen: Aunque
opino y creo que hay crímenes que esclarecen
las conciencias, de generaciones enteras   Es el
contraste en todo, como la sombra al objeto.
Nada puede despreciarse, ni elevarse en grado
sumo. A veces, una deformidad humana es necesaria y provoca grandes reflexiones y produce
bellezas. (Cuasimodo) Como una gran belleza puede producir la ruina, el desastre. (Febo).
Leyendo y escribiendo, ví en el papel un punti-
to luminoso que brillaba, que me hizo detener
la pluma Lo observo. Era una pequeña arruga;
y díjeme. Lo deforme brilla. Y acordéme de Cuasimodo y eso me detuvo, y me hizo pensar mucho, y analizar más. A veces lo indescriptible
se sumerje en la nada. Las ondas van y vienen
sin desbordar el océano. Como puede la lluvia
fecundizar la tierra, y producir una derrota. Lo
mismo las olas bañan y golpean la arena de las
playas, que á las rocas. Sin embargo estas se caen de su base y ruedan por la arena, y
estas siempre están en el mismo sitio, no bajan.
Estas juegan con las olas, aquéllas se resisten,
se revelan á moverse al compaz, al vaivén de las
aguas. Son rocas, por eso caen. Simbolizan
la terquedad, la aspereza. En la arena se su-
merjen los piés como en el agua. Simboliza la
suavidad, la tolerancia. Es el eterno enigma
de la naturaleza, donde el sol alumbra y da vida
de un modo igual á la dulce malva que á la
venenosa orquídea, igual se posan sus rayos en

la cumbre que en el llano; se mecen á su calor
la mas olorosa flor que la insípida dalia.
Es volcán aterrador y nieve perpétua, se-
duce y domina. Canta y llora. Gime y sonrie.
El eterno contraste de la vida soberana. Contraste que es armonía, luz y sombra, agua y
fuego, amor y olvido, cielo ó infierno. Eleva
lo más torpe y hunde lo más grande. Se eleva
á lo infinito y baja al fondo del abismo.
Es libélula azul y terroroso mónstruo Brillante y tenebroso. Sube á las cumbres crista-
linas de las montañas del Polo y desciende á las
bajas estepas asoladoras de la Arabia. Gorgea
en el pajarillo, brama y ruge en el león ó pantera.
Es hiena, y es cordero, besa y muerde y ruje
y canta. Miel y ácibar. Atrae y repele. Esa
es la vida humana, incomprensibles destellos de
contrastes que producen armonías. No destru-
yen, queman.
Por la misma calle y acera pasa el criminal,
que el abnegado, el uno va al presidio, y el otro
á la cátedra.
Sinembargo muchas veces salen de la cátedras
y universidades bandidos y criminales, y de los
presidios apóstoles y sabios.
Es que el camino, el derrotero, no va debajo
de los piés, va en el cerebro. Marchan con la
cabeza. Por eso se ha dicho que el reinado de
Cristo, lo lleva cada cual en su alma, es la justicia. Dos pueden vivir juntos, beber la misma
agua, aspirar igual brisa. Sinembargo uno vi-

ve en el «cielo» y otro en el «infierno.» La
exasperación y la tranquilidad. La justicia y la
desesperación madre de la venganza.
¿Quién ha creado al soberbio y al pacífico?
La naturaleza visible é invisible. Lo han hecho
de luz y sombras. Juguetea en la superficie de
las rizadas aguas ó rueda al fondo de los abismos. Así hay muchos corazones humanos hun-
didos en tristezas y alegrías, llantos y risas.
¿Por qué? No se puede explicar y se adivina.
Es la musa creadora de las auroras-boreales y
de las resplandecientes madrugadas, no necesitan explicaciones, creadoras de imposibles. La
luna y el sol. Uno ilumina suavemente, el otro
quema brillando fuertemente.
Es el Todo.
En la apariencia de la nada está el Todo. Bu-
lle en el polen de las flores y brilla en el insecto. ¿Cuál es más, el insecto ó la flor? De la
flor brota el fruto, son iguales, y el insecto,
puede dañarla. ¿Dañarla? ¿Por qué? porque
la prueba, la muerde, la saborea y se alimenta
con aquella pequeña parte, es insecto y no la
necesita toda. Tiene derecho á alimentarse de
eso, vive entre ellos. El hombre no investiga,
cree que el insecto daña el fruto; que no tiene
derecho á tocarlo y quiere, destruir los insectos, y á veces destruye muchos. ¿Pero, quién
tiene más derecho á comerla, el hombre ó el insecto? Yo creo que los dos, si el insecto tomó su
parte, el hombre debe aceptar la suya Vive
más en armonía con la natura, el insecto, que el

hombre. Pero éste quiere fabricar leyes absurdas, las ha fabricado. Aquel las acepta como están establecidas, como leyes que no podrán variar jamás.

¿Cuál es más sabio el hombre ó el insecto? (in sectun) Si el hombre sin variar ni alterar el orden natural hubiera inventado y estudiado, sería un Dios. Seríamos dioses. Pero aunque haya establecido leyes estúpidas, siempre vendremos á terminar la tan decantada civilización, con las costumbres primitivas, con la verdad y razón.

Y es que, lo que el hombre no puede fabricar, no puede destruir. Puede detener el curso de las aguas y el movimiento de los astros? Podrá hacer variar el curso de las aguas ó inmovilizar en un papel los astros y los sistemas, pero no puede dirigirlos. Y variar el curso de las aguas lo ha hecho la natura. No es nuevo. Lo ha hecho mejor, sin utilizar mano humana alguna. Son las grandes equivocaciones. A veces luminosas y á veces tenebrosas. Es la equivocación del símbolo de la cruz, en mano de curas y frailes, hombres también, pero que no han debido llamarse representantes de Jesús, ni educadores de la humanidad. No hay que destruir las iglesias, ni expulsar los crucifijos, este es el recuerdo de un hombre que murió porque predicó la justicia, no hacer daño; lo que hay que hacer es conseguir que los curas, frailes y monjas huyan de los conventos y las iglesias y pueblen las talas y el hogar triste....

¿De qué manera? Procurando que la humanidad no los acepte como representantes de una idea sublime, que han tratado de sustituir queriendo deformarla. Pero se han deformado ellos, y la idea cada día es más hermosa, más humana y se acerca á la realización. ¿Qué culpa tienen las imágenes, las paredes y el recinto de las iglesias y los crucifijos? Ninguna. Vamos á conducirnos de modo que los demás vean lo que nosotros vemos. El obstáculo no está en los crucifijos y las láminas; ¿que haya quien prodigue besos á ambos? Bien podemos decirle que la infeliz huerfana, triste y sin cariños necesita de esos besos prodigados á una efigie inerte. Que eso es idolatría. Y persuadir que lo que estorba y fanatiza es la práctica perniciosa de los falsos representantes que engañan, no para servir á Jesús ni á sus ideas sino para adquirir fabulosas riquezas y extensos dominios. Procurar conseguir que no hayan curas ni frailes.

Las iglesias se pueden utilizar en escuelas y bibliotecas. Y las imájenes que sean obras de valor, serán conducidas á los museos. ¿Y cómo se hará? Oh, la palabra escrita y hablada es la piqueta demoledora que destruye obstáculos. Y nada más? En último extremo, de todos modos había que hacerlo. Acaso después de las innundaciones no está el terreno más fecundo? Después de los movimientos terráqueos surgen nuevas islas en el medio de los mares. Así también, al limpiar de fanatismo y ridiculeses nuestras viviendas ó nuestro mundo, el ambiente estará más sano,   Esto es todo.

Lo deforme brilla.

Para los reyes todos los hombres que presten ebediencia son buenos ciudadanos.

Para los curas todos los que acepten sus doctrinas y dogmas, son buenos cristianos.   De modo que el trono y el altar se dan la mano, se sostienen, se ayudan.

Cuando el rey ordena ir en nombre de la patria á la guerra, el cura lo afirma en nombre de Dios.

Ninguno de los dos saben lo que dicen, ambos son criminales ante las leyes naturales.

Ambos conducen á la humanidad por caminos errados, enseñando costumbres perniciosas. Esas dos instituciones viven y se mantienen con la ignorancia del pueblo que dominan á su antojo.

La Mujer en la época primitiva.

En la época primitiva. Siempre fué considerada como un objeto de poco valor, hasta que se le concedió ser esclava, y de esa esclavitud surgió su reinado doméstico. Considerándola tan sumamente necesaria que no se podía prescindir de ella en ningún caso. La comunidad fué comprendiendo más el valor de la esclava reina en el hogar, que llegó á ocupar altos puestos y á conseguir privilegios no obtenidos. Aquí empezó á triunfar la mujer en el seno de las familias; y en el poder. Se le concedió educara sus hijos y esta es la base fundamental de la educación; y en el poder, tuvo grandes influencias, salvando pueblos de matanzas, y evitando y provocando guerras.

En Roma tuvo en una época más libertades que actualmente en los países de más importancia. ¿Por qué perdió esos derechos? Cambio de costumbres, mezclas de razas y naciones ocasionaron pérdidas en sus libertades y derechos adquiridos.

Luego desde la era cristiana hasta la edad media, fué adquiriendo privilegios, que fueron beneficiosos y perjudiciales. En esa época ya era considerada por el hombre como reina y señora de su pensamiento, de su alma y su vida. Estaba siempre dispuesto á sacrificar su honor, su valor, su vida por su dama. Escalaba los más altos puestos, y ponía su vida en constante peligro por halagar á su dama. La mujer en esta época fué idealizada, pero esclava aún. Esta época fué para España, Francia, Italia, Inglaterra. Pero en Rusia, en Turquía, en la China y el Japón no. Luego el progreso de la mujer tiene varias etapas, y varía según los países, las épocas y las costumbres.

En la edad moderna se le han concedido derechos y privilegios, pero aun es esclava. Esclava, no en inteligencia ni en el trabajo, si por el sexo.

En inteligencia rivaliza con el hombre, en el trabajo igual en actividad, en iniciativa y en perseverancia; para todo tiene libertad y derecho, menos para amar, para elegir con entera franqueza y libertad. Eso, aun el egoismo del hombre, no se lo ha concedido. Podrá hacerlo alguna, pero con la desventaja de ser conceptuada mala y viciosa, ó infinidad de adjetivos injustos y exagerados.

¿Pero continuaremos consintiendo que el hombre se imponga y trate de aminorar el valor de las que tomen la libertad que deseen?

Las mujeres no debemos tolerar que se hable mal jamás dé ninguna mujer, al que lo haga en presencia de un grupo de nuestro sexo, debemos

aislarlo si continúa haciéndolo; y de igual modo
con la joven ó vieja que se atreva á criticar á
otra mujer, en lo que atañe á su libertad de
sexo, de la cual es responsable. Dije que el
hombre no nos concedía libertad, pero ¿qué derecho tiene el hombre de concedernos más libertad ó de restringirla, ó de criticar la que
disfrutamos?

La mujer que ha sido durante siglos considerada inferior, y se ha estado otros tantos en discutir, sostener, afirmar y dudar su inferioridad.

Hoy terminan los hombres por reconocerla y
conocederla superioridad

Dice Marius de Zayas en «América,»—refi-
riéndose á los espectáculos teatrales, en los cuales, «los empresarios se esmeran siempre en hacer
variar los espectáculos, porque la mujer es más
fuerte en emociones, y ésta forma el mayor público.»—«Esto demuestra un vez más, la superioridad de la mujer sobre el hombre.» No
afirmo, ni dudo, ni niego; reservo mi opinión,
pues la mujer tampoco quiere ser superior al
hombre, podrá serlo pero no gusta demostrarlo
para no herir. Y no podía menos la mujer en
ser generosa con quien ha de compartir los honores, las glorias y el amor! que es la mayor de
las glorias y á la que aspira la mujer con vehe-
mencia. Por sentirse más satisfecha en ser la
gloria de su amado, que ser una gloria científica
ó artística. Y en esto superamos á los hombres,
nos preocupa más ser amadas que admiradas.
De admitir que somos superiores hoy, tenemos

que suponer que admitan que lo hemos sido
siempre. Esto no pueden negarlo, sin confesarse culpables de nuestra ignorancia y esclavitud, aprovechada por ellos, sin grandes beneficios hasta la fecha. De modo que hoy canta-
mos nuestra libertad, que teníamos adquirida
por derecho natural. Pues de igual modo nace
un hombre que una mujer. Y la cantan y desean más nuestros antiguos "amos," sin temor
á perder sus derechos.

De lo que no habla M. de Zayas es de las faldas pantalón ó de la nueva costumbre de vestir-
nos, pues luego que se utilice el pantalón, no
vuelve la falda. Puede esta usarse en el teatro
y en los bailes de mariposas y serpentinas que
usan muchos colores y entre los pliegues y vo-
lantes del traje no se divisa la artista en el ver-
tiginoso vals.

Esta costumbre de pantalón se adapta perfectamente á la época de progreso femenino. Y
esta costumbre hará que vayan variando las te-
las desde las más gruesas á las más finas y delicadas y terminaremos en usar solo un velo ó ga-
sa para cubrirnos. Y en esa futura época la
mujer en general procurará no engordar mucho,
mejor será delgada que gruesa. Y será tan natural y artísticamente bello, que esa época se
acerca con rapidez, con igual rapidez que los
progresos en sociología. Que todo tiende á ser
comunista en la práctica. De modo tal, que no
extrañamos que nos tomen un libro, ó dinero ó
ropa, y se queden con todo.

Es el progreso sociológico, comunista, anarquista que se impone. Fundamos sociedades y hacemos reuniones sin la bendición del clero, y sin permiso del juez ó alcalde. Sin darnos cuenta hemos prescindido de las autoridades eclesiásticas, civiles y políticas, que tanto aclamamos.

Y á este desarrollo sociológico se adapta admirablemente la mujer. Esperamos de esas ideas nuestra completa emancipación y todos nuestros derechos y deberes esclarecidos.

El ser humano por naturaleza es anarquista, y hacia la anarquía comunista vamos de un modo sorprendente sin bombas ni incendiarios, ni terrorismos inútiles.

No quiere esto desaprobarlas, supresiones de algunos tiranos, ¿qué derecho tienen ellos para matar á Ferrer en España, Kotoku en el Japón (Tokío,) y los otros en Chicago y otros más en otras partes. Los tiranos monárquicos, imperiales ó republicanos son iguales en todas partes. En América se cosechan muy buenos preguntadlo á Méjico y la Argentina que están en el siglo décimo en procedimientos. Y aún así no quieren explosivos ni supresiones. ¡Si son necesarios que se utilicen! ¿Acaso los gobernantes solos tienen derecho á matar? Que empiecen ellos por dar el ejemplo ya que se hacen llamar directores y padres de pueblos y aplaudir como generosos y "caritativos." Que no mantengan en pié ejércitos de infelices dispuestos á destrozarse, á la menor orden; que no legislen disparates y contradicciones. Que gandı la verdad, que no compren ni vendan acusaciones, que no tengan cárceles y presidios para los hambrientos, en vez de escuelas de artes y oficios y depositos de comestibles. Que no derrochen en sus vicios y bestialidades, mientras hay descalzos y desnudos. Que no degraden á la mujer, para luego despreciarla; y por qué soportar sus desprecios, en vez de lanzarlos á sus rostros, llamarla inferior. Unicamente así tienen derecho á pedir la abolición de los atentados individuales y colectivos.

Hacedlo gobernantes, de lo contrario no os quejeis, siempre estareis amenazados. No soy partidaria de los atentados, ni los del gobierno á los del pueblo.

Mientras existan unos, existirán otros. "That is the question." ¡Resolvedlo soberanos y presidentes!

Resumiendo finalmente, la mujer es apta para todo.

A JACINTO TEXIDOR.

RECUERDOS.

Que impresión me produjo vuestra bellísi-
novela «Los Culpables», impresión indescriptible, amigo mío.

Cual cinematográfica escena reprodujo en
mi mente todos los recuerdos pasados envueltos
en lágrimas y suspiros de lejana época.

Conocéis bien todos los defectos de esta sociedad de moralistas sin moral.

Habéis dicho:

"El que cause el daño repárelo, el que sea
culpable de la caída de una mujer, levántela; y
levántela del fango, si al fango la lanzó".

¡Cuántos tendrían que reparar sus errores!....

Las mujeres esperamos llegar á una época
en que esos abusos hayan terminado. No es
justo que si dos infringen una ley se castigue á
uno solo.

Además el hombre que exige una joven virgen debe estar en iguales condiciones.

¿Qué ley, qué privilegios y qué moral es esa,

que empiezan por no cumplirla los que la legislaron y la proclamaron?

Para mí todas las leyes son inútiles, no sirven para el fin que fueron creadas. Las leyes naturales son las únicas que deben regir entre los humanos.

Si vuestro libro fuese verdaderamente estimado en lo que vale, tendría un altar en cada paisano de ambos sexos y un sitio en cada hogar.

Como moral más hermosa y real, que la de los llamados libros sagrados.

Pero á todos los que piensan altamente le dicen «Locos» que se han adelantado un siglo.

No importa, continuad estimado amigo, exponiendo esas verdades que terminarán reinando en el futuro.

Así nos ayudaréis á derribar los obstáculos, y vencer las dificultades que en nuestro camino encontramos, la mayor parte de las mujeres.

Y tendremos orgullo en contaros como sincero defensor de nuestras futuras libertades.

Sinceramente os felicito por vuestro oportuno libro, pues con las verdades que encierra es oportuno en todas las épocas. Dejará de serlo cuando los hombres no digan embustes y no engañen á las mujeres. ¿Y eso tardará algún tiempo ó durará siempre?

Espero que terminará cuando termine este injusto sistema social, que estamos derribando poco á poco ó imponiendo nuevas costumbres. Y esto si contáramos que con elementos ilustra-

dos y valientes como Vd. seguramente que ade-
lantaríamos mucho más, y apresuraríamos la tan
esperada época, sin escándalos, sin grandes ó
inútiles discursos políticos, de sabi-hondos su-
perficiales y alborotosos que no inician nada
práctico.

Yo desearía continuara su obra, pues tiene
Vd. buen temple para eso. Y esta es labor de
anarquistas, que no temen nada y desafían vien-
tos y tempestades de cualquier clase que sean:
políticas, religiosas, económicas, sociales; resulte lo que resulte.

Es Vd. de esos, y esos son los que hacen
falta.

San Juan, 1910.

ELISA TAVAREZ DE STORER.

Esta gentil artista, excelente pianista y distinguida dama, es una de las más cultas y finas de nuestras compatriotas. Es orgullo de nuestro país.

Pocas veces se podrá admirar la hermosura, el talento, la distinción .y el arte, en armonía tan perfecta. Ahora en otro ramillete sus bellas cualidades como esposa amante y cariñosa y madre abnegada y tierna.

Con su maestría y gentileza admirable comparte sus aptitudes entre su hogar y su arte.

Su amena conversación, á la cual da variados matices é impresiones, hace olvidar las horas á su lado.

Vayan estas líneas á rendir mi humilde tributo pero sincero, como demostración de admiración y simpatía de la amiga que la distingue.

Casada con el laborioso y culto joven David Storer, estimado amigo y compañero de ideas, pues está afiliado en la «Federación Libre.»

Estimamos en lo que vale tan digno joven. Felicidad eterna!

San Juan, Enero de 1911.

A M. MARTINEZ ROSSELLO,
Arecibo.

Las Postales.

Son bellas y sugestivas, cuando llevan grabadas algún paisaje poético ó ramo de flores de
colores delicados, unidos con armonía.

Y son útiles y hasta necesarias, cuando se
graban sobre su cartulina, frases de amistad y
sincero afecto conservando en ellas un recuerdo
de amigos estimados.

Y al volverse á leer lo que en ella se expresa, se evocan la figura, el porte, el estilo del autor de la memoria.

Y es un gran auxiliar para conservar latente el recuerdo de los que sinceramente se aprecian y distinguen Y produce una gran satisfacción el poder contemplar en ellas grabada
una demostración de amistad y simpatía.

Yo he sentido un gran consuelo, una tarde
de tristeza indefinida para mí, recordando estas

frases de un muy distinguido y respetable amigo de quien conservo una postal, que dice:

« Oh! bendita amistad, pasión sublime
Que de el amor redime
Y enjuga en la tristeza nuestro llanto.
Cuando mi alma gime
Hallo en la mano amiga que comprime
mi franca diestra lenitivo santo.»

. . . .

Bella y sugestiva postal que me trae recuerdos imborrables de situaciones difíciles.
Son muy bellas, muy bellas, cuando llevan
impresas en ellas frases de amistad sincera. He
visto infinidad de postales y me he conmovido
al leer en ellas una expresión de cariño; un
mensaje de amistad enviado de allende los mares
de la persona amada y estimada.
Cuan agradable es recordar los amigos que
se estiman. Y qué tristeza infinita é inexplicable me embargaba abstrayendo mi alma que
gemía; y exhalando un suspiro de angustia dije:
¡Ay, mi alma gime. . . . . . y entonces recordé:

. . . .

«Cuando mi alma gime
hallo en la mano amiga que comprime
mi franca diestra lenitivo santo. »

. . . .

San Juan.—Octubre, 1909.

A TOMAS CARRION.

Al escribir tu nombre, evoco nuestro viaje rápido á Juana Diaz estando en Ponce, y el otro á Cabo Rojo estando en Mayagüez, en este último nos acompañó nuestro estimadísimo amigo Ramón Irizarry, al que envío mi cariñoso y leal afecto.

Tuve la suerte que me acompañaras á esos dos pueblos y me ayudases en mi labor de propaganda por obtener suscriptores para la revista *La Mujer*. Abnegado, valiente, desinteresado, noble y leal, en tan alto grado que te asfixias en esta atmósfera de iniquidades é injusticias; y haces oir tu vigorosa y elocuente palabra, llena de conceptos verdaderos, exentos de la hipocresía actual, sin temor á la crítica. Lanzas tu opinión por sobre todo los convencionalismos, estruendosa, formidable, cual otro Mirabeau. (¿serás él?).

Amigo mío, en la lucha por la libertad humana me he despojado de formulismos y ridículas exageraciones. Y ante la opinión somos lo-

cos, sí; locos-cuerdos, cuya locura es decir la
verdad. Tú no estás dentro de nuestra causa,
..... no sé por qué, pero hombres como tú
que tienen formado un concepto de la moral y
la verdad tan hermoso, no debían estar susten-
tando ideal político que beneficie solamente á
unos pocos. ¡Aquí á nuestro lado en las filas li-
bertarias! de frente al sol, en defensa del proletariado universal!

Ven á ayudarnos á libertar á la humanidad
de la explotación del hombre por el hombre.

Presta tus energías á la propaganda liberta-
ria que beneficie á todos, sin distinción.

¡Hasta luego!

MI PROFESION DE FE

A Manuel Ugarte.

PARIS

Socialista soy, porque aspiro á que todos los adelantos, descubrimientos é invenciones establecidos, pertenezcan á todos, que se establezca su socialización sin privilegios. Algunos lo entienden con el Estado, para que este regule la marcha, yo lo entiendo sin gobierno No quiero decir que me opongo á que el gobierno regule y controle las riquezas, como lo hará, pero yo mantengo mi opinión de sentirme partidaria decidida del no gobierno. Socialismo ácrata. (1)

Bien yo aquí afirmo y declaro solemnemente, que para ser socialista es necesario haber analizado y comprendido la Psicología.

---

(1) Anarquista.

291

Está en un error el que se crea socialista y acepte los dogmas, ritos y prácticas fanáticas de las religiones, pues el Socialismo es la verdad y las religiones impuestas son errores.

Está equivocado el que se crea socialista y es ateo, excéptico ó materialista.

El Socialismo no es una negación, ni una violencia, ni una utopía. Es una verdad real y tangible. En el socialismo no está la astucia para vivir, no! de un modo cómodo aun á costa del trabajo ajeno. No está el engaño, no está la imposición ni el imperialismo para con los débiles é ignorantes. El socialismo persuade con verdades, no hiere. En él está la razón pura, la armonía entre todos, la dulzura de carácter, la igualdad en todo. Es la verdad no la mentira. La sinceridad no la intriga. He dicho la dulzura de carácter y habrá quien diga, eso lo predican las religiones. Pues bien, analicemos mejor. La razón es recta, serena, apacible é impasible. Jesús fué racionalista. Una persona que tenga por norma la razón no se violenta, no huye, no burla, no se alegra del mal de su enemigo ó adversario.

Pues una persona razonable no tiene enemigos, aun teniéndolos no los odia. ¿Qué resultado obtiene? Si lo insultan ó lo abofetean con la mano ó con frases hirientes, y corresponde en igual forma, ¿qué consigue? (Yo no puedo aceptar que sin un motivo se abofetee ó maltrate á alguien.) Me dirán, pues,—desquitarse, vengarse. Pero la razón es serena, dueña de sí

mismo, no es vengativa, ni injuriosa, y un socialista por el bien y la emancipación humana
debe ser razonable. El que tiene la razón por
norma, es dueño de sí mismo, no es instrumento
de la venganza y su consecuencia el crimen, la
violencia y todas las pasiones brutales.

El socialismo está en el luminoso cristianismo que socavó los cimientos del poder de los
Césares, por la fraternidad. Y la fraternidad
universal sera la implantación del socialismo que
es abnegación, dulzura, modestia, templanza,
«Uno para todos y todos para uno.» Seguros
escalones que conducen á la perfección humana,
para la libertad y el progreso espiritual indefi-
nido aun por la pluralidad de mundos habitados
superiores.

Instruyámonos para purificarnos. eduque-
mos nuestra voluntad para el ejercicio del bien,
y dejemos consumir bajo el influjo de la razón,
el fuego de la pasiones, en holocausto á la emancipación bumana, para la persecución del progreso espiritual.

Impresiones de viaje Julio 1909.

Salí de Arecibo á las diez de la mañana para Isabela: partió el tren y en el trayecto, por
entre las campiñas próximas á ese pueblo, entre
las plantaciones, en la tierra preparada para recibir las semillas, ví una niña que con una mano
recojía su pobre falda, en la que estaba la semilla, y con la otra la regaba entre los surcos
abiertos en la tierra. ¡Bella y poética figura!

Hermoso símbolo de la constancia en el trabajo, que el implacable egoismo esa insaciable
hidra de la explotación, axficia en sus monstruo-
sos brazos, aniquilando la belleza y salud de
aquella pobre criatura dejándola escuálida y miserable sin un sostén para sus futuros y postri-
meros días. Y después de una existencia entera
de privaciones y dolorosa miseria, recurre á pedir limosna, ó camina al hospital, único refugio
de los que todo lo producen y nada disfrutan.

¡Ah! ¡bello símbolo del trabajo y la perseverancia, yo te saludo en nombre de la fraternidad universal! Y tú, mónstruo explotador,
mide tus pasos; no vayas á caer en el precipicio
de tus egoismos, en el abismo de tus errores.

Camina con cuidado. que la Justicia, en nombre de la Libertad, ajustará tus errores.

Tiembla! estremécete de horror ante el final terrible de tus días, debido á la indiferencia para con tus hermanos, á quienes sacrificas del modo más inicuo é injusto, sumiéndolo en la más degradante miseria. Pero todo tiene término y el tuyo se aproxima. ¡Temblad tiranos de todas las épocas y edades que la Revolución Social se acerca para igualaros al nivel social que os corresponde!

Alerta!

. . . .

En Isabela permanecí algunas horas, pues por la noche salí para Aguadilla; en esta ciudad tuve ocasión de saludar con gran satisfacción á varios trabajadores carpinteros que están organizados, es la única sociedad obrera que allí existe, la política en ese pueblo no permite á los obreros pensar en la defensa del salario. La esclavitud del salario es la esclavitud moderna, que oprime y ha hecho y hará más hambrientos y criminales, que la esclavitud de razas y la de la época feudal. Es más cruel, más injusta. Si en pasadas épocas la esclavitud de la compra y venta de carne humana era despiadada, si á la imposición del Sr. Feudal, dueño del castillo, y de las tierras, y del derecho, á todos los privilegios, al extremo de que no podía el infeliz colono campesino vender ni un trozo de madera, ni una fruta, ni cederla sin permiso del amo, ni ceder su hija en matrimonio, sin antes conceder la primera noche de bodas al Sr., ni comprar algún objeto necesario que entre el fizco y los curas absorvían al infeliz dejándolo sin voluntad. Si la esclavitud, en aquella época llegó á estrujar tan cobardemente al trabajador y la usura de aquellos tiranos no dispensó ni de un paso, que no fuera esquilmado bárbaramente. si la dignidad humana se pisoteó y se acorraló ignominiosamente, en la época actual varían poco las circunstancias. Hoy se permite la compra y venta al campesino, se permite que tome mujer, sin exigirle la primera noche de bodas. Se les deja libremente ir y venir, comprar y vender. Reunirse en asambleas, si, todo. ¡Ah! pero su esclavitud es más difícil, está cubierta con el velo sutil de la hipocrecía.

¡Trabajadores!

Pero al observar esa tan elogiada libertad, palpaba la realidad en vuestra miseria que de familia á familia, de generación en generación, no tencis donde extender vuestro adolorido cuerpo, y con lo que os pagan no podeis alimentaros. ¿Donde está el producto de vuestro trabajo? La hermosa riqueza que producen el tabaco, el azúcar y el café, donde está? En las arcas del que os explota que se ha hecho capitalista mientras careceis del concepto de ser humano. ¿Vuestro trabajo no produce? y de donde extrae el que os explota tantos miles de dollars? ¿Qué es lo que produce? (Ellos son tan cínicos que te dirán: la naturaleza); pero vuestro trabajo nada vale, la naturaleza no necesita la ayuda del hombre ¿verdad? Serían capaces de negarlo.

Trabajadores, estais en un estado de esclavitud peor que la antigua, ¿no teneis prisa en salir de ella? No olvideis que teneis en vuestras manos la redención que necesitais.

Si no cedeis hoy, como en pasadas épocas, lo mejor de vuestros productos para el amo. Si no os piden la primera noche de boda de vuestras hijas. En cambio os morís de hambre y degenerais visiblemente, sin derecho á disfrutar de los inventos y producciones científicas del progreso moderno.

¡Campesinos! de generación en generación pasais sin ver más abundancia en vuestros hogares, ni más instrucción. Aun no ha desaparecido vuestra esclavitud, antes os mantenía el amo, privandoos de vuestra voluntad; hoy os deja libre la voluntad, pero os priva de los medios de poder utilizarla. La misma esclavitud, con distintos procedimientos. ¿Que os oprimen, que os humillan y os atan á la tierra, á la máquina, al trabajo humillante que os aniquilan y embrutecén perdiendo de ese modo el concepto de hombres libres, sirviendo de obstáculos para la redención universal? Y aun así, no os preocupáis de otra cosa que de la política, que nada os brinda, ni defiende vuestros derechos, únicamente utiliza vuestra ignorancia para ataros y rendiros siempre en contra de vuestra libertad.

**
* *

Salí de Aguadilla y llegué á Mayagüez entre las 2 y 3 de la tarde. Visité la imprenta «Unión Obrera» y conocí al distinguido periodista y escritor amigo Rafael Martínez Nadal.

En esta poética y singular ciudad permanecí algunos días, Celebróse en esos días la reunión del Consejo Ejecutivo y la del Cuerpo Consultivo Conjunto de las Uniones de tabaqueros organizados, á las que asistí. Celebramos un «meeting» público en honor al 14 de Julio, organizado por Julio Aybar, Director de la «Unión Obrera, uno de nuestros más entusiastas compañeros.

Disfruté una temporada deliciosa, con una división de días placenteros y divertidos, junto á mis compañeros de labor, luchas, fatigas é ideales.

En grupos íbamos al paseo, á la mesa, á las sesiones, y como hermanos pasamos horas muy agradables y divertidas.

Rocuerdo que en plena sesión salieron nuestros camaradas Alejandro Escalet, Alfonso Torres y Antonio Olavarría, con sus maletas, á cumplir los sagrados deberes que imponía la valiosa y estimada «Cruzada Ideal,» á difundir ·los hermosos ideales de la redención obrera por villas y ciudades, campos y aldeas, Sembrando la hermosa y fructífera semilla que dará en el futuro óptimo frutos, creando los elementos del proletariado instruidos, puedan apreciar la hermosa labor que aportaren nuestros valientes,

adalides, sin otra recompensa que la del bien
general de los trabajadores.

En malos caballos, y bajo los rayos de un
sol radiante, iban de pueblo en pueblo, llevando
la buena nueva de los ideales redentores ; y á la
media noche aun se oían los últimos toques de
alerta dados á los trabajadores, desde la roja
tribuna.

Dichosos los pueblos que oyen propagar la
verdad sin fines especuladores! ¡Felices los hombres que comprendan tanta valentía y recojan
en la brillante concha de su inteligencia las sugestivas frases de concordia que cual nítidas
perlas brotaron de labios redentores.

Ah ! vosotros, honrados propagandistas que
sin haber estudiado en altas escuelas, sin haber
ambicionado títulos ni distinciones, sabéis decir
la verdad con más lealtad, que los que han cur-
sado lucrativas profesiones y tienen medios más
á propósito y mayor comodidad para ilustrar al
pueblo.

A vosotros no se os conceden honores, ni
diplomas, ni menciones honoríficas, ni os levan-
tan estatuas. ¿Para qué?

Vosotros no deseáis eso; concurrís á vuestra
labor diaria, y vuestro descanso és agitaros en
la tribuna.

¡Mártires de la verdad, heroicos defensores
de la libertad humana! ¿por qué no sembrar de
flores vuestro camino? Dejad que yo las vier-
ta para consuelo de vuestras angustias y decepciones... La hora solemne llegará para disfrutar

de los dones que con tanta prodigalidad produce Natura. Vosotros habéis cumplido vuestro deber, y ante vosotros se descubrirá la humanidad entera.

* * *

Salí de Mayagüez para San Germán. En esta ciudad bellísima, con sus encantadoras lomas, permanecí una noche y un día. La noche de mi llegada, visité el centro «Amor y Caridad.» Celebrábase reunión, y conocí al señor Celedonio Carbonell, y después que hice varios elogios de la Anarquía, por su síntesis igualitaria, terminaron por decirme que yo era materialista.....
Materialista yo? ¿Por qué? No lo sé. Sólo sé que me siento humana, altamente humana.

¿Materialista?..... bien y qué; sería yo la única; son despreciables los materialistas? Acaso porque no esté sofísticamente hablando de Dios de modo embrutecedor, que diga por ejemplo; ¡Oh Dios, Tú estás en todas parte, Sublime Creador, tu Nombre está escrito en el espacio con luminosos astros; te agitas en las profundidades del mar y en los misteriosos abismos! ¡Oh! Tú, Creador Celestial que bulles en el cáliz de las flores, y la brisa gemidora, al besarlas, pronuncia tu Nombre.

En el microbio que vive en la gota de agua, estás ¡oh Dios! y en el bacilo que destruye miles de existencias también estás! Te ciernes poderoso como el águila que cruza majestuosa los ai-

res, y estás en el león que hace estremecer selvas
con su rugido.

La tórtola te canta en la enramada y el rui-
señor en el bosque ; y en la pantera y el tigre,
que acechan la útil oveja, también estás.
Eres luz y sombras. Te revuelves en el calor y te estremeces en el frío. En todo eso estás
Tú, ¡oh Dios! y por no dejar de estar en todo,
en el ignorante que vela la oportunidad de clavar
el puñal en el pecho del hermano para sustraer-
le el reloj y la bolsa ; estás de igual modo en los
hipócritas inteligentes que há siglos engañan á
sus hermanos en tu Nombre, también estás. Y
los átomos y moléculas te pregonan Poderoso
Señor de sus dominios, y el aura dulcemente
pronuncia tu Nombre!

Y las avecillas vuelan alegremente, entonan-
do himnos á Tí, Poderoso Creador increado!

Bien ; decidme ahora que he alabado y en-
salzado y adorado á Dios. . ¿he hecho algo sublime?......

¡Ah, tontos! y os llamáis racionalistas. El
infeliz que carece de todo lo necesario, ¿qué obtiene alabando á Dios? La explotada lavandera
que se priva de comer para pagar el casero, y
que por su mal nutrido organismo, tiene los ner-
vios en mal estado, y por cualquier insignifican-
cia se desespera. ¿Para qué le sirven las alaban-
zas á Dios? Las mías ¿qué falte le hacen á Dios?
Cualquiera se figura que Dios se nutre de elogios
y que existe por las oraciones.

Yo no acepto esa forma de ignorancia. Yo

soy racionalista, y la razón es severa : no necesita de elogios.

La verdad no exige tales prácticas. Esas
costumbres son el residuo de pasados errores establecidos para someter las muchedumbres bajo
el dogal de la tiranía y el despotismo..

Los racionalistas somos los demoledores de
todas las costumbres perniciosas que no permi-
tían á los pueblos, pensar con entera libertad,
sin temor á supuestos castigos en desconocidas
regiones que la ciencia investigadora no ha lo-
grado encontrar.

Todos los seres humanos son libres, de vivir
de acuerdo con las leyes naturales, no las impuestas por los errores humanos. Entiendo que
el que desea viajar en globo ó en vapor no tiene
que encomendarse á nadie, pues todas las peticiones que haga son inútiles.

Hay seres que poséen el presentimiento de
que nada les pasará aun en los mayores peligros.
No hay poder humano que pueda destruirlos,
inaccesibles á toda tentativa de destrucción.
Cuántos hay que se ocupan de dirigir oraciones
para dañar á otros, cuántos que rezan con fines
para su prójimo, si fueran escuchados qué sería
de la libertad y la vida de cada uno de nosotros?
estaría al capricho de cualquier furioso mal in-
tencionado, y mal dirigido, y mal dirigido por
su ignorancia. No niego, ni dudo de que en
múltiples casos hayan intervenido espíritus para
proteger ó salvar de un accidente á un amigo
encausado pero. Hay infinidad de casos de esta

índole, pero que no han necesitado oraciones
muy lejos de la intervención humana

Recuerdo haber leído en «El Buen Sentido»
un caso muy afortunado para un cura que iba
en un tren, y quería llegar á todo trance á un
punto determinado en que el tren no hacía pa-
rada, para asistir á una fiesta. Poco antes de
llegar al sitio el pito de alarma sonó, porque
había en la vía algún obstáculo, todos los viaje-
ros asustados, y al llegar al sitio designado se
detuvo el ferrocarril y el joven ministro bajó.
Se informaron los pasajeros del motivo de alarma y el maquinista dijo que había en la vía dos
personas con el hábito de monjas: se observó
donde estaban y nada había. Sólo el maquinista las vió. Esto no lo dudo, jamás he dudado
de tales relatos por encontrarlos muy naturales.
Pero esto no me decidera creer en la eficacia de
la oración. Si me dijeran por la educación de
la voluntad, sí yo acepto, la perseverancia en
desear un objeto, á fin determinado, pues la
fuerza mental es poderosísima.

Pero pedir, como he oído yo en varias sesiones, al Padre Celestial que envíe buenos espíritus, es una simpleza. Es dirigir de un modo
incierto el pensamiento. El mejor medio de
para obtener relaciones espirituales de buenas
influencias, es ponernos en condiciones de obtenerlas. Pero si Vd. es colérico es perezozo,
vicioso y mal humano, así ruegue toda la vida
al Padre Celestial no logrará Vd. lo que desea.
Colóquese Vd. en vías de prácticas útiles á Vd.

y sus semejantes, a lo demás vendrá por añadi-
dura. Es consecuencia lógica que el que beba
con exceso se embriaga: el que otro maldice, á
sí mismo se maldice. No creáis en supercherías:
todo sale de nosotros mismos; somos tan libres,
que la justicia está en nosotros mismos.

Hay un adagio ó máxima que dice: «Tu misma conciencia ha de ser tu juez, por lo que ahora
hagas, no sufras después.»

Pero podéis hacer muchos cosas ignorante-
mente, y en este caso podéis luego reformaros.

Bien se ha dicho y se dirá, que la ignorancia
es madre de los mayores crímenes.

Ilustrémonos bien, y luego recostémonos á
meditar; y después practiquemos nuestras reflexiones, que tienen que ser mejores que ante-
de meditar.

La humanidad siempre se ha precipitado
por caminos errados, por excesos de amor propio sin análisis.

El exceso de amor propio es egoísta, y el
que es aturdido por él, va errado.

Por exceso de amor propio se cometen crímenes, por una equivocación de lo que es dignidad y honor, que quieren superarlo á las leyes
naturales.

El amante celoso, que no puede consentir
que su amada pueda dejarlo, y llega al crimen
para vengarse por un exceso de amor propio que
es egoísmo.

Se pueden tolerar los egoísmos que no da-
ñen otra individualidad, ni estorben ajenas vo-

luntades. Lo contrario es perverso y sólo produce acerbos dolores.

Por exceso de amor idolátrico, puede una madre en beneficio de sus hijos dañar hijos ajenos ; esto no debe consentirse ni practicarse: «lo que no quieras para tí, no quieras para otros.» Todo el que se guíe por máxima tan sublime, tiene el verdadero concepto de la libertad, igualdad y fraternidad.

He procurado dominar en mí todo lo que tienda á perjudicar á otro aún indirectamente.

La indiferencia es criminal: el indiferente no puedo ser humano.

Es necesario que el verdadero concepto de las leyes naturales sea comprendido, en beneficio de todos. El que falta á las leyes naturales perjudica á la humanidad.

Lo que se entiende por honor y honestidad, de acuerdo con las fórmulas sociales, son aberraciones, equivocaciones de la humanidad ignorante.

Nada hay en las leyes naturales que sea deshonesto ni deshonroso.

Todo es invención del egoísmo humano, en contra la ley natural, por un error de lo que es beneficio propio.

Pero todas esas equivocaciones desaparecerán; todo el sistema social de la familia, consti· tuido tal como está ; el sistema comercial todo, desaparecerán para dar curso á la familia libre, el comercio libre, dentro de la ley natural, ó sea el libre albedrío en beneficio de todos.

Las costumbres establecidas en contra de la
expontaneidad de la naturaleza, desaparecerán.
El sistema de educación irá sustituyéndose
por otro más de acuerdo con el bien común.
La instrucción se adaptará sin banderas ni
en determinado estado ó nación; el respeto ab-
surdo é idolátrico de los gobiernos será abolido
del futuro sistema educacionista.
La fraternidad como ley suprema, sin fronteras ni divisiones de razas. color é idiomas,
será el ideal religioso que se establecerá en las
escuelas.
El interés común como divisa, y como lema
la verdad, por sobre todas las cosas.
El único ideal religioso: «Amáos los unos á
los otros» imperará en todos los corazones.

* * *

De San Germán á Yauco. En este pueblo
conocí á la insigne escritora y poetisa Dª Fidela
M. de Rodríguez ; tuve el alto honor de salu-
darla Muy correcta siempre, expresión genuina
de la distinción sugestiva de los poetas.
Vaya mi cariñoso saludo á tan distinguida
amiga y compañera
De Yauco para Arecibo,en mi pueblo, con-
feccioné, unas cuartillas (1) que leí á mís hijos
con el fin de interesarlos en los dolores humanos.
Y en Agosto salí para San Juan en época tan

_____

(1) «Verdad y Justicia,» que volverá á editarse por segunda
vez.

poco afortunada para el director entonces de
«El Carnaval,» mi caro amigo J. Barreiro que
estaba preso ó en vísperas, pues no lo encontré
en su oficina varias veces que fuí: pero tuve la
suerte de encontrar y conocer á mi estimado
amigo culto novelista José E. Levis, quien me
acompañó á varias imprentas, entre ellas la del
gallardo escritor y gentil caballero, J. Pérez
Lozada y al no menos distinguido y culto Sr.
S. Dulmau Canet la de la buenisíma y atta. Sra.
Timothée; y se me olvidaba, en la del viril
poeta, y compañero eximio, Luis Muñoz Rivera,
que no tuve la suerte de encontrar por hallarse
en New York; pero tuve la gran satisfacción de
conocer y saludar al fecundo escritor Mariano
Abril, que ansiaba conocer há tiempo, y no
recuerdo á quién más. Ah!.... en la de «La
Correspondencia» en la que saludé á Blandino y
al oportuno cronista Joaquín Pujals (Semper) y
quién nadie más? nadie más. Luego fuí donde
mis camaradas y amigos E. Sánchez López, Rafael Alonso y Santiago Iglesias, propagandistas
y luchadores incansables,en beneficio del proletariado. Los que sustentan las ideas más avan-
zadas dentro del régimen actual. Los que dirigen la única institución que defiende la clase
trabajadora de un modo enérgico y perseverante.
Al llegar á San Juan yo llevaba el propósito de quedarme, bien colocada, ó de cualquier
modo; y me ví precisada á imprimir otra edi-
ción de mi primer folleto, para ver el modo de
colocar en la fábrica y marchar á Cáguas y á

Juncos y se agitaba aún la Cruzada Ideal, por
J. B. Delgado y J. Ferrer y Ferrer, iniciada
por la Federación Libre y tuve oportunidad de
asistir y contribuir con mi humilde ayuda á las
conferencias para los obreros en Cáguas, Juncos y Gurabo, y al volver á San Juan, ir á Arecibo para ayudar en la propaganda á los Tabaqueros en Utuado donde estuvimos varios días y
dimos varios meetings en los que tomaron parte
David Storer, que fué un cáustico en su oratoria
fogosa por sus verdades, Nicolás María de Jesús
y la que escribe. Yo ataqué el fanatismo católico
enérgicamente y debido á eso, se publicaron algunas hojas sueltas de un tono algo descortés é
insolente según me informaron; yo no pude juz-
garlas, no lo censuro, creo que hacen bien en
defenderse pero dentro de lo razonable y lo
científico; por ejemplo que me replicaran si es
justo que siendo creencia de muchos, la UTILI-
DAD del bautismo por qué no bautizan al que no
aporta un dollars, aunque el infeliz no tenga
que comer, se lo exigen al creyente. Si es útil
é ilustrativo que infinidad de jóvenes que pueden ser padres de familia, hayan formado una
congregación llamada de San Luis, y obstenten
bandas verdes; y en vez de estudiar la situación
obrera y su miseria, pierdan el tiempo en arro-
dillarse y resar en la que pretenden los curas
sea casa de Dios.

No he podido volvor á esa población. Iré
á sostener enérgicamente mi propaganda anterior; es decir, á exponer la síntesis de la única

y verdadera religión : »Amáos los unos á los otros,» bendecid á vuestros enemigos, orad por los que os calumnian y os persiguen.

No explotes, no usurpes á tu hermano el producto íntegro de su trabajo ; no engañes, no adulteres los artículos de primera imporiancia para la salud y la vida.

No engañes ni finjas amor por mujer alguna, sin sentirlo. No hagas del acto sexual de la procreación humana, el más hermoso y sagrado, objeto de placeres impuros y viciosos, que perjudican las futuras generaciones.

No tomes la mujer como objeto de placer simplemente ; respeta en ella la representación de la madre del género humano.

Sé útil y justo y serás feliz. No mientas.

Por fin terminé mi viaje. Me detuve en Arecibo, y volví á este S. Juan de mis alegrías.

Me hice Agente de «Unión Obrera,» y luego fundé una revista: «La Mujer.»

Naturalmente que estando saturada de lo que adolecía la sociedad, no tuviera inconveniente alguno en presentar al desnudo los crímenes y vicios que produce ese fardo de preocupaciones estúpidas, en el desarrollo de la mujer.

Empecé á tratar la cuestión sexual bajo el punto de vista de «Amor Libre,» como lo explica Magdalena Vernet, y no hay una mujer, por mística y pudorosa que se haga, que al leer esa explicación no la encuentre razonada y prudente; pero el obstáculo que han establecido las fórmulas sociales, la hacen enmudecer.

Sé de uno que se cree correcto caballero, que
no tiene mujer, ni utiliza mujeres según él, que
se atrevió á criticarle á una señorita que estuviera suscrita al periódico. La aludida señorita no
deseó volver á recibir el periódico porque le dijeron que era inmoral. Y no se lo llevé más, ni
quise tocarle el motivo para evitar disgustos.
Ese señor que se cree correcto caballero está en
un error, si no se une á una mujer. Así como
lo oye, señor mío.

El artículo no inducía á ninguna mujer que
se fuera con su amante ó novio; únicamente
explicaba el error y lo esclavitud de la mujer.

Y una señorita graduada como Doctora, re-
chazó el periódico muy indirectamente, pero yo
no acepto paliativos de este género. Y ahora yo
me pregunto, ¿á tal grado conduce el fanatismo
de esta comedia de la honestidad, que aun con
los libros de la ciencia en la mano que aboga por
su sexo, se niega á admitirla, y se hace cómplice
del sinnúmero de errores que produce esa equivocación respecto á los sexos.

Si el acto de la procreación no estuviera con-
fundido como un placer en vez de una necesidad
reglamentada por la ciencia y el estudio y el dominio de la voluntad, seguramente no habrían
tantos locos, idiotas, contrahechos, criminales y
lujuriosos. Pero la mayor parte tienen hijos por
casualidad, por pasiones bestiales, en estado de
embriaguez, y en estas condiciones ¿qué generación se puede procrear, siendo el acto genési-

co una sentino de vicios, abusos y contamina-
ciones? ¿Se puede educar una generación que
no comprende el ejercicio de sus deberes ni el
fin para que es creada?

Infinidad de jóvenes que creen han nacido
única y exclusivamente para satisfacer sus ins-
tintos carnales, sin importarle la forma como los
ejecute.

Que desde muy temprana edad quiere disfrutar de los derechos concedidos á la edad co-
rrespondiente, con perjuicio de su salud y con
detrimento de la generación que han de procrear.

Decidme, si los que deben hacer luz no la
hacen porque es deshonesto ó «inmoral,» ¿quién
se ocupará de dirigir y decir la verdad sin rodeos?....

¿Qué se puede esperar de una juventud que
á los doce y catorce años conoce en sus menores
detalles el acto genésico en la práctica?

La falta de centros ó sociedades que se ocupen de juegos científicos y gimnasia, contribuye
á aumentar esta costumbre.

Es sumamente higiénico y necesario que las
personas de estudios humanos científicos, se ocupen de estirpar este mal, en beneficio de las generaciones futuras. Que se establezcan centros
de estudios, y juegos y gimnasia para prevenir
el desgaste y la degeneración de la raza.

Los médicos, profesores y los padres de familia, son los señalados para este asunto de importancia suprema para el porvenir.

✦✦✦✦✦✦✦✦✦✦✦✦✦✦✦✦✦✦✦✦✦✦✦✦✦✦✦✦✦✦✦✦✦✦✦✦✦

Para M. L.

Arecibo.

PENSANDO EN TI.

Oh! la luna, ¡qué bella! sí; cuantas veces la
he contemplado allá en mi juventud, casi noches
enteras, en contemplación muda, frente á un
pequeñísimo huertecillo, en el que habían algunas plantas y flores, por mi cultivadas

Allí sentada horas interminables, de eterna
espera, viendo pequeñas nubecillas pasar, que
no ocultaban la belleza de su esplendor ni la
limpidez del cielo, aquellas nubes blancas, ador-
naban el horizonte al pasar. Allí tenía gran
placer en sentarme á esperar el objeto amado.

Ay!... aquella luna, y en la forma como la he
contemplado no la he vuelto á contemplar jamás.

Y ahora al recordar aquella intranquilidad
amorosa, que descanzaba en mi ignorancia, de
las luchas de la vida, y de las mentiras y trai-
ciones humanas, brotan lágrimas dolorosas;....
recordando á quien esperaba en aquellas noches

interminables en una soledad increible, y en la
cual me envolvía para poder así estar á mis
«anchas» para pensar y esperar que la pequeña
aldabita de bronce sonara, para que cesará mi
eterno afán, afán que destruyó mis ilusiones y
me mortificó cruelmente, el deseo de tener á mi
lado, al dueño de mi pensar y sentir, el que hizo germinar en mí la vida, reproducida en dos
seres, producto de mi amor expontáneo, sin
trabas, sin rodeos, sin hipocrecías, sin interés.... solamente maleado por un obstáculo....
una mujer-madre, que simbolizaba para mí las
fórmulas sociales.

Mas no importa si ella se oponía, y se opuso
siempre. La gran satisfacción que siento es que
no poseo bienes, sólamente guardo de él, el recuerdo imperecedero de la libertad conque lo
amé (sin desear perlas ni brillantes, coches ni
palacios), en mis dos hijos.

Hé aquí la única herencia de mi amor. Há
tiempo vivo de mi trabajo ; él quizás creyó tener
la obligación de sostenerme, y realmente la tiene. A mí no me molestaba eso, pero he querido
demostrar que podía sostenerme, produciendo
algo, sin ridiculeces ni exageraciones.

Y aquí estoy con mi eterno dolor por compañía. Esto lo escribo, mas nadie lo admirara
el que lee esto, lo olvida al verme, pues no de-
muestro tristeza.

Y sin embargo, cuando estoy sola, sin saber
por qué, me siento triste, y necesitando disipar
esta tristeza, me pongo á leer y á estudiar, y le-

yendo unos párrafos de Castelar á la una, recordé aquella luna bella que contempló tantas veces
esperándole á él... y las lágrimas humedecieron
mi rostro, y me levanté á escribir estas mal tra-
zadas líneas de recuerdos imborrables, eternos
compañeros de mi alma angustiada, cual «tórtola herida».... es que aún te amo.... «apesar del
tiempo y la distancia, guardaré en mi corazón
vuestra memoria, como una flor de singular fra-
gancia.»

He querido volver á impresionarme.... he
querido amar.... pero no es posible.... no puedo amar como lo amé á él....

Aquella ilusión hermosa por la cual yo des-
variaba, ¿do está?.... ¿Qué se me hizo aquella
ilusión querida, que alimentaba en mi alma, que
forjó mi vida entera, que luche por conservarla,
se deshizo cual espuma que forman las olas y
se deshacen en las playas.

Y traté de alimentar nuevos sueños para mi
alma, fuegos nuevos en mi mente, y traté de so-
ñar, y busqué impresiones para aliviar mi triste
soledad y... se borraban. ... No podía enga-
ñarme.

Libé nuevos néctares de amores para apa-
gar mi sed y para olvidar mi dolor, pero el néctar se extinguía, y la sed no se apagaba, ni el
dolor desaparecía.... Y con la sonrisa en los
labios, en una suprema lucha y con una suprema calma, esperaré, me decía, á la existencia
próxima.

Volviendo á leer ¿diré como Pierrot? «¡Oh!
Luna, blanca y pálida Luna, ¿cuando volveré á
extasiarme contemplándote y esperando á aquel
objeto de mi amor?....» ó decir como Castelar:
«¡Que argenteos dan sus rayos á las ondulacio-
nes del arroyo! ¡Como se deslizan sus resplan-
dores mustios entre las ramas de los olmos!»
Hasta Bryon se inspiró con sus rayos, y rezó
él, el exceptico! «¡La Luna lo iluminó con sus
rayos suavísimos!»

. ..., ...